CHINESE ANIMATION

CHINESE ANIMATION

A History and Filmography, 1922–2012

Rolf Giesen

McFarland & Company, Inc., Publishers

Jefferson, North Carolina

All photographs courtesy Liuyi Wang from his Chinese book series
March: Chinese Animation Enters a New Century.

LIBRARY OF CONGRESS CATALOGUING-IN-PUBLICATION DATA

Giesen, Rolf.
Chinese animation : a history and filmography, 1922–2012 / Rolf Giesen.
                    p.   cm.
Includes bibliographical references and index.

ISBN 978-0-7864-5977-3 (softcover : acid free paper) ∞
ISBN 978-1-4766-1552-3 (ebook)

1. Animated films—China—History.   2. Animated films—China—Catalogs.
I. Title.
NC1766.C6G54 2015   791.43'340951—dc23   2014041907

BRITISH LIBRARY CATALOGUING DATA ARE AVAILABLE

On the cover: Poster art for the 1999
animated feature film *Lotus Lantern*

Printed in the United States of America

McFarland & Company, Inc., Publishers
Box 611, Jefferson, North Carolina 28640
www.mcfarlandpub.com

Table of Contents

Acknowledgments

Special mention must be given to CAA, the China Animation Association, founded in 1985, and the kind support of its chairman, Mr. Yu Peixia, and his assistants Zhang Yixiang and Cai Zhijun. The CAA is a national non-governmental organization and the only national corporate body in China's animation industry. The China Animation Association not only is a bridge between the government and the national animation industry but also works to link animation enterprises and public institutions as well as animation practitioners nationwide to develop coordinated service. It also supports intercultural research between East and West, academic research and scholarship, education, and consultation. The China Animation Association annually convokes a nationwide convention since 1996 and collaborates with other organizations to jointly host or sponsor grand animation festivals, exhibitions and contests.

Grateful thanks are also due to Mr. Jin Delong (the State Administration of Radio, Film and Television); Mr. Fu Tie Zhang (secretary-general, CTVAA Cartoon Commission) and his former assistant, Ms. Tina Yang; Mr. Wang Ying (former general manager, CCTV Animation, Inc.); Mr. Cai Zhijun (general manager, CCTV Animation, Inc.) and his associates, Mr. Zhou Xiang and Ms. Dong Hang; Madame Zhou Fengying (general manager, China International TV Corp. Beijing Glorious Animation Co.) and her staff; all former colleagues and students of the Animation School of Communication University of China (CUC Anima) in Beijing, including Mr. Liao Xiangzhong, Mr. Shengzhang Lu, Mr. Li Zhi Yong (Vincent), Ms. Viviana Gao (Gao Weihua), Mr. Wang Lei, Mr. Song Ge, Ms. Ding Li, Ms. Zhao Bing, Mr. Cheung Xiaowei, Ms. Ji Ling, and Mr. Dong Yan; Mr. Zheng Liguo (president, Jilin Animation Institute), his charming wife and his staff: Mr. Luo Jianglin, Mr. Xiaodong Yuan, Ms. Xu Man, and Mr. Harvey Lee; Mr. Sun Lijun and the staff and students of the Animation School of Beijing Film Academy; the grand old masters of Chinese animation: the late Mr. Zhang Songlin, Ms. Duan Xuao Xuan, Mr. Zhou Keqin, Ms. Lin Wenxiao, Mr. Yan Dingxian, Mr. Wang Borong, and particularly the kind Mr. Chang Guangxi; Mr. Qian Jianping, Su Da, and Chen Zhihong (Shanghai Animation Film Studio); Ms. Jane Li and Ms. Sookie Xia (The Walt Disney Company Shanghai Ltd.); Shanghai Media Group; Li Jie (deputy director, CCTV Animation Department); China Film Animation, Ltd.; Sunchime Group; Mr. Jung Chi Gwang and his wife, Zhou Hui (3DAnimagics Entertainment Co., Ltd., Beijing); Mr. Zhang Tianxiao (Fantasia Animation Shanghai Co., Ltd.); Mr. Robin Shen (StarQ Animation Studio); Ms. Jane Wu (chairman and president, Zhejiang Zoland Animation Co., Ltd.); Mr. Baolu Han (Zhejiang Pro&High Culture Industry Co., Ltd.); Mr. Vincent Wong (HaoXi Culture Creative Co., Ltd.); Ms. He Weiping (Zhejiang Provincial Department of Culture); Mr. Zhang Jun (executive secretary-general,

Zhejiang Association of Promoting Zhe-shang Culture); Mr. Fred C. Y. Wang (Salon Films Hong Kong, Ltd.); my fellow scholars and historians, Mr. John A. Lent, Mr. David G. Ehrlich and Mr. Giannalberto Bendazzi; Mr. Chen Jun; Mr. Junxin Dong; Jokelate; Mr. Nelson Shin (president, ASIFA, Seoul); Bordo (Mr. Borivoj Dovniković) and his wife, Vesna (general secretary, ASIFA); Mr. Kevin Geiger; Mr. Martin Brandes; Ms. Anke Redl (German Films, Beijing branch office); Mr. Jeffrey Katzenberg (Dream-Works); Mr. Mark Osborne; Mr. Luca Raffaelli (I Castelli Animati, Rome, Italy); Mr. Heinz Hermanns and Mr. Christian Gesell (Interfilm, Berlin); the late Thilo Graf Rothkirch and Maya Rothkirch (Cartoon-Film, Berlin); Mr. Jakob Bosch; Mr. Piet De Rycker; Mr. Herbert Schramm; Mr. Stefan Thies (NFP, Berlin); Mr. Wolfgang Lukschy; Dr. Michael Schoemann; Prof. Wolfgang Tumler; Prof. Frank Geßner (HFF, Potsdam-Babelsberg); Prof. Ulrich Weinberg (Hasso Plattner Institute); Mr. Andreas Lange (Computerspielemuseum, Berlin); Dr. Alexander Voegele; Dr. Martin Zimper (ZHdK Zurich University of the Arts).

I have to acknowledge the friendliness, advice and kind help of Mr. Wang Liuyi. Mr. Wang not only supported my work and introduced me to various parties, he also let me select from the vast photofiles he collected for a book of his own.

Last but not least, many thanks to Anna Khan. Without her caring, persistence and always welcome help I never would have succeeded in building the nucleus of a Museum for Animation, Comics & Games in Changchun, China.

Introduction and Overview:
A Strong Nation of Animation

Originally known for inexpensive and limited animation, mostly for TV, Asian producers are in a process of developing their digital animation industry and aesthetically competing with products from the Western world with the clear objective of pleasing domestic audiences as well as entering foreign markets and the global scene. Highly popular and acknowledged round the world are the achievements of Japanese manga and anime, which have become industries in themselves. Indian producers are becoming strong as well, but the real success story is going to happen in China. This is what Chinese government is hoping for. Despite many problems and shortcomings, there is evidence that the persistence in building an infrastructure will pay off someday. According to *China Daily*,

> Real estate and manufacturing are passé. For businesspeople and policymakers, the next gold mine lies in the animation and cartoon industry. Being a high-profit and emission-free, creative industry, animation has received strong government support and been blessed with large capital injections for its development in China in the past two years. More than 20 national-level and hundreds of provincial- and regional-level animation clusters cradling the industry have cropped up in these two years, while Beijing and a dozen-odd cities along the country's coast have declared their ambition to be China's "animation and cartoon capital." Welcome to the changing business priorities of 21st century China.[1]

In 2004, the State Administration of Radio, Film and Television (SARFT) in Beijing stated, "The development of the cartoon industry already has become an important symbol to deduce the current state of our education system and the comprehensive national strength. Therefore it is necessary for the government to conduct a policy that protects and supports the development of the national cartoon industry."[2]

People tell of a high Chinese official who found his grandson watching Japanese animation and, upset by this, asked for a change. Apparently the story is true. It was Premier Wen Jiabao who complained during a visit to the South Chinese Jiantong Animation Studio. This is what he said: "There are times when I watch TV anime with my grandchild but all he ever watches are foreign works like *Ultraman* and the like. He should watch more Chinese cartoons. We should be cultivating a domestic anime industry." Then he advised the assembled animators: "Your work is meaningful. You should play a leading role in bringing Chinese culture to the world.... Let Chinese children watch more of their own history and their own country's animation."[3]

What a Chinese politician recommends usually is taken as a dictate, and so a whole industry went ahead and expanded to gigantic dimensions to fulfill the premier's commands. Let's try to interpret his words:

1. Chinese anime—*Manhuna Anime*— should become stronger than Japanese anime,

1

2. therefore a strong domestic animation infrastructure has to be established, according to the model of the Japanese, to show the former aggressor a thing or two.

3. The target audiences are Chinese children, who should be raised to be aware and proud of their own culture (requiring national education), and patrons abroad, who should start to appreciate what the Chinese have to say and pay for it, as they have paid the Americans for what some call cultural imperialism.

By the end of the 1980s, as the previous "planned economy" was gradually replaced by market-oriented ways, with China, in breathtaking speed, opening up to the capitalist world, Chinese TV animation was indeed dominated by foreign companies, notably American and Japanese. Chinese companies had almost no chance against this powerful competition, whose product seemed to be more attractive to domestic audiences starving for new and different content. Suddenly, established Chinese producers were losing money on their own territory. Nobody cared back then, but a decade later it became known that animation, cartoons and digital art could make the tills ring too. Domestic producers, however, didn't participate. Not to reach even domestic audiences was tantamount to losing face.

This, of course, sounds just like psychology, but there are more than superficial political reasons for the revived interest in cartoons and animation. There is capital at stake. The case of Walt Disney shows that animation sells best through merchandising. Chinese experts calculated that the average output of 30,000 minutes of animation per year (before 2004) should be increased to 250,000 minutes to counter foreign imports. (Up till then Chinese animation only covered 10 percent of the domestic market. Chinese officials hoped for 75 percent.)

Quatech Market Research has surveyed people of ages 14 to 30 in Beijing, Shanghai and Guangzhou and found out that they spend over 1.3 billion RMB ($163 million) every year on cartoons, cartoon products and merchandising. But more than 80 percent of the revenue flew out of the country. Therefore, the Chinese government postulated a "strong nation of animation."

Highly important to the Chinese government are the youngest citizens. In China so far there are 370 million children—a clear target group for the biggest toy manufacturer in the world. The Chinese government wants to keep the high license fees from being paid to Disney and other American or Japanese cartoon suppliers and create their own brands. But up till now no true cartoon star who might compete with Mickey Mouse, the Simpsons or Garfield has been created in the Middle Kingdom. In television they are going for mass-produced series like *Blue Cat*, created by the Sunchime Cartoon Group of Hunan. More than 7,500 minutes' worth of episodes have brought the Disney-inspired cat (that remotely resembles a blue version of Felix the Cat) to prominence in the *Guinness Book of Records*. Wang Hong, general manager of Sunchime, had high hopes for *Blue Cat* to be distributed in foreign countries, but so far there has not been much interest.

With the demand of the industry to churn out increasing standardized quantities with the chance of billion dollar grosses, however, there is a general lack of quality. In 2007 China mass-produced a total of more than 100,000 minutes of animation, in 2008 over 130,000 minutes. The final objective of 250,000 minutes annually has been reached in the meantime. At the International Comics, Cartoon and Games Forum at Jilin Animation Institute in Changchun (with now almost 10,000 students, the biggest private animation school in China and perhaps the world), Ding Wei, the assistant to the minister of culture, complained in front of a number of illustrious guests from a dozen countries about the poor quality of domestic animation.

Government has provided safe conditions, he told the audience: a solid infrastructure of more than 5,000 animation companies, subsidies, real estate for high-tech industrial development zones, and education for tens of thousands of animation students in universities and colleges. With gestures in the protectionist direction, SARFT, the powerful State Administration of Radio, Film and Television, has banned popular American and foreign series from Chinese prime-time TV (between 5 p.m. and 8 p.m.), but not even Chinese children like to watch domestic animation.

In the audience was Mark Osborne, co-director of DreamWorks' *Kung Fu Panda*, which broke house records in China—without any Chinese involvement in the process of production. Therefore, some hardboiled Chinese tried to boycott the *Kung Fu Panda* series:

> Panda-crazed artist Zhao Bandi started his own boycott campaign in 2008 and attracted much attention through the internet. Zhao believed that the animation series "distorted Chinese culture and serves as a tool to 'kidnap' the mind of the Chinese people." Controversial Peking University scholar Kong Qingdong supported Zhao's effort and criticized Hollywood for using "a Chinese symbol" to "brainwash and conquer" Chinese people. Yet many other Chinese people regard the politicization of this children's film as outlandish and an excuse for China's own lagging animation industry. Furthermore, the box office of *Kung Fu Panda 2* reached 40 billion RMB (6.17 billion dollars) in half a month, signifying the defeat of boycott efforts.[4]

When asked by this author a few years ago, Jeffrey Katzenberg, co-founder and CEO of DreamWorks Animation SKG, gave a sniff at the very thought and said that he would never like to produce in China, and would never even consider doing so, but would rather go to India, for the Chinese tend to copy things cheaply while the Indians are highly innovative and imaginative; in addition, there would be no language barrier. In the meantime Mr. Katzenberg seems to have changed his mind, however, and did a 180:

> Dreamworks Animation and Xi Jinping have announced a joint venture to build a major production center in Shanghai.
>   Oriental DreamWorks plans to develop film, TV, games and live stage productions for the Chinese and international market. It will create original animated and live action content, has $330 million in assets and will be open for business this year. China's vice-president Xi Jinping, probably their next president, met Obama in Washington and later flew to Los Angeles on his visit to the U.S. He said it is "the most significant deal to involve a Hollywood studio in China."
>   DWA's CEO Jeffrey Katzenberg has been an aggressive industry leader seeking his company's growth. DWA which has 45 percent interest in the new studio (Oriental DreamWorks owns 55 percent) should be able to take advantage of China's strong economic, population and box office growth to offset sluggish film industry momentum in the U.S. China restricts the number of foreign made films shown there each year, so by creating new product in China, DWA hopes to increase profits. China is already the third-largest cinema market in the world with a box office gross of $2.09 billion, up 29 percent from last year, putting it behind the U.S. and Japan. It is forecast to be the world's biggest cinema market within the next decade. The country is adding new movie theaters at a rate of about three screens a day, the fastest growth rate in the world.[5]

In the meantime Mr. Xi Jinping was elected general secretary of the Communist Party and president of the People's Republic of China. The fact of an official of his caliber dealing in matters of animation demonstrates the importance of the issue. Glendale-based DreamWorks SKG's plans to build a studio in Shanghai are being hailed as a landmark agreement. In the long run, one might speculate which partner will have the upper hand, with the Chinese interested in buying American corporate know-how and the Americans clearly interested in Asian funding and markets.

Oriental DreamWorks is a joint venture with China Media Capital and Shanghai Media Group, in concert with Shanghai Alliance Investment—an investment arm of the Shanghai municipal government—to establish a family entertainment company in China. According to the *Wall Street Journal*,

> The battle for market access in the Middle Kingdom is proving to be more challenging than Po's quest to defeat Lord Chen in DreamWorks' "Kung Fu Panda 2."
>
> For one thing, Beijing has failed to fulfill its promise to lift a quota on foreign movies, currently set at 20 per year, from its 2001 agreement to join the World Trade Organization. Since cultural products are particularly sensitive, the U.S. and other trading partners have muted their criticism. But the commercial consequences of censorship have been severe for American companies such as Google and Facebook, which have failed to garner a market share comparable to those they enjoy in other foreign markets.
>
> Another way that China protects its markets is by forcing foreign companies to transfer technology and know-how to domestic players through joint ventures. And once Chinese companies are ready to compete on their own, the door swings shut....
>
> DreamWorks' partners are state-controlled companies, Shanghai Media Group and China Media Capital. Political protection is their main contribution to this endeavor, and they will supervise production to make sure that nothing offends the delicate sensibilities of Beijing's leaders. No doubt they will also use the new state-of-the-art animation capabilities to produce propaganda pieces, much as China's live action studios are now forced to do.[6]

Disney in the meantime didn't want to be left behind and followed hard on the heels of their former executive employee Katzenberg. In April 2012, "Walt Disney Co. said it would join an initiative to develop China's animation industry, making the latest push by Hollywood to expand into the world's most populous country. The agreement ... unites the Burbank entertainment giant with an animation arm of China's Ministry of Culture and China's largest Internet company, Tencent Holdings Ltd."[7] And, besides that, Disney has a deal with state-owned Shanghai Shendi Group Co. to build its first mainland China theme park. Located in Pudong, the Shanghai Disney Resort is targeted to open at the end of 2015.

For these players, quantity is what matters. Quality comes second.

There was a time, however, when China created quality animation. And, in a way, single-frame animation was invented in China. While the Europeans invented the Zoetrope in 1833, Chinese inventor Ting Huan had invented a revolving device already, around AD 180. And there were comic books long before the Europeans and Americans started the trend: 300 years ago.[8] There also were so-called magic mirrors creating fantastic imagery, forerunners of today's holographic techniques: "Image formation using a specially designed mirror under sunlight illumination, similar to holographic imaging, can be traced back to Chinese scientists as early as the Tang dynasty in the 700s. This particular type of mirror is known as the Chinese magic mirror." Among these mirrors is a type that

> produces an image such as the image of Buddha on a wall when it is illuminated by sunlight. However, there is no sign of any such image at the surface of the mirror and it differs from the relief image on the back of the mirror. It is speculated that this Chinese magic mirror forms an image through interference among multiple beams reflected by parts of the mirror that have unequal curvatures. Although nobody knows exactly how it works because the knowledge for making a magic mirror has long been lost, the Chinese magic mirror indeed acts like a modern hologram.[9]

But when the first moving images were screened at the Forbidden City in the early

20th century, Cixi, the dowager empress, became so upset by this Western black magic that she had the Chinese cinematographers decapitated (while she let the European entrepreneurs escape). The movie industry, and animation itself, eventually found a niche in Shanghai, which luckily had a polyglot culture. While Germany released its first feature-length Arabian Nights animation in 1926, *The Adventures of Prince Achmed* by Lotte Reiniger (patterned after Asian shadow plays and even including a Chinese episode), Shanghai filmmakers produced their first short films on a low level that was clearly inspired by Max Fleischer's *Koko the Clown* and the *Out of the Inkwell* series. The pioneers were the famous Wan brothers, who paid their tribute to the American way of filmmaking: Wan Laiming, Wan Guchan, Wan Chaochen, and Wan Dihuan.

In 1935 the Wan brothers made China's first sound cartoon, *The Camel's Dancer*, and in 1941 during the Japanese occupation, their Shanghai-based studio produced an ambitious animated feature, *Tie shan gong zhu* (*Princess Iron Fan*). But after the war China's most famous mythological tale, part of their cultural heritage, *Monkey King* Sun Wukong and his *Journey to the West,* was made into a Japanese animated feature film, *Saiyu-ki* (U.S.: *Alakazam the Great*), co-directed by *AstroBoy* inventor Osamu Tezuka. This was a national disgrace. By 1957 China had established its own state-controlled animation studio in Shanghai, and by 1961 was able to do the first part of its own Monkey King version, *Da nao tian gong,* with the second part finished in 1964. *Havoc in Heaven* or, as it is also known, *Uproar in Heaven,* was screened for the first time as a single picture in 1965 and clearly showed the influence of Soviet Russian animators (Ivan Ivanov-Vano, among others) with a mix of Disney and Fleischer. But that *Monkey King* didn't please Chairman Mao Zedong. In the Shanghai version of Sun Wukong he saw a caricature of himself creating "havoc" in the "heaven" of China. The chairman had a lot going for him, but humor and self-irony were not among those virtues. If animation existed at all it should be propaganda controlled by the party. He could make this happen, as Shanghai

Ting Huan's Chinese Zoetrope.

was no longer polyglot. China had become again what it had been for many centuries—a closed society.

During the Cultural Revolution the Shanghai animation outfit was shut down, like other film studios, and its personnel were sent to the countryside for re-education. The country was hermetically sealed off and isolated. Mao Zedong died on September 9, 1976, after having welcomed both Nixon and Kissinger, and other politicians from the Western world, and under Deng Xiaoping the Middle Country opened up again. In the 1980s the once prestigious animation studio reopened, but the days of glory were over, although in 1999 the company was still able to take a third place in box-office charts with its fairy-tale feature *Lotus Lantern* (box-office receipts: 26 million RMB = U.S. $2.6 million). At this time the average age of personnel in the studio was 50 years. They simply were not able to compete with modern Chinese capitalism, the challenges of an open economy and the speedy development of new and cross media.

Today Chinese animation is cheap and produced mostly for TV (including three satellite channels devoted to cartoons). According to Sun Lijun of the Animation School of Beijing Film Academy, this is the biggest disadvantage. Even the large-scale *Lotus Lantern* only cost 12 million RMB or $1.45 million, a mere fraction of what Disney's *Mulan* had cost.

Nevertheless, the Chinese care for cross-media, particularly media for mobile phones. In 2004 an article was published by a German magazine, *Film-dienst*, titled "ChinAmation."[10] A year later a company with that very name was founded (they took the name from the article, which they had located on the Internet). With the solid backing of some well-to-do investors they secured the worldwide rights to Mordillo's cartoons and released them exclusively for

cell phones. The new media and mobile content will play a key role in the development of animation and digital art and in China's return as supreme commander of all images moving.

For no money at all, the Chinese provide webtoons and Flash animation for the Internet with only a little ingenuity. There are, however, more and more exceptions. In 2001 the *Xiao-Xiao* series, starring kung fu stick figures, created a phenomenon receiving more than 50 million hits.

Besides poor production values, Chinese animation suffers from sometimes unintelligible storytelling and story concepts that are unprogressive but, for odd reasons, seem to make money. Apart from some lovely Hong Kong animation, such as the cute cartoon pigs of *My Life as McDull* (2001), Chinese animation usually lacks in story, character and originality. Chinese artists mostly think in symbols and have a peculiar way of storytelling that avoids any drama or conflict. They often prefer mundane solutions, and the bulk of their animation is stiff and impersonal.

The number one box-office hit of China—produced for both TV and cinema—is *Xi Yang Yang yu Hui Tai Lang* (*Pleasant Goat and Big Big Wolf*), a simple Flash animation about a gray wolf who is ordered by his queen wife to get some tasty little goats for dinner but constantly is outsmarted by them (with 1,000 episodes and four feature films until now, a modest pendant to America's Wile E. Coyote and Road Runner series). Even the Chinese wonder why the series is so successful. In early 2009 the first feature done after the TV series made 100 million RMB. At the same time, the release of James Cameron's 3D animated *Avatar* was drawing large audiences and breaking house records even in China, although the flat version was withdrawn in favor of stereoscopic screenings.

The future of Chinese animation is somewhere between the controlled standardization of cheap mass production and the new age of virtual industries. Currently, the Chinese animation industry is still suffering from poor income from broadcasting rights, advertising and sales of cartoon related products: "CCTV usually spends 10 Yuan ($1.2) on buying the broadcasting rights of one minute of a domestic cartoon, while the cost of such production is 15,000 Yuan ($1,807)."[11] The sale of merchandise, the name of the game, which dominates the income of the foreign animation industry, is still at a fledgling stage in China. Nevertheless, in 2011 China's animation industry reported a record-high box-office revenue of 320 million RMB ($50.6 million):

> According to "The Report on the Development of China's Animation Industry," a total of 24 films and 435 TV series with a total running time of 261,224 minutes were made in 2011, making a year-on-year increase of 18.5 percent.
> However, the report, which was released by the Social Science Academic Press, noted that the quality and production value of these products remain far below those of similar products made in developed countries.
> The report urged more policy support as well as the industry's own efforts to overcome various development obstacles in order to achieve a boost in quality in the upcoming years.[12]

Indeed, the government bowed again and "has pledged to offer more favorable financing policies to boost the country's domestic animation industry":

> The plan [released by the Ministry of Culture] says private investment will be encouraged to enter the industry in various forms, while the government will direct its policy-based banks to give financial support to qualified enterprises.
> The new policies will apply to both State-owned animation companies and private entities, according to the five-year development plan (2011–15) on the animation industry.
> Official figures indicate that the production value of China's animation industry hit an estimated 60 billion yuan ($9.4 billion) in 2011.
> However, the plan warned that the country's animation sector remains weak, proposing a list of stimulating policies.
> The plan calls for domestic animators (by 2010 roughly 8,300 producers and studios were registered in the field, with approximately 25 of them really important and able to achieve bigger things) to churn out 30 animated films annually by 2015, as well as sets goals for building industrial parks and cultivating new animators and brands.[13]

Film books mainly are an account of things that have happened. I believe a film book can achieve more. This one is intended in part and to tell about the complex way of Chinese thinking.

When I accompanied a group of top Chinese animation experts who after attending Annecy Animation Festival in June 2012 traveled through various European cities, including Berlin and Potsdam, I was astonished to find that, instead of exchanging polite phrases, Mr. Jin Delong, who on behalf of the State Administration of Radio, Film and Television is monitoring all Chinese animation products, directly asked members of the University of Film and Television HFF in Potsdam-Babelsberg how they dealt with creativity, which right now is a big topic in China. The German partners became a little nervous and didn't respond properly. Creativity training is high on the Chinese agenda, and they told me that they are going to build a new educational platform for animation. They will find out that creativity cannot be indoctrinated but only experienced, and once they have done so they will be on the path of success because there is almost nobody in the world who is *not* interested in China.

One cannot create new things if one is not a creative individual: "The key is innovation. Science and technology must be emphasized and commercialized, education must infuse society with creativity, and intellectual property rights must be protected," writes Dr. Robert Lawrence Kuhn:

> Paradoxically, creativity in China often begins with copying. In Dafen village, more than 2,000 artists, working on oil-painting assembly lines, mass-produce classical masterpieces of Van Gogh, Picasso, Monet, Raphael and Da Vinci, such as Da Vinci's *Mona Lisa*. Dafen controls 60 percent of the global oil-painting market.
>
> But when the financial crisis hit, painting factories lost foreign orders and many went bankrupt. Painters had to turn to China's domestic market. Only a few could transform themselves from duplication to originators, but that transformation is the big test for China itself.

Innovation, Dr. Kuhn postulates, "requires freedom. For China to become an increasingly innovative society, China must become an increasingly free society. China must also enforce IPRs and rethink the essence of education. China's new leaders face the challenge of innovation. The Chinese people are watching."[14]

The future of animation, games and cross-media ventures lies in China. And as in the past, future imagery will be Asian and Chinese. The pendulum of history will swing back. But to reach the intellect and the hearts of Western audiences, they have to be on the same wavelength.

Capitalism has gone global, as Karl Marx envisioned. It's a challenge and at the same time a curse. Money respects neither national borders nor the heritage of national culture. The same is true for the billions of images on the World Wide Web that are not protected by any kind of copyright.

All of this is destroying societies and their individual cultures, and it may end in a big clash. The worldwide financial crisis will have its impact on China, too: "A looming hard landing in China will bring the financial and economic crisis of the past five years to a climax in 2012, one of the City of London's leading analysts has

warned. Albert Edwards, head of strategy at Société Générale and one of the UK's leading 'bears,' said the next 12 months would be the 'final year of pain and disappointment.'"[15] My personal guess is that the disastrous chain reaction will take longer, but China may recover sooner from it than the Western world and rebuild and reshape its society and economy. There is a saying that Shiva, a major Hindu deity, has to destroy to transform and rebuild properly. Maybe, without being aware of it, we are living in a change of eras, on the threshold of virtualization.

One may hope that China's monied industry leaders sooner or later will make room for young, creative entrepreneurs who will understand and use the advantages of interactive media, which are cross-media and therefore cross-cultural or intercultural. This is one of the reasons why I have given considerable focus on recent work and students' films in the present work. Young talent will have to introduce new content and new style.

The Chinese welcome and at the same time fear globalization and the effects it might have on the national culture, including the effects cultural globalization and foreign animation might have on the education of children.

In a positive sense, however, cross-media communication may help to create an awareness of what's wrong in the world and contribute to the raising of children and their education.

Cross-media, if thoughtfully linked, helps us to understand where we live. It's going to widen our horizons.

Chinese, other Asians, Russians and Europeans may find out that they all share one and the same continent: Eurasia (an idea German artist Joseph Beuys promoted at the end of his life), a continent that is rich in nature, culture, tales, and resources. We have a lot to learn from the peoples of the East. We did so in the past. Why not in the future? Where does the idea of paper money come from? What kind of imagery inspired our mythology? For instance, the well-known fairy tale of Cinderella, to us a mix of Charles Perrault (*Cendrillon, ou La petite pantoufle de verre*), Brothers Grimm (*Aschenputtel*), Ludwig Bechstein (*Aschenbroedel*), and Walt Disney, who released his successful animated version in 1950, originates from China, where it was called *Yeh-Shen* (or *Ye Xian*). It was conceived in the Tang dynasty, predates any Western version by almost 1,000 years, and more or less offers what all Cinderella versions have in common. It's about the initiation of a young girl to womanhood. A girl who is literally living in the ashes and feels neglected by her cruel (step-) mother and sisters will grow up and marry, as is common practice in fairy tales, a prince. In the Chinese version of the tale it is a mysterious fish with golden eyes that does the transformation by the gift of golden slippers. On the Silk Road, the famous tale found its way to the West to enrich the imagination of generations of youngsters, with its origin sadly forgotten. All over the world it is known as *Ashpei, Ashpitel, The Brocaded Slipper, The Jewelled Slipper, The Broken Pitcher, La Cenerentola* (Italy, transformed into an opera of the same title by Gioachino Rossini), *Cenicienta* (Spain), *The Cinder Maid, Conkiajgharma, Essy Puttle, Finette Cendron, Grattula-Beddattula, Katie Woodencloak, The Little Red Fish and the Clog of Gold, Papalluga, Pepelyouga, Rashin-Coatie, Rosina in the Oven, Sodewa Bai, Solushka* (Russia), and *Soushka* by Sergei Sergeyevich Prokofiev (1945).[16] Looking for international markets, Chinese producers could turn it into a co-production, for the basics of the tale are internationally known.

In all of Eurasia, there are many stories that could repeat the miracle of Cinderella. China is rich in stories but still lacks in intelligible narratives, as we have already noticed: "Sergei Vladimirovich Bodrov, a two-time Academy Award–nominated Russian-U.S. film director, uses a metaphor to say that Chinese filmmakers need to learn proper story-telling languages that are accepted by the West. 'Filmmakers are like street musicians—you have to attract passers-by in a few seconds to let them throw money to you.'"[17]

However, Wen Jiabao reminds us that spreading Chinese culture is at least as important as money-making:

> Some film insiders point out that the importance of developing China's film industry is not just to earn bigger box office receipts.
>
> "The biggest meaning of Hollywood films is that every year, thousands of millions of people around the world watch them, through which they learn about American values, culture and way of life," said Zhou Tiedong, president of China Film Promotion International.
>
> However, as more Chinese cultural products make inroads in the overseas markets, there should also be awareness that such kinds of products need a longer time for success.[18]

In short, for the Chinese it's also about propaganda. For others it's about intercultural values. Maybe we can convince filmmakers that mutual understanding is the best propaganda in the world of new media.

It all is about the right mix of cinema, television, mobile phones, computer games, and the Internet with respect to the grand achievements of past generations. A Silk Road of animation through Eurasia might be the right vision for the rest of the world too.

Note: *For some films, the only information available about them is the title. Even without further information, it was decided that their inclusion in this book would be valuable to readers. Generally, there are no accepted English translations of many Chinese film titles. The author has tried to use the most prevalent translations he could find.*

CHAPTER 1

The 1920s: The Wan Brothers and the Origin of Shanghai Animation

The first American cartoons screened in China fit ideally with the Asian feeling of shadow plays. Most of the early cartoon characters were created in solid black shapes, which were easier to animate.

One of the series that attracted cinema-goers in Shanghai was titled *Out of the Inkwell* and was created in 1919 by Max Fleischer, a Vienna-born cartoonist: "The title *Out of the Inkwell* was used for want of a better name. The pictures were done in pen and ink. In addition, there are so many things that can come out of an ink-well."[1]

The cartoons featured a mischievous clown, Ko-Ko, who was a rotoscoped duplicate of Fleischer's brother Dave. Max Fleischer's son, the late Richard, recalled the series fondly: "Dipping his pen into an inkwell, he'd [Max Fleischer] draw KoKo the Clown, ... and lo and behold, it would come to life, jump off the drawing board,

The famous Wan brothers; from left to right: Wan Chaochen, Wan Laiming and Wan Guchan.

and crawl all over him. Together, Max and KoKo would have all sorts of adventures in real-life settings, and at the end KoKo would dive back into the inkwell and my father would screw the top of the bottle into place."[2] Fleischer continues:

> The cartoons were marvels of invention, imagination, and charm and were also hilariously funny. No two cartoons ever started the same way. Ko-Ko makes his entrance in an almost infinite variety of brilliantly conceived ways: in one cartoon, a drop of ink drips off Max's pen onto a sheet of paper, the blot that it makes transforming itself into the figure of the clown; in another, a half-finished Ko-Ko grabs the pen and draws the rest of himself after Max is called away from the drawing board. The Fleischer trademark of surrealism and morphing is very much in evidence in all the cartoons.[3]

It was one of these Ko-Ko cartoons that the Wan Brothers had seen in Shanghai. The Wan Brothers are Wan Laiming, Wan Guchan, Wan Chaochen, and Wan Dihuan. They all came from the shadow play theatre (so Fleischer's inkwell fit), worked in the fine art departments at Shanghai Commercial Press and had entered the film business by designing and painting sets for live-action films. Laiming and Guchan were twin brothers, born on January 18, 1900, in Nanjing. Wan Laiming worked for the Shanghai Commercial Press and held positions in the Department of Fine Arts and the Department of Activities Movie Service as early as 1919. His brothers joined him as soon as they had graduated from art schools.

Their first glimpse of Zoetrope technology and an animated cartoon changed it all. They started to train themselves in animation techniques, made some advertising films and, in 1926, joined Great Wall Film Company and created their first animation short to copy what they had seen on the screen. If a Chinese person copies, it is a tribute to a master (although the master might not always acknowledge it).

Thus begins what might be called the exploration stage of Chinese animation.

The Films

1922

Shuzhendong Chinese Typewriter (Shuzhengdong Huawen Daziji)
Shanghai Commercial Press
Directors: Wan Laiming, Wan Guchan

Comment: An advertising film featuring China's premier animation. Most likely *object animation*, in which things move as if by an invisible hand, but it's also possible that the film uses only graphic art. (According to some sources, it was released in 1925, which would make more sense, as the Wan brothers began to focus on animation at that particular time.)

For the original title there are two possible translations: *Comfortable Zhendong Chinese Typewriter* or *Comfortably Raised Eastern Chinese Typewriter* (referring to the town of Zhendong, north of Shanghai).

1924

Dog Treat
Chinese Film Company
Directors/Producers: Wan Laiming, Wan Guchan

Comment: The original Chinese title translates as *Dog Treating Guests* or *Dog Entertaining Guests*.

New Year
Directors/Producers: Wan Laiming, Wan Guchan

Comment: An advertisement film for Shanghai Tobacco Comany (British American Tobacco Company).

1926

Paperman Makes Trouble
Directors: Wan Laiming, Wan Guchan

Comment: In a 1985 essay Marie-Claire Quiquemelle stated that two similar films were produced in 1926, one being the copy of *Out of the Inkwell,* the other with a Chinese approach.[4]

According to different information, this short may have been finished in 1930.

Uproar in the Studio/Studio in a Row (*Da Nao Huashi*)

Great Wall Film Company
10–12 Minutes
Directors: Wan Laiming, Wan Guchan

Synopsis: After the artist has left, one of his painted figures comes to life and fools around with paint and brushes.

Comment: One can call this the first copied Chinese animation. It follows exactly the pattern set by Max Fleischer and KoKo the Clown. It deals with an artist who is disturbed by a small paper person jumping out of the page and causing some chaos. Max Fleischer used his brother Dave to play KoKo; Wan Laiming asked his brother Wan Guchan to substitute for the paper person. His movements were recorded on film and traced by the animator. When a Chinese person copies it is not meant to be plagiarism or piracy but an homage to the original artist, which is an attitude difficult to understand for Westerners.

CHAPTER 2

The 1930s: Japanese Invaders and the Dancing Camel

In the following years the Wan brothers did a number of cartoons for various companies. When the youngest of them, Wan Dihuan, left in 1935 to open his own photography business, the remaining brothers set up an animation department for the Mingxing Production Company.

As an article they wrote for the journal of that production company[1] reveals the brothers were not influenced only by American cartoons but also by artistic qualities of German animation and the educational efforts of Soviet cartoons.

These years also saw the Japanese invasion of China. The Japanese invasion of Mongolia in 1937 led to the Second Sino-Japanese War in 1937. The Wan brothers participated by doing anti–Japanese propaganda.

 **The Films**

1932

Citizen, Wake Up! (Tongbao Suxing)

The Police Dog/Detective Dog (Gou Zenthan)
Comment: According to other sources, made in 1937.[2]

The Price of Blood (Xueqian)
Comment: A patriotic film condemning the Shanghai Incident, the Shanghai War of 1932.

1934

The Motherland Is Saved by Aviation/ Aviation Saves China (Hang-Kong Jiugui)
Mingxing Company
Comment: Promotes the Chinese air force.

The Painful Story of the Nation/The Sad Story of the Nation (Xiangcao Meiren)
Mingxing Company

The Year of Chinese Goods (Guohuo Nian)
Mingxing Company

1935

The Camel's Dance (Luotuo Xianwu)
Mingxing Company
Directors: Wan Laiming, Wan Guchan, Wan Chaochen
Synopsis: A clumsy camel entertains other animals by dancing and singing.
Comment: China's first sound cartoon.

1937

Anti-Japanese War Posters Cartoons (Kangzhan Biaoyou Katong)
Mingxing Company

Anti-Japanese War Songs Collection (Kangzhan Geji, aka Kangzhan Gefu)
Mingxing Company

* * *

Mingxing Film Company was closed in 1937 by the Japanese occupation forces.

1938

The Wan brothers relocated in Wuhan province and worked for China Film Production.

Go to the Front (*Shang Qian Xian*)
Director: Wan Chaochen

The River Is Red with Blood (*Man Jiang Hong*)

Wang Laowu Became a Soldier (*Wang Laowu Qu Dangbing*)
Director: Wan Chaochen

Comment: A propaganda film that promotes resistance against the Japanese occupation and asks all patriots to join Chinese troops.

CHAPTER 3

The 1940s: Shanghai, Changchun and Back

Before they left Shanghai the Wans created the first feature-length Chinese animation.

⇒ The Films ⇐

1939–1941

Princess Iron Fan (Tie Shan Gong Zhu)
Xinhua Film Company
73 Minutes
Released by Cinema Epoch on January 1, 1941
Producer: Zhang Shankun
Directors: Wan Laiming, Wan Guchan
Assistant Director: Wan Chaochen
Voice Actors: Wan Laiming (Sun Wukong), Wan Guchan, Wan Chaochen, Wan Dihuan

Synopsis: The fan of a vengeful princess who is married to King Bull is desperately needed to quench the flames that surround a peasant village. The Monkey King gets it for the villagers and also overcomes the revenge of the fierce Buffalo King, whose rampage is stopped between mighty trees.

Princess Iron Fan (1941).

Comment: In 1937, after Japanese invasion and beginning of total war, the Wan brothers went to Wuhan and continued work there. Two years later the oldest, Wan Laiming, returned to Shanghai where he saw Walt Disney's first feature-length Technicolor extravaganza, *Snow White and the Seven Dwarfs.*

So impressed was Wan Laiming by this experience that he gathered a new team of animators to start on what became China's first cartoon feature while Shanghai was under Japanese occupation. As animated star he selected their biggest national icon, the Monkey King, Sun Wukong, who became sort of a Chinese Mickey Mouse.

The film illustrates an episode from *Journey to the West,* one of China's most important novels, with the Monkey King and his companions, Zhu Bajie and Friar Sand, accompanying Buddhist monk Tang Xuanzang and outsmarting the fearful Buffalo King.

Princess Iron Fan was three years in production, with 237 artists working on it.

Production conditions in the French concession of Shanghai were difficult. Technically, *Princess Iron Fan* is not up to Disney standards but is somewhere between Van Beuren and Max Fleischer. It borrows from Fleischer, including the technology of rotoscoping in case of the human actors, who move quite smoothly thanks to the animators, who apparently traced, frame by frame, over previously filmed live-action movement as they had done earlier in *Uproar in the Studio.* Considering the period of origin and the circumstances of the Sino-Japanese War, however, *Princess Iron Fan* is nothing short of a masterpiece.

This was the film that inspired 16-year-old Japanese Osamu Tezuka to become a comic artist and later make his own version of the *Monkey King.* Tezuka Osamu and Wan Laiming met at the end of their lives. It is said that Mr. Tezuka was very interested in cooperating with Chinese artists but death intervened.

After finishing the movie, the Japanese entered the foreign concessions, and the brothers left and went to Hong Kong.

While *Princess Iron Fan* was in production, the Wans also made *Happy Peasants* and *Lao Bengou Edu Ji* (below).

1940

Happiness in Peasant Family

Director: Qian Jiajun

Comment: The year 1940 also marked the debut of Qian Jiajun as an animation filmmaker. *Happiness* follows the same pattern as *The River Is Red with Blood,* made by the Wans in 1938. The creator, Qian Jiajun (1916–2011), graduated from Suzhou Fine Arts College and joined the Chongqing Educational Film Animation Studio. He also was involved with an animation school in Hong Kong and served as director of China Film Production

Factory in the Republic of China. Later he became an outstanding filmmaker of the Shanghai Animation Film Studio.

Happy Peasants (Nong Jia Le)

Comment: Made during the production of *Princess Iron Fan.*

1941

Lao Bengou Edu Ji

Comment: Made during the production of *Princess Iron Fan.*

* * *

During the war there was not much going on in animation in China, but right after, animation would play a prominent role.

Te Wei's camerawoman, a retired but still dynamic and highly energetic woman by the name of Duan Xiao Xuan, whom I met in Shanghai, reminded me that the origins of animation that would lead to a new beginning of animation in the People's Republic of China are not to be found in the South but the Northeast of China and were based on the leftovers of the defeated Japanese occupants.

On October 1, 1946, a northeast motion picture company was established in Nenjiang Province, known today as Heilongjiang Province. And it was a woman who would spearhead animation over there.

Duan Xiao Xuan, camerawoman extraordinaire, in 1959.

1947

Emperor's Dream/The Dream of an Empire (Huangdi Meng)

Northeast Motion Picture Company
35 Minutes
Director: Chen Bo'er
Animator: Fang Ming

Synopsis: Chiang Kai-shek, like Pu Yi before him, in this animation literally becomes a wooden puppet in the grip of American puppet masters and string-pullers who are going to use him as a marionette to claim the imperial throne, which prominently features a Swastika-shaped ornament. Although a tra-

東北解放區合江省省長張聞天（左1）視察東影，與夫人劉英（左4）和東影領導人袁牧之（左5）吳印咸（左2）陳波兒（左3）合影

Chen Bo'er (center) with visitors at the Changchun Film Studio.

ditional symbol in Buddhism, in this case the Swastika should clearly recall Hitler's Third Reich.

Comment: Pu Yi, the puppet emperor, ruled the puppet state of Manchukuo from 1934 to 1945. So why not have puppets to act out scenes of contemporary history? In the fall of 1947 the Communist Party in Manchuria commissioned a female director, Chen Bo'er, to do a film against the Nationalists and Chiang Kai-shek.

Originally, the filmmakers were shown a caricature of Chiang Kai-Shek and a photograph of G. E. Marshall, U.S. Secretary of State, for the purpose of making a live-action puppet film using actual marionettes. Fang Ming, the chief animator, decided against string puppets and chose stop-motion models instead. Alas, the animation is crude. The puppets move like wood. But as propaganda for the simple-minded it seemed to have been effective.

Everything was arranged for Chiang to act like a king in the Peking Opera, but he failed despite powerful injections by "Doctor" Marshall.

The end title suggested that Chiang was going to lose and would die soon. (In fact, he passed away in 1975, and even his rival Mao Tse-tung, who survived him by a year, lamented his death.)

1947–1948

Go After an Easy Prey/Turtle Caught in a Jar (Wengzhongzhuobie)

Northeast Motion Picture Company
Director-Animator: Fang Ming
Assistant: Mochinaga Ayako

Synopsis: Another anti–Chiang film: Marching out of his spiderweb castle, located somewhere in the forest where he has received in-

Anti-American *Go After an Easy Prey.*

structions from his U.S. string-pullers, Chiang sends three diminutive marionette soldiers against Communist territory, but a giant member of the People's Liberation Army stops their ambitions.

Comment: The Chinese in the North didn't know much about animation back then. Their first animated films were done by Fang Ming. But Fang Ming was no Chinese. Actually, Fang Ming was the Chinese name (translated "Bright Direction") of a Japanese animator, Mochinaga Tadahito. Tadahito had traveled to Manchuria in 1945 to work for the Manchuria Film Association. Later, after his return to Japan, his Puppet Animation Film Studio in Tokyo would be associated with client Rankin/Bass' Animagic stop-motion specials, such as the perennial Christmas favorite *Rudolph the Red-Nosed Reindeer* (1964) and the horror spoof *Mad Monster Party* (1967), which featured the voice of Boris Karloff. Rankin/Bass billed him as Tad Mochinaga. According to *Animation World Magazine*,

Born in Tokyo in 1919, Mochinaga moved to Manchuria with his family, since his father worked at the South Manchuria Railway Company. Mochinaga spent his elementary

school days in China where he became familiar with the Chinese people and their culture. Although his father was stationed in Manchuria, other members of the family, including Mochinaga, made trips back and forth between Japan and China from time to time. When he was 10 years old, he saw a Mickey Mouse animation short at a movie theater in Tokyo which left a strong impression on him. During his junior high school days in Tokyo, Mochinaga saw another Disney animation: *Water Babies* from the *Silly Symphony* series. Made in Technicolor, the lotus flower pond in the film captured him with its beauty. Due to this, he was determined to become an animation filmmaker.

During his three years as an art school student in Tokyo, Mochinaga devoted his time to studying the techniques of animated filmmaking. In 1938, he surprised the school instructors by making a short film titled *How to Make Animated Films* as his graduate work. After graduation, he was employed as a member of the animation department at Geijutsu Eigasha (GES) or Art Film Company.[1]

Mochinaga was the first Japanese person to build a multiplane camera (4 levels). He also participated in Japanese war propaganda. His first directorial assignment, *Fuku-chan's Submarine* (1944), showed an attack on an enemy cargo ship.

In 1945, accompanied by his faithful wife Ayako, he left for Chang Chun (meaning "Eternal (or Long) Spring," which only could be meant ironically, as the city is located not far away from Vladivostok and enjoys hard winters), the capital of Manchuria, where he was asked to join the art department of Man-Ei (Manchuria Film Studio), with 2,000 employees the largest film studio in Asia in those days. Under Japan's surrender on August 15, 1945, Man-Ei was disbanded, and the company was handed over to the Chinese.

Animation World Magazine continues:

Since a film studio was a valuable asset for both Mao Tse-Tung's Communist Forces and Chiang Kai-Shek's Nationalists, they fought over the ownership. Even the Soviet forces showed their interest in this studio, because of its scale and latest equipment. The whole of China plunged into civil war. When the Nationalists' attack on Chang Chun became intense in 1946, the studio staff, including Mochinaga, escaped and went further north. Arriving in the mining town of Hao Gang, they started the "new" Tong Pei Film Studio from scratch. The shooting crew set out to the front lines and concentrated on making news films to inform people about the status

of the civil war. Thus, this became the starting point for filmmaking in what is later referred to as New China.[2]

Go After an Easy Prey is very crude 2D animation that looks like something from the 1920s, but it was well received by Chinese audiences.

* * *

Animation (as film in general) at that time was used according to Lenin's words, "You must remember always that of all the arts the most important for us is the cinema."[3]

It was mainly used as weapon of propaganda.

Chen Bo'er, who finally had become head of the studio in Changchun, which was to blossom into what was called "the Cradle of New China's Cinema," was convinced that they should continue to do animation.

Her choice for heading the new animation division of the art department was a political cartoonist, Te Wei. Born Sheng Song (on August 22, 1915) to a family of limited economic means, Te Wei finished only two years of middle schooling, then worked

Members of the Changchun Film Unit in 1950: Te Wei (front row, fourth from left, next to the child), Duan Xiao Xuan (standing, far left).

in a Shanghai advertising company. He began to draw cartoons in 1933 and two years later started a career as a professional cartoonist for magazines and newspapers.

To delegate Te Wei to Changchun was a political decision. When Japan invaded China in 1937, Te Wei had become a prominent member of the anti–Japanese cartoonist propaganda group that traveled from city to city boosting the spirit of resistance. Talking to historian John A. Lent, Te Wei said, "We had exhibitions in and out of doors, printed our cartoon works as posters put on walls, and published journals against the Japanese. We did everything ourselves, and though economic conditions were very difficult, we found ways to survive."

Chen Bo'er seemed to like Te Wei's political view and approach to cartooning and caricature. So she asked for him, although Te Wei was not at all experienced, neither in filmmaking nor in animation. "I like animation," he said, "but I didn't like to do production. I liked doing cartoons, not all those monotonous frames. But, it was an order and I had to do this job."⁴ The order was submitted by the Ministry of Culture, following a directive from Zhou Enlai.

So in 1949, joined by Jin Xi (Jin Shi, 1919–1997, by real name Zeng Diping), a painter and intellectual, Te Wei headed to the cold north of China to start work and learn the new craft from Japanese animator Fang Ming.

All that counted was that Te Wei seemed to be true to party principles. And while the best of Western animators are primarily interested in movement of characters, Te Wei's priorities were caricatures and paintings.

This period marks what one writer called the "stable stage" of Chinese animation.⁵

CHAPTER 4

The 1950s: The Classic Period—Watercolors, Cut-Paper, Origami and Puppet Animation

In the 1950s began the so-called golden era of Chinese animation, which lasted from 1957 to 1966 and from 1977 to 1988. Under the planned economy, the newly founded Shanghai Animation Film Studio turned out some aesthetically pleasant films. Given unlimited time and plentiful resources, animators experimented with various materials, techniques, and approaches, such as brush painting, folded paper, paper cut, cel, and puppets, and employed Chinese artistic techniques, literature, proverbs, and folklore.

In 1950, Te Wei and his group, including technical expert Fang Ming, who was kept as an advisor and technical instructor, were asked to resume their work in Shanghai.

Art by Te Wei.

22

The Films

1950

Thank You, Kitten/Thank You, Kitty (Xiexie Xiao Huamao)

13 Minutes
Director-Animator: Fang Ming

Synopsis: A cat keeps night watch to protect the villagers from a bunch of nasty rodents.

Comment: The prototype or blueprint of the famed Chinese cartoon character Inspector Black Cat. Preproduction was finished in Changchun before the animation unit was transferred to Shanghai. Research was done in the countryside.

At the same time the Culture Division issued a new policy that all animated films should be healthy entertainment for children. Since then not much has changed, and this is one of the reasons for the temporary stagnation of Chinese animation art.

1952

Little Cat Goes Fishing (Xiaomao Diaoyu)

14:25 Minutes
Supervising Director: Te Wei
Screenplay: Jin Jin
Musical Score: Huang Zhun

Synopsis: Two little cats, Miaomiao and Mimi, go fishing. Miaomiao does it right. She watches her mother keenly to see how she

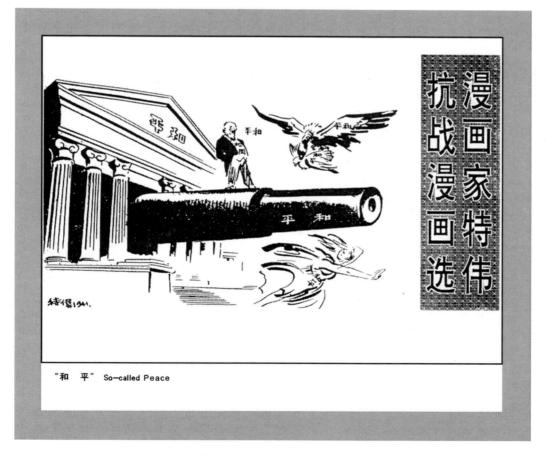

"和平" So-called Peace

Political caricature by Te Wei.

handles the task. Mimi, however, is impatient and therefore isn't as successful as Miaomiao.

Comment: A family cartoon asking the kids to follow parents' advice. The cats are anthropomorphic and act completely human.

* * *

In 1954 Wan Laiming, the pioneer of Chinese animation, and his twin brother Wan Guchan returned from Hong Kong, where they had worked on film settings, to join Shanghai's new animation department. From the United States came Wan Chaochen, the youngest of the Wan brothers, who in 1946–48 had studied animation technology and methods in Hollywood and most likely had been in touch with Disney. By that time, in 1953, Mochinaga, who had finished the tests for China's first color cartoons, had left for Japan. (After the Cultural Revolution he would return occasionally as consultant. From 1985 to 1986, he lectured animation technique at Beijing Film Acad-

四十年代的特伟: 特伟在他创作的画前
Te Wei in the 1940s   Te Wei and his Works

Te Wei, 1940s.

emy. He passed away on April 1, 1999, at the age of 80.)

In a speech to a closed session of party leaders, on May 2, 1956, after eight years of self-imposed isolation, Chairman Mao Zedong proposed the "double hundred" policy of "letting a hundred flowers bloom and a hundred schools of thought contend." Mao also urged party members to learn more about the West and study foreign languages.

In the fall of the same year, out of the small team of animators that started in the northeast of China, at the Chang Chun Film Studio, and then was transferred to Shanghai, grew the Shanghai Animation Film Studio, controlled by the Ministry of Culture and supervised by Te Wei.

In October, a film studio factory manager meeting was held in Beijing by the Film Bureau of the Ministry of Culture. Under the reform program, the reorganization of Shanghai Film Studio was put on the agenda. The former dubbing department and photo printing department, which had been directly affiliated with Shanghai Film Studio, were separated from it. Instead Shanghai Animation Film Studio, Shanghai Film Dubbing Factory, and Shanghai Film Equipment Factory were set up.

The sign of the Shanghai Animation Film Studio or Shanghai Fine Art Film Studio was put on the gate of the official residence of former Shanghai mayor and Taiwan refugee Wu Guozhen on April 1, 1957.

Te Wei, appointed studio head, presided over a number of famous artists, animators, and writers such as Wan Laiming, Wan Guochen, Wan Guhan, Qian Jiajun, and Yu Zheguang Zhang, who all had joined the Shanghai Fine Art Film Studio.

Shanghai Fine Art Film Studio consisted of animation (2D), puppets (3D) and paper-cut production departments as well as photography, editing, sound recording, scoring, production management and other business sections. In the beginning there were 200 employees, 380 before the Cultural Revolution and more than 500 employees well into the 1980s, who contributed to an annual output of 14 to 15 animated films, short and occasionally feature-length.

According to David Erlich, "In addition to the tremendous credibility given the Shanghai animators in 1957 by their new official status as the state 'Studio,' there was an influx of additional state support, new artists, equipment, and the encouragement for them to abandon the Soviet model of animation, to study animation being done throughout the west and to develop their own animation models that were more truly Chinese."[1]

The late premier Zhou Enlai pointed out, "Animation films are rather outstanding with their special and unique style in the Chinese film industry."[2]

On the occasion of the 30th anniversary of the studio Te Wei wrote,

It is said that Chinese animation has two characteristics; the first is healthy content with rich aesthetics and educational value. The second is that Chinese animation has a unique national style with various expressions, especially ethnic expression. In spite of the animation that is imported from abroad, we create animation with Chinese art characters and establish our own Chinese animation school. Our animation absorbs the forms and techniques of traditional Chinese painting. Our puppets draw the rich experience of local puppetry. Our Paper-Cut film learns from folk paper-cut and shadow play. We establish this Chinese animation school with unique and various styles. Our animation is appreciated and recognized and enjoys reputation in the world. Shanghai Fine Art Film Studio is the cradle of Chinese animation. A large number of Chinese artists and experts as well as animation producers have emerged from the studio in the past four decades.[3]

1953

Little Hero (Xiaoxiao Yingxiong)

Director: Jin Xi (Jin Shi)
Comment: The first color film of this genre, it set the pattern for kids' entertainment.

1954

The Dream of Xiao Mei (Xiao Mei De Meng)

Comment: China's first synthesis of puppets and live recording.

1954–1955

Good Friends (Ye Wai De Zao Yu)

10 Minutes
Directors: Wan Laiming, Shishun Shang
Writer: Yuan Song
  Comment: Another color short.

1955

The Magic Brush (Shen Bi Ma Liang)

20 Minutes
Directors: Jin Xi (Jin Shi), You Lei
Screenplay: Hong Xuntao
Writers: You Lei, Zhou Qin
  Synopsis: Ma Liang, a peasant boy, wants to learn painting and asks for a brush. The officials of the village can't believe it: "What? Learn painting? A cattle boy wants to learn painting?" The officials laugh off the very thought: "Just concentrate on feeding your cow." The boy, however, won't give up his artistic ambitions, and he practices by drawing on the soil using a stick. "Ma Liang," another kid asks, "if you learned painting, would you draw for nobilities and lords?" "No way, my art will belong to poor people," replies Ma Liang.

After that, Ma Liang never ceases to practice painting in his spare time. One year later the paintings of animals he does on rocks are so good that even huntsmen are fooled and mistake them for the real thing. But Ma still needs a good paintbrush. All of a sudden, the spirit of an old man appears in his hut with a precious gift: "Little Ma Liang, you are awarded this brush as you aren't afraid of difficulties and you are diligent. Remember what you said—that you would paint for poor people." Then the benign ghost vanishes and leaves Ma Liang with the brush, which turns out in his hand to be a magic brush.

As Ma Liang believes in the new tool, it performs miracles. And true to the boy's belief, what he paints becomes reality: first a rooster, then a sheep for a girl whose own sheep was taken away by force, and an ox for an old man whose cow died and who is too weak to pull the plough himself. Seeing what kind of magic Ma Liang achieves with his painting tool, a greedy local officer forces him to render similar service for him: "Ma Liang, paint a gold sycee for me." "Don't know how to paint it as I have never seen one before." "Show him a gold sycee." A servant brings a sycee. "There you go, now you know what a sycee looks like. Paint one." "Why need to draw a sycee as you already have one?" The official gets very upset: "If I ask you to draw it, you will draw it! Understand?" "No way." "Guard, take him to prison!"

In prison Ma Liang meets fellows in misery: "Folks, what crimes did you commit? Why are you being held here?" "They put us in prison just because we can't afford exorbitant taxes and levies, that's all." The prisoners tell Ma Liang that their families are starving, as they are unable to support them. Quickly Ma Liang draws a door on the cell wall that opens to freedom. The guards follow them on horse but they cannot find them. Painting on a rock, Ma Liang creates a magic, white horse and escapes from his hometown. But they search for him: "Reward for the capture of Ma Liang. This prisoner has an evil brush that can draw birds and make them alive. Now Ma Liang has committed a felony prison escape. Anyone who will inform the authorities of his whereabouts will be rewarded."

Some time later a severe drought hits the village and makes survival for the poor even more difficult. Ma Liang returns and offers to draw them a water wheel to water the fields. The villagers are endlessly grateful: "He helps us regardless of his own safety. What a hero!" But his return has been discovered by the authorities and he is arrested. The villagers protest to no avail: "You can't take him away. He is a good man." The supreme official rejects the request and threatens them: "Who dares to stop me will spend the rest of his life in prison like him."

Eventually Ma Liang is sentenced to death. His brush is confiscated. But as the local officers are unable to use the tool correctly they ask Ma Liang to come out of prison and paint a golden mountain. Ma Liang does as told but also paints a big ocean around it. When the officer and his servants sail across the sea, Mia Liang waves his brush and the boat and people sink due to the squall.

Comment: Te Wei's associate, Jin Xi, would mainly focus on puppet film animation.

Award: First Prize for Excellent Films, issued by the Ministry of Culture.

First Prize for Excellent Melodramas for Children aged eight to twelve, Eighth Venice International Film Festival, 1956.

Excellent Children's Film Award, First Yugoslavia International Children's Film Festival.

First Silver Medal for Short Films, Third Damascus International Film Festival, 1956.

Special Excellent Prize for Puppet Films, Second Warsaw International Children's Film Festival, 1957.

Certificate of Merit, Stratford Shakespeare International Film Festival of Canada.

1955–1956

Why the Crow Is Black/Why Is the Crow Black-Coated?/Wuya Weishenme Shi Hei De

10 Minutes

Supervising Directors/Producers: Wan Laiming, Wan Guchan

Directors: Qian Jiajun, Li Keruo

Screenplay: Yi Fan (Liu Quan)

Photography: Chen Zhenxiang, Duan Xiao Xuan

Synopsis: A gorgeous bird entranced by its own beauty sings and dances all day long in the forest, not caring enough to prepare for the winter. When winter finally comes, the bird has no place to go. After a while, there is a fire, and the freezing animal wants to limber up but in the end all his colorful feathers are singed and turn black as coal. And thus the once so beautiful bird has transformed into a black crow.

Award: Certificate of Merit, Eighth Venice International Children's Film Festival.

1956

Plumpy Aunt Goes Back to Her Parents' Home

10 Minutes

Director: Yu Zheguang

Synopsis: When Plumpy Aunt, who has just made a new dress for her sleeping baby, receives a letter telling her that her mother is seriously ill, she prepares to leave that very night but is so scatterbrained that she starts forgetting things.

Comment: Puppet animation comedy.

The Proud General/The Conceited General/Jiao'ao De Jiangjun

23:37 Minutes
Supervising Director: Te Wei

Synopsis: The premise of the story deals with a self-obsessed general who has won a single battle. Everybody applauds the victory: "Our general has won a great battle! It's really terrific! He destroyed ten thousand enemies with one blow!"

"General," they ask him, "do you think the enemy will dare to attack us again?"

"Nonsense!" The general laughs and points to a vessel outside: "All of you, look! How heavy do you think this vessel is?" "It must be four or five, perhaps six or seven, or even eight hundred pounds!" The general approaches and to prove his strength lifts the heavy vessel, then throws it up to the sky and catches it again.

"Amazing, amazing! As long as our general is here, death is waiting for anyone who dares to attack."

"Bring me my bow! Look!" The arrows don't fail a single time.

"Bravo! Wonderful, wonderful, really wonderful! The general really is a skilled marksman! Let's drink to him!"

From then on, being rewarded by the king, the general thinks he is entitled to rest on his laurels and so starts to get idle, wining and dining and as a result losing all his abilities and interest in martial arts. He believes that all enemies will be intimidated by the sheer mention of his name: "Say, who do you think is the greatest hero?" "The greatest hero?," the sycophant, who surrounds him, reassures him, "You, General, of course!"

"We won," the yawning general persuades himself and tells everybody who wants to hear. "We don't need to practice anymore." Soon his once conquering spear is covered by spiderwebs.

Over the next months, the general becomes fat and loses all his strength and skill in archery. Suddenly the old enemy, whom the general believed had been defeated for all time, returns and, as one expected, the feisty general is unable to prevent the downfall of the nation. He even doesn't believe at first that the message is correct because nobody would challenge the number-one hero of the country: "That's stupid! Find out what's really happening! They wouldn't dare to attack me!" A second messenger arrives with a new report: "The enemy is only fifteen miles away!" "My spear! Where is my spear?" The old weapons, however, have become useless. In the end, everybody, the soldiers and with them the sycophant, prefer to leave the sinking ship.

Poster for *The Proud General* (1956).

The Proud General (1956) by Te Wei.

Comment: Te Wei: "We had a clear idea to draw useful things from the traditional arts—local opera, drama, Peking opera. From the models to the movements, we followed these operas. Most importantly, we invited opera teachers to the film studio to show us how to move."

The film was first received skeptically but eventually was hailed as a Party allegory, reminding audiences that even the highest in rank must be humble and watchful, as China still thought itself surrounded by enemies.

We shouldn't forget that in February 1956 Khrushchev in Moscow had delivered his "Secret Speech" and soon was to join the list of enemies.

As Shanghai Animation Studio hadn't been established at the time, the production, which resembles the work of Ivan Ivanov-Vano, was probably completed at Shangying Studio.

1957

Pull the Radish

10:14 Minutes
Director: Qian Jiajun
Screenplay: Guo Liang

Synopsis: A cute, white rabbit looking for food finds what turns out a giant radish, but he cannot pull it out himself. Only with the help of many others, including a monkey, a pig and a bear, is the rabbit able to achieve his goal: *Together we preserve.*

Comment: Pull the Radish was the first animated film produced by Shanghai Animation Film Studio after it was officially established. Although it was an animation short, it embodied the Chinese art style of entertainment with an educational background. It is also indicated that Chinese animation would gradually break away from the influence of the Soviet, Czechoslovakian, Polish and other East European styles, although it still looked just like them. Over the next years a Chinese animation school was formed.

1958

Across Monkey Mountain/ Crossing Monkey Mountain

10 Minutes
Director: Wan Guchan
Animation: Wan Guchan, Hu Jinqing,
    Dai Tielang
Screenplay: Wang Zheng Zhong
Photography: Wang Sheng Rong

Synopsis: An old man, selling straw hats, takes a nap under a tree on the Monkey Mountain. A gang of monkeys watches him. They are greedy for the straw hats. They steal them and take refuge in the tree. The old man wakes up and gets angry when he sees what has happened. The naughty monkeys wearing the straw hats imitate the old man's every move. When he realizes this, the old man devises a stratagem. He deliberately throws his hat to the ground and hopes that the monkeys will do the same. Eventually he takes out a gourd full of wine and starts to drink. As a result the monkeys become drunk too. While the drunken monkeys are sleeping it off the old man collects the hats and gets away.

***Across Monkey Mountain* (1958).**

Comment: This was the first funny, Chinese animation that was based genuinely on Chinese humor, which is quite different from Disney style.

Date Tree of Old Lady
10 Minutes

Synopsis: Little animals help an old lady harvest dates.

Little Carps Jump Over the Dragon Gate/The Small Carp Jump Over the Dragon Gate

Director: He Yumen
Animation Design: Duan Jun, Wang Zhengzhong, Jiao Yesong, Hang Zhixing
Screenwriter: Jing Ji
Scenic Art: Gaoyang, Jiang Aijian
Musical Score: Zhang Yun Qing
Photography: Duan Xiao Xuan

Synopsis: The carp grandmother tells the little carps the story of their ancestors, of those carps that jumped over the Dragon Gate. She says that behind this gate are Heaven and Paradise. But she also says that only the bravest of carps can do it. After listening, all little carps are eager to volunteer and want to jump over the gate. They start to look around for the fabled gate, under the leadership of a big black carp. They swim across river and rapids, overcome difficulties, and finally arrive at a grand reservoir. They are very happy, as they think this is the gate they were looking for. However, they are unable to jump over it and are washed away by the current. Finally the black carp has an idea and has the carps jump over it one by one. When they reach the reservoir, they are surprised by the modern construction with illuminated factories, high-rise buildings and running cars. They ask a swallow to tell them where they are. The swallow tells them that this is the Dragon Gate Reservoir, so the little carps believe they really jumped over the Dragon Gate. They ask the swallow to carry a message back to Grandma and invite her to join them at this wonderful place.

Award: Silver Medal for Animated Films, First Moscow International Film Festival, 1959.

Little Carps Jump Over the Dragon Gate (1958).

Pigsy Eats Watermelons/Zhu Bajie Eats Watermelon/Zhu Bajie Chi Xihua

15 Minutes
Director: Wan Guchan
Consultant: Wan Laiming
Animation: Hu Jinqing, Chen Zhengong, Zhan Tong, Liu Fengzhan, Xie Yougen, Chen Hui, Du Chunfu

Synopsis: When Tang priest Xuanzang asks his faithful escort, Sun Wukong, to find something to eat, Pigsy insists on accompanying the Monkey King. Having found a tasty watermelon Pigsy cuts it into four pieces, one for the Buddhist monk, one for Sun Wukong, and one for Friar Sand, but in the end he eats all by himself. To teach him a lesson Sun Wukong transforms himself into a piece of watermelon peel that is going to fool Pigsy.

Comment: Pigsy is no other than the pig character, Zhu Bajie, also named Zhu Wuneng, who starred alongside the Monkey King in *Journey to the West* and, as with most pig characters, is associated with greed.

This was the first Chinese cut-paper animation and has been recognized for its distinctive folk-art characteristics. It opened a new venue for the development of cut-paper animation in China. Since then, cut-paper animation has been understood as relatively independent form of animation art. Although the volume of production was not that large, it was well received by audiences domestically as well as abroad.

It was Wan Guchan who introduced the technique when he returned to Shanghai. His idea coincided with the studio's plan to develop animated films that had a clear national style and so was approved by studio head Te Wei. A unit was formed with Wan Guchan in charge, assisted by Chen Zhenghong, Zhan Tong, Liu Fengzhan, Xie Yougen, Chen Hui, Du Chunfu, and Hu Jinqing, who later would himself become an accomplished director of cut-paper animation. Their first test animation failed, but a year later they were able to finish this film, which received great critical acclaim.

1959

The Carved Dragon/Inscription of Dragons

Directors: Wan Chaochen, Yan Lei, Zhang Chaoqun

Synopsis: The tale of a carpenter who carves a dragon in order to defeat a monster.

Comment: Puppet animation.

Pigsy Eats Watermelons **(1958).**

Chuang Tapestry/Chwang Tapestry

60 Minutes
Director: Qian Jagun
Screenplay: Gan Xiao Niu

Synopsis: For three consecutive years, day and night, Mother Tanja of the Chuang family is found weaving a precious tapestry. One day a heavy storm blows the tapestry away. Mother Tanja is heartbroken and becomes very ill, her hair turning grey. One of the children, a teenage boy by the name of Kam Tong, dares to travel to the dangerous mountains of Tibet to get the tapestry back. Magic makes the stone statue of a huge tiger alive and transforms it into his faithful riding animal. Together they pass many dangerous places and overcome a fierce fire dragon. In Tibet, Kam Tong is welcomed to a place of noble females who are producing copies of the precious tapestry. While the young man sleeps, the head mistress weaves her own image into the pastoral scene that the tapestry depicts, then returns it to him. On his tiger, Kam Tong returns home with the tapestry to save the life of his mother. Using the healing power of the tapestry, the woman recovers and her grey hair turns black again. And the very scene that we see in the tapestry becomes reality, includ-ing the image of the noble maid the hero has met in Tibet. Only the tiger turns to stone again.

Comment: First feature-length cartoon to be produced in the People's Republic. The same year the movie was made, in March 1959, the PLA finally broke Tibet's uprising and forced the Dalai Lama to flee.

Award: Karlovy Vary International Film Festival, Czech Republic, 1960, nomination only.

Cricket Fighting by Ji Gong/Ji Gong Dou Xishuai

23 Minutes
Director: Wan Guchan
Screenplay: Wu Lun

Synopsis: Set in the Southern Song Dynasty. The son of Prime Minister Luo has won a lot of money from cricket fighting. Accidentally, while removing the lid from the jar, Zhang Yu, a carpenter, lets the prize-winning cricket escape. The prime minister's son fumes and requires compensation within three days. Zhang Yu returns with a half-dead cricket he has acquired from Ji Gong. Ji Gong asserts that this cricket could beat a rooster. In the end, the cricket defeats the rooster, and the prime minister's son buys it for 500 ounces of silver. The cricket, however, upturns the whole residence, and the prime minister's son is buried under the ruins.

Comment: Cut-paper animation not only appeared very Chinese in style and so became the standard for many films to come, but was also cheaper than full animation. It was certainly a variation on limited animation techniques.

Cuckoo Is Late

Director: Quin Jiajun

Comment: At Shanghai Animation Film Studio, Quin Jiajun was regarded as a master in Chinese water painting and was always happy to try out new things in art.

Fisher Boy/Fishing Child/Fishing Boy/ Yu Tong

22 Minutes
Director: Wan Guchan
Character and Action Design: Hu Jinqing, Qian Jia, Shen Zuwei

Synopsis: After the Opium War, the imperialists who have occupied China's harbors prohibit fishermen from doing their work. One night an old, white-bearded fisherman ventures through the blockade line in stormy weather, but what he finally catches on a rough sea is not a fish but a white jade fish jar engraved with the image of a fisher boy. At midnight, the painted fisher boy jumps out of the fish jar. He starts fishing from the jar with his fishing rod, conjuring very large pearls. Next day a surprised but happy fisherman sells the pearls on the market and hopes to buy a new fishing boat. But a nasty foreign Jesuit unravels the secret and claims in front of imperial authorities that he is the rightful owner of the fish jar. Infuriated, the old fisherman smashes the jar in public to prevent it from falling into the dishonest priest's hands. Suddenly the magic fisher boy appears again, creates turmoil and throws the lying priest into the sea. The fisherman and the other poor Chinese, however, will keep the precious jar in honor.

Comment: Cut-paper animation based on a popular story from the so-called Boxer rebellion.

Award: Second Prize, Second National Teenage Art Creation Competition, 1980.

CHAPTER 5

The 1960s: Havoc and the Cultural Revolution

The period 1957–1965 became the first prosperous time for Chinese animation, as it tried to find its own style. This period ended with the Cultural Revolution.

All productions in this chapter are by Shanghai Animation Film Studio (Shanghai Fine Art Studio).

 **The Films**

1960

The Clever Ducklings/Congming De Yazi
7:39 Minutes
Director: Yu Zhenguang

Synopsis: Three ducklings that play around wake a cat. The cat chases them, but they outwit it and crawl into a stove pipe, becoming totally black. This shocks the cat to no end and frightens it away.

Comment: This short film for the first time adapted the folk craft technique of folded paper, a forerunner of Japanese origami. It was made in the aftermath of the Great Leap Forward, when the Shanghai Studio experimented with different animation techniques and styles. The technique was only used in a few other films.

Coy Nightingale
Director: Jiang Aiqun

Synopsis: A nightingale, although a good singer, never dares to sing in public because it is too timid and shy. To encourage it, its mother consults with a Chinese bulbul and then asks the child to find a learned teacher. Where is the experienced teacher? The little nightingale finally overcomes the psychological hurdle.

1960–1961

Where Is Momma?/Little Tadpoles Looking for Their Mother/Little Tadpoles Look for Mamma/Little Tadpoles Look for Their Mummy/Xiao Ke Dou Zhao Ma Ma
14 Minutes
Directors: Te Wei, Tang Cheng
Animation Design: Tang Cheng, Wu Qiang, Yan Dingxian, Xu Jing-Up, Dai Tielang, Lin Xiao, Duan Jun, Pu Eric, Lu Jin, Yang Suying, Ge Zhiyuan
Musical Score: Wu Ying-Ju
Photography: Duan Xiao Xuan, Yu Yung
Background Design: Transnatured such as Fang Peng
Technical Guidance: Qian Jiajun

Synopsis: Little tadpoles that just have been born are curious to find their mom. In search of their "mama" (and identity), they meet other creatures in the pond: "Uncle Shrimp," a goldfish, the white belly of a crab, a tortoise and even a large catfish, all mistaken for their mom. Eventually, after suffering a series of twists and turns, they find their real mother—a frog.

Comment: Encouraged by Vice President Chen Yi, who, while visiting an exhibition dedicated to film animation, suggested Te Wei animate the work of contemporary painter Qi Baishi (1864–1957), who was famous for his illustrations of fish and shrimps,

Where Is Momma? (1960–61)

Te Wei did as he was told and made this little film in the traditional form of brush-painting. The tedious animation process was supervised by Te Wei's associate, Ms. Tang Cheng, with Te Wei claiming almost all credit for himself. Tang Cheng (1919–1986) was born in Anhui, the daughter of a teacher and a painter, and grew up in Shanghai. A protracted illness led to her being trained as a painter by her father.

With *Where Is Momma?* the Shanghai studio started a trend of ink animation. The film begins with simple and elegant Chinese paintings on screen, just like opening a book. The audience is led into a beautifully lyrical inked world. The small tadpoles themselves are lively and lovely, just like a bunch of innocent kids.

Awards: Best Animated Movie Prize at the First Chinese "Hundred Flower" Festival, 1962 (the Annual Awards were established by *Popular Movies Magazine*).

Silver Sail Award for Short Films, Four-

teenth Locarno International Film Festival, Switzerland.

Children's Film Award, Fourth Annecy International Animation Festival, France.

Honorable Prize, Seventeenth Cannes International Film Festival, France.

First Prize, Third Zagreb World Festival of Animated Films.

Second Prize, Fourth International Children and Youth Festival, Centre Georges Pompidou in Paris, France.

1961–1962

Ginseng Baby/The Spirit of Ginseng
Director: Wan Guchan

Synopsis: Huzi (literally, "Tigerskin") who is sold as a child laborer to a landowner named Hu Guapi (literally, "Skinner"), overthrows the moneybag with the help of a ginseng plant's spirit.

Comment: Cut-out animation.

Opposite: *Where Is Momma?* (1960–61).

Ginseng Baby (1961–62).

Awards: Honorary Prize, Fourth Leipzig International Documentary and Short Film Festival, GDR, 1961.

Silver Mermaid Award for Best Children's Film, First Alexander International Film Festival, 1979.

1962

A Cabbage
Comment: Another folded paper animation.

Scatterbrain and Crosspatch
20:46 Minutes
Director: Zhang Songlin
Animation: Chang Guangxi and others
Synopsis: There are two boys. "Scatterbrain" (Meitounao) usually forgets things and is careless, while "Crosspatch" (Bugaoxing)

Director Zhang Songlin near the end of his life.

has a horrible temper, is always querulous and constantly grim-faced. Temporarily both of them are turned into adults to overcome their respective weaknesses. After bringing so much trouble on themselves and others, they finally master their flaws.

Comment: This film shows Director Zhang Songlin's unique and creative understanding of animation, says Zhang's former student, Chang Guangxi: "The film tells a modern story with a humorous tone at a time when animation was basically adapted from folk stories and myths."[1]

Scatterbrain and Crosspatch (1962).

In style, reminiscent of the Polish TV series *Bolek and Lolek*, which incidentally started the same year.

Wait for Tomorrow/Let's Wait for Tomorrow

14 Minutes
Director: Hu Xiong Hua
   Synopsis: When it begins to rain all the animals seek shelter in their houses. Only the monkey was too lazy to build one, and wouldn't do so even in the future. As a result he is poured on again.
   Comment: Cut-paper animation.

1961–1964

Havoc in Heaven/Uproar in Heaven/Da Nao Tian Gong

Originally released in two parts.
First Part: 50 Minutes
Second Part: 70 Minutes
Director: Wan Laiming
Co-director: Tang Cheng
Animation Design: Yan Dingxian, Duan Rui, Pu Jiaxing, Lin Wenxiao, Guan Guanyun, Zhang Shiming, Yanshan Chun, Duan Jun, Lu Qing, Yan Shanchun, Wang Shirong, Ge Guiyun, Duan Xiaoxuan
Voice Actors: Qiu Yiefeng (Sun Wukong), Fu Runsheng (Emperor Jade), Shang Hua (Taibaijinxing)
Screenplay: Li Kerou, Wan Laiming
Art and Design: Zhang Guangyu, Zhang Zhengyu
Photography: Duan Xiao Xun
Editor: Xu Zhenzhu
Musical Score: Wu Ying-Ju
Shanghai Film Orchestra, Shanghai Peking Opera Theatre
Conductors: Chen Chuanxi, Zhang Xinhai, Wang Yupu

   Synopsis: The heavenly adventures of the Monkey King, Sun Wukong.
   One day atop the Flower-Fruit Mountain, a magical monkey called Sun Wukong is born out of magic stones that fell down to Earth long ago when Goddess Nuwa mended the broken sky.
   With his magical powers, Sun discovers the Water-Curtain Cave and is hailed as the Monkey King by the other monkeys. But he agonizes over the lack of a good weapon and decides to visit the underwater palace of the Dragon King of the Eastern Seas to seek something suitable. The arrogant Dragon King lets Sun know that he can borrow and take away anything that he is able to pick up. To the king's surprise, Sun manages to pick up the massive pillar used by the Dragon King to pin down the sea. This heavy golden-banded staff *Ruyi Jingu Bang* or "Golden-As-You-Will Cudgel" (which also can change to any size) the Monkey King is going to convert into a mighty weapon to challenge Heaven itself.
   The infuriated Dragon King turns to the Celestial Jade Emperor to accuse the Monkey King of robbery and to petition for the return of the pillar. Following the advice of the God

Poster art for *Havoc in Heaven*, starring Sun Wukong, the Monkey King (1961–64).

Both photographs: Original Designs for *Havoc in Heaven* (1961–64).

of the Great White Star, the Jade Emperor entices Sun with the official post of "Protector of the Imperial Horses" to keep him under close supervision in Heaven.

When the Monkey King discovers the plot, the revolutionary monkey wrecks the imperial stables and returns to Flower-Fruit Mountain. The Jade Emperor sends Heavenly King Li, his son Nezha who has three heads and six arms, and the huge God of Mighty Miracles to capture the defiant monkey, but after a fierce battle they all are defeated by the Monkey King's acrobatics.

Again, the Jade Emperor sends the Great White Star to entice the Monkey King, granting him the coveted title "Great Sage Equaling Heaven" and appointing him guardian of the imperial peach orchard.

But he soon starts eating the forbidden peaches and learns from the Seven Fairies that he is not even invited to the empress' annual "Peach Banquet." Realizing that he has been tricked again, he creates havoc in heaven, eats the Pill of Immortality Lord Lao has made for the emperor himself, and steals the Immortal Wine.

Jade Emperor is so furious that he sends the entire celestial army to catch the mischievous monkey. The quick-witted Sun uses all his cunning and artfulness to overcome the 100,000 heavenly warriors. Finally Lord Lao captures him but the Monkey King cannot be executed by the Demon-Beheading Plat-

form. Lord Lao locks him up in his furnace and tries to burn him, which only adds to the Monkey's magic power. When the Monkey King fights back and heads for the celestial court, even the Jade Emperor has to run for his life.

Comment: The most ambitious project of Chinese animation marked Wan Laiming's

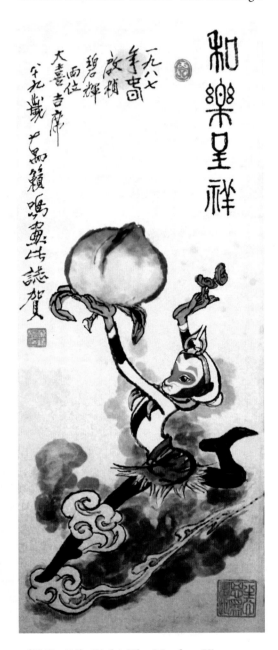

Left: **Original Designs for *Havoc in Heaven* (1961–64).** *Right:* **The Monkey King.**

万籁鸣 口述   万国魂 执笔

我与孙悟空

WO YU SUN WU KONG

return to *Journey to the West,* one of the four great classical novels of Chinese literature, written in the 16th century (during the Ming Dynasty) by Wu Cheng'en. This time Wan Laiming adapted the incidents that happened before the Monkey King's punishment (creating havoc against the old-age authorities in heaven).

It took four years, from 1960 to 1964, to finish *Havoc in Heaven.* Apparently, the decision to make the film was taken after Japan's Toei Company released their own version of the classic Chinese myth (*Sa-yuki,* released in 1960), transforming the Monkey King into a cute, boyish little ape that had nothing to do with the Chinese original.[2]

Wan Laiming later recalled the massive production:

> Li Kerou and I were asked to write the story. The first thing we worried about was whether we would dare to present

Top: Havoc in Heaven *(1961–64).* *Left:* **Wan Laiming,** Havoc in Heaven *(1961–64).*

Havoc in Heaven (1961–64).

the story as it was told in the book. It was a sensitive issue at the time. We studied the first seven chapters of *Journey to the West* and believed it to have profound significance—the sharp contrasts of conflict and struggle between the oppressor and oppressed within the mythological context. In *Uproar in Heaven,* the dramatic conflict is mainly between the Monkey King and the rulers headed up by Emperor Jade. Throughout a series of adventures, the Monkey King matures, and uses his courageous ingenuity, unyielding character and tenacity to prevail.

The Monkey King has the characteristics of a real monkey. He's a lively and nimble prankster. But he is also a God who will change 72 times, or become invisible at will. Human beings certainly do not have these features. He is also thoughtful and upright, so in the shaping of the character, it was necessary to exaggerate some aspects and use our imagination. Zhang Guangyu, the main designer, together with Yan Dingxian and Lin Wenxiao made the characters in the film come vividly to life, and they deserve a great deal of credit for the success of the movie.

For each scene, we paid particular attention to the setting and atmosphere in order to unify the scenes with the personality and style of the characters. We absorbed the best essence of Chinese folk art tradition, and added to it our own imagination. As a result, the film has a very special flavor. Because of the fantasized atmosphere of the myth, we strived to construct a unity of rich colors, refinement towards simplicity and a shaping of the images that is more "vague" than "real." By doing this, we achieved a greater artistic effect.

The pacing of the film adopted many techniques of montage, so the story develops quickly, avoiding a slow unfolding of the plot. We made use of typical Chinese folk music—the drums and percussion instruments commonly used in Pekling opera. This added a strong sense of rhythm to the action of the figures.[3]

Duan Xiao Xun, who also photographed Te Wei's work, handled the cinematography and accomplished a lot of colorful effects: "The Monkey King's weapon is called the 'Jingu Bang.' It looks like a glittering red stick with yellow on both ends. In order to make it glow and sparkle, we employed multiple exposures, and it proved to be a very successful technique in the film."[4]

Nearly 70,000 drawings were done. The

first part was officially released in 1961 to great critical acclaim and with much success. The second part was finished in 1964 but could not be released due to a change in the politics of art and culture that led to the so-called Cultural Revolution. During this period, Shanghai Animation Film Studio was amongst the institutions criticized. *Havoc in Heaven* was accused of being directed against Chairman Mao. The Monkey King was seen as a rebel not only against Heaven but against Mao's authority although, in a way, he was leading a sort of Cultural Revolution himself. The original painting, animation, and film prints were damaged and would disappear. (Ironically, this is very similar to what had happened to Eisenstein's second part of *Ivan Grozny* in Soviet Russia.)

Havoc in Heaven (1961–64).

Background art, *Havoc in Heaven* (1961–64).

Only a few drawings were left; these became very valuable relics of Chinese animation art. The artists did not escape persecution either. Wan Laiming, the director, was detained. The co-director, Ms. Tang Cheng, and Yan Dingxian were sent to the countryside for re-education and reform through hard labor.

In 1978, eventually, *Havoc in Heaven* was released as a whole domestically and abroad and found recognition all over the world.

Mr. Jin Guoping, the formal head of Shanghai Animation Film Studio, analyzes the reasons for the success as follows:

First, this part of Chinese mythology is a good topic for animation. It can be naturally expressed by means of animation.

Second, the main character, Monkey King, was described and created as a vivid and attractive being. The character design was very impressive. It can stand the test of time.

Third, the quality of production was on a high level. Everything in the film was arranged very well.

Fourth, the atmosphere during production was creative. The Studio supported a very good team helmed by the director, Mr. Wan Laiming, and mobilized excellent artists to work on the film.[5]

Interestingly, some years later there was a short paper-cut animation about a boy sitting in front of a TV set watching clips from the original *Monkey King*; the character suddenly comes out of the TV and takes the boy to the world of imaginative science, travelling to outer space as well as underwater.

Awards: Best Art Film Award, Second Chinese "Hundred Flowers" Festival, 1963.

Special Award for short films, Thirteenth Karlovy Vary International Film Festival.

Third Prize, Fifth Quito International Children's Film Festival, Ecuador.

Jury Prize, Twelfth Figueira Da Foz International Film Festival, Portugal.

Screened at Locarno Festival, 1965, and awarded at the Twenty-second London International Film Festival, where it was regarded as the most stirring and moving film in the festival in 1978.

Once again, it was well received in Paris. Twelve cinemas jointly premiered this film and screened it for more than a month in 1983. It was released worldwide to more than forty countries and regions, creating the record of Chinese film export.

Selected by *Asia Weekly* magazine from over 10,000 Chinese films to be one of the "100 best Chinese films in the 20th century."

Mr. Cheng Huangmei, a famous Chinese film critic, wrote in his preface to the book *I and Monkey King* by Mr. Wan Laiming:

The internationally acclaimed *Havoc in Heaven* finally put Chinese animation on the peak of global animation film history. When this film was shown in America where animation occupies a prominent position and is world market leader, Associated Press reported: "American people showed greatest interest in *Havoc in Heaven,* because the film is vivid and colorful, just a bit like *Fantasia.* It was even more exciting than the works of Disney. For America it would have been impossible to produce such a film."[6]

Kane Ruskin, an American reviewer, believed that *Havoc in Heaven* "can be compared with Biblical myths and Greek legends. They all are filled with boundless originality, fascinating events, heroic deeds and wonderful wit. We are moved by outstanding art design. It is an inspiring and exciting film. By this film director Wan Laiming is ranked into the history of international animation film."[7]

* * *

Havoc in Heaven was restored and re-released in 2012.

92 Minutes
Directors: Su Da, Chen Zhihong
Presented and Produced by Ren Zhonglun
Executive Producers: Frederic Rose, Wang Tianyun
Producer: Qian Jianping
Chief Production Supervisor: Zhu Yuping
Voice Actors: Li Yang (Sun Wukong), Chen Kaige (Dragon King of the Eastern Sea), Feng Xiaogang (Lord Lao), Liu Ye (Heavenly King Li), Zhang Guoli (God of the Great White Star), Chen Daoming (Celestial Jade Emperor), Liu Xiaoqing (The Empress Queen Mother), Yao Chen (Eldest Fairy), He Ling (Nezha), Chen Peisi (Local Guardian God), Zhou Libo (Lord of the Imperial Stables)
Supervisor of Restoration: Tom Burton
3D Conversion Director: Pierre (Pete) Routhier
3D Version Consultants: Yan Dingxian, Lin Wenxiao, Chang Guangxi
Production Design: Zhang Guangyu, Zhang Zhengyu
Sound Design: Wong Ken
Composer: Wu Yingju
Sound Recordist: Liang Yingjun
Editor: Xu Zhenzhu

Dubbing Director: Di Feifei
Digital Restoration and 3D Conversion: Technicolor, Los Angeles

Half a century after they had started the ambitious project, Shanghai Animation Film Studio and producer Jianping Qian restored the colorful epic—celebrating the Year of the Dragon—in stereoscopic 3D, thanks to the labs of Technicolor in Los Angeles. They even had to change the aspect ratio (the original was made in the old Academy ratio) which means that for every scene set extension had to be executed perfectly matching the color and style of the old movie. By the way, new adventures of the Monkey King are waiting in the wings from Shanghai Animation (although the box-office receipts of the re-release didn't meet exactly with the expectations).

The directors commented on the restoration and 3D conversion:

Fifty years ago "The Father of Chinese Animation"—Wan Laiming—made his masterpiece "The Monkey King—Uproar in Heaven" which was based on the first seven chapters of the classic novel "Journey to the West." The film had spectacular and vivid colours, distinctive characters, grand sets and a unique Chinese flavor. All the key creatives who worked on the film, like the character designer, background designer, composer, conductor and voice-over artists are all masters in their profession at the time. The film not only made over 100 million yuans at the box office within a few years, it also created a big splash in the international animation world....

Fifty years later, we have worked with the world's largest post-production company Technicolor to combine tradition with new technology, in order to give a new life to the ultimate masterpiece of Chinese animation—"The Monkey King—Uproar in Heaven." We have used the latest and most advanced technology in the world to create a brand new 3D version of the classic. We have also condensed the original 110 minutes that were made up of two episodes into an 86 minutes theatrical version. With the latest technology from our U.S. specialists, a massive amount of work was undertaken in the digitization, repair and restoration of the original negative, color grading as well as the conversion from 2D to wide-screen 3D.

Our guiding principle in the creative process is respect for our classics and the continuation and future development of our heritage. In order to retain the original flavor of the classic, artistically "The Monkey King—Uproar in Heaven 3D" has preserved the traditional Chinese style. The rhythm for both the film and the actions has also become tighter. In order to achieve a three-dimensional look and the unique sensation of 3D viewing, we have specifically designed and drawn by hand the special treatments needed for an "out-of-the-screen/at your face" sensation for over 20 scenes. The original music score and voice-overs were brilliant additions to the film but due to technological limitations at the time, all the sound was recorded on a single track only and so cannot be recreated. That is why in the 3D version all the composition, accompaniment, performance, voice-overs and sound effects have to be totally created again.

Musically we have retained the original Chinese characteristics by preserving the percussion style of Peking Opera, but we have also drawn on Western harmonic techniques and popular modern rhythms. In addition, we have utilized Western instruments to achieve a bigger and more powerful surround sound for the cinema, which is different from the singular operatic sound utilized for the entire film in the past. With regard to choice of musical instruments we have adopted a mix and match approach. We continue to use typical Chinese instruments—like "suona" (a small Chinese trumpet), Chinese flute, "sheng" (a wind instrument), the Chinese dulcimer or "yangqin," string instruments like "pipa," "sanxian," "daruan," "banhu" and "erhu" etc.—as the key instruments for the melody, while adopting Western instruments as accompaniment to add more weight and substance to the sound.

Percussion music will also be another highlight in this film. Peking Opera drums and gongs will be matched with Western percussion instruments like timpanis and base drums. The special digital 5.1 sound system will also make the film more dramatic and realistic while making the viewing experience more enjoyable. Musical themes for the different scenes are another important aspect of the score. Modern electronic music has opened up many more possibilities for scoring the background themes. It is no longer hard to differentiate between "Heaven" and "Earth," "Fairies" and "Human," with electronic instruments playing a big role in portraying the different sounds. For the voice-overs we have chosen to work with the most accomplished and experienced actors to re-create the roles, with the aim of perfecting the image of each character. We do not just want to sound like the characters, we also want to strengthen each individual character's personality.

We hope that the current 3D version of "The Monkey King—Uproar in Heaven" is not merely a replay of the old classic, but a brand new and dramatic experience of sight and sound. The film shall show the world the charisma of a new style of "Modern Chinese" animation. The life-force and aesthetics of classic Chinese animation shall become a continuing legacy that may flourish with even more splendor.[8]

The Cowherd's Flute (1963).

1963

Cowherd's Flute/Mu Di

20 Minutes
Supervising Director: Te Wei
Technical Director (Animation): Qian Jiajun
Screenplay: Te Wei
Photography: Duan Xiao Xuan
Background Design: Franciscan Congregation
Animation Design: Wu Qiang Jiao, Lin Xiao, Dai Tielang
Art Director: Fang Peng
Composer: Wu Ying-Ju

Synopsis: A cowherd, good at playing the flute, grazes his water buffalo in the morning and takes a rest under a tree, falling asleep. In his dream he sees himself waking up but cannot find his water buffalo. Still dreaming, he searches, walking along the mountain road, then turning into a ravine wilderness. On the way, he keeps asking about the whereabouts of the cows: he asks some urchins, the woodcutter and the fisherman. Under their guidance he finds himself in a beautiful scenery. There are magnificent waterfalls pouring down from the cliff on the rocks directly toward the clear pools. There is a splashing score composed of the wonderful sounds of nature. The cowherd finds the buffalo enjoying the beautiful lakeside. He wants the animal to return with him. The water buffalo, however, disobeys and even fights him. This makes the cowherd angry. Suddenly he remembers the flute. He picks up some bamboo and produces a simple bamboo flute. Playing soft tunes, he manages to pacify the buffalo and gets him back. The cowherd is delighted to embrace the beloved animal. When he wakes up and realizes that it all was a dream, he leads the buffalo back into sunset.

Comment: An homage to Li Keran, famous for his paintings of the countryside south of the Yangtze River. At the first glimpse, there is not much of a story, just a boy and his flute, a water buffalo and nature, all in perfect harmony.

Production was started in 1961. The film was completed and released in 1963. Several famous Chinese artists were involved in the creation. It was an idyllic work that reflected the tradi-

Cowherd's Flute (1963).

Cowherd's Flute.

tional Chinese philosophy of harmony between heaven and human beings.

The innocent cowherd, babbling brooks and swaying bamboo always convey the delicate and subtle feelings of Chinese aesthetics. It was entirely in a Chinese art style. Each shot looked like a painting in itself. From then on, Chinese propaganda considered good painting the most important art aspect in animation, not movement. Te Wei, although highly influential in art style but being not interested in the technique of animation, left a rather stiff view of animation.

The animation and background art were created by ink painting. The relationship between form and meaning in Chinese painting has been discussed for centuries among Chinese artists and scholars. One of the great painters named Qi Baishi said that when he paints a reality subject, he does not try to copy it but rather to express the very spirit of it. Chinese ink animation combines the meaning of Chinese poetic painting with Western animation narrative and provides a new kind of artistic expression.

Award: Gold Medal at the Danish Third Odense International Fairy Tale Film Festival 1979.

Golden Conch/Jinse De Hailuo

40 Minutes
Directors: Wan Guchan, Qian Yunda
Screenplay: Bao Lei

Synopsis: The golden conch, caught by a young man by the name of Aniu who lives by the sea, miraculously transforms into the blue sea fairy Hailuo, a snail girl who has fallen in love with the handsome fisherman and changed into gold out of admiration for him. The girl starts to clean his house. Aniu wants to know why she is caring for him. The girl explains her nature and tells him that she wants to make friends with him. After a series of trials and tribulations, Aniu and the fairy marry and live happily ever after.

Comment: In style, a variation on Chinese shadow puppets and the ancient art of paper cuts.

Award: Lumumba Prize, Asia-Africa International Film Festival, 1964.

The Peacock Princess/Peacock Flying Southeast

Director: Jin Xi (Jin Shi)

Synopsis: Located in Xishuangbanna, China's tropical rain forest. The king of Peacock Kingdom has seven daughters, each more beautiful than the last, but the most beloved is the seventh. Her name is Nan Muluna. All Peacock princesses could fly. One day they flew to the Golden Lake, where Nan Muluna caught the attention of the Prince of Mengbanzha. Soon they married and became a couple. The romantic love story of Princess Nan Muluna and the prince of Mengbanzha, however, is interrupted by an evil vulture who has transformed himself into a magician. The vulture-turned-magician hates the prince and does everything to cause him grief. The prince is given a bow that only superhuman strength can flex to fight for his love and reunion with his beloved wife.

Comment: First feature-length puppet animation that was based on a legend of the Thai People, something like the *Swan Lake* of the East.

1964

Almost/More or Less

10 Minutes

Director: Hu Xiong Hua

Synopsis: Xiao Lin, who had been careless in learning archery, is almost eaten by a wolf.

Comment: Cut-paper animation.

The Cock Crows at Midnight/Midnight Crow/Le coq chanté à minuit (France)/ Ban Ye Ji Jiao

Director: You Lei

Screenplay: Yu Ho-King, Zhang Songlin

Synopsis: The landlord who Kao Yupao, a little peasant boy, works for is especially sly and greedy. This mean exploiter, whose name is Chou, is the "skinner" of his laborers. He makes the farmhands work very hard and gives them little to eat. Naturally, they hate him. Apparently, the landlord's rooster has a strange habit: it doesn't crow at dawn, it crows at midnight. And when it starts to crow, the landlord, who begrudges his people any rest, shouts: "Get up, you lazy-bones. Get

The Cock Crows at Midnight (1964).

The Cock Crows at Midnight (1964).

up and go to work." One night Kao Yupao sees the landlord steal into the courtyard and start to crow at midnight, just like a cock would do. So that is the trick. When Kao Yupao tells the other farmhands, they decide to teach the landlord a lesson. The next night, as soon as the landlord appears, Kao Yupao cries out: "Stop thief! Stop thief!" Immediately all farmhands turn up, knock the supposed "thief" and give him a whipping. From then on, the cock would nevermore crow at midnight and the farmhands would have their deserved rest.

Comment: This puppet animation is based on an episode in the autobiography of Red Army fighter Kao Yupao, who grew up in Taiping in the bleak province of northeastern China. He was denied the chance to attend school but at age twenty, as an illiterate Communist soldier, enrolled in a new kind of class that enabled him to eventually write his life story and publish it in forty chapters: "Kao Yupao: Story of a Poor Peasant Boy."

Award: Second Prize, Second National Teenage Art Creation Competition, 1980.

New Things on the Roadside
15 Minutes
Synopsis: A boy takes a bus to the countryside and joins the peasants.

Comment: Puppet film starring Young Pioneers wearing red scarves and idealized peasants working in the commune.

Red Army Bridge
Director: Qian Yunda

Synopsis: Set in Hunan province. A bridge is being destroyed by fleeing landlords but repaired by soldiers of the People's Liberation Army and defended against the Kuomintang troops by a collective of peasants.

Comment: Cut-paper animation by Qian Yunda, who had studied with Jiří Trnka.

Singing and Dancing on the Lake

Comment: Folded paper animation.

1965

Diary of Xiao Lin
10 Minutes
Director: Hu Jinqing

Synopsis: Stories from the diary of a Young Pioneer who has just entered school and is joined by an illiterate adult.

Little Sisters of Grassland/Heroic Little Sisters on the Grassland
40 Minutes
Directors: Qian Yunda, Tang Cheng

Synopsis: Two Mongolian teenage sisters, Long Mei and Yu Rong, risk their lives to protect their commune's sheep herd during a sudden snowstorm. The older sister saves the younger one.

Comment: "To protect the sheep," Yu Rong sings, "we fear neither the cold nor the blizzard. Ah, the beacon of revolution is shining in the hearts of the little sisters. To protect the property of the collective, we fear neither frost-bite nor hunger. Ah, Communist thoughts are beaming over the little heroes."

Little Sisters of Grassland is supposedly based on a true story that happened in Inner Mongolia in the 1960s. Films such as this and

Both photographs: *Little Sisters of Grassland* (1965).

The Cock Crows at Midnight, Red Army Bridge and *Diary of Xiao Lin* foreshadowed the so-called Great Proletarian Cultural Revolution (Wenhua Dageming, 1966–1976).

Luckily, apart from the inevitable Mao portrait on the wall and some dialogue, the picture is less propagandistic than its companion features and today still holds a certain charm thanks to the characterization of the heroic sisters.

*   *   *

During the Cultural Revolution, Shanghai Animation Studio was closed down by the Red Guards. Te Wei recalls:

Little Sisters of Grassland (1965).

They demanded I write self-criticism, not only pertaining to my own film, but all the films they thought were not right, because I was, after all, the director of the Studio at that time. I really didn't understand what they were after and why. I wrote the self-criticism I felt I could justifiably write, but they were not satisfied. They asked me to write it again and again, and I grew sick, with a stomach disease. In the end they wrote it instead of me. All this happened even before the Cultural Revolution. When I came back, I was "welcomed" by a multitude of banners spread over the walls of the Studio, all of which were criticizing me. My crimes were named. "The person who walked on the Capitalist Road" and "Reactionary intellectual."[9]

And Yan Dingxian, who would become head of the studio from 1985–1989 and was married to female director Lin Wenxiao, recalled:

For eight years, from 1965 to 1973, we couldn't do animation. We were laboring, separately, often in different parts of the countryside. My specialty was feeding the chickens and Lin's was planting vegetables. We were afraid of being criticized. We worked for one year, separately far from Shanghai and then came back to work, separately again, in the countryside outside of Shanghai. When we were first sent out, our younger son was only six months old, our older one was eight. For two years, others were taking care of our children. We could come back to Shanghai from the countryside every month for a day or so to see them. After the Gang of Four fell, we both came back to the studio in 1975. We continued the same film we had begun before we were sent away.[10]

CHAPTER 6

The 1970s: The Aftermath of the Cultural Revolution

The Cultural Revolution in fact put an end to traditional Chinese art and culture. During the Cultural Revolution Te Wei was maltreated and, together with fellow artist A Da, sent to the countryside to raise pigs for about a year. After his return to the studio he was put in charge of the library. Finally the studio opened again and Te Wei was allowed to direct a film about Tibet (1975).

In 1976, after Chairman Mao's death and the fall of the unlucky Gang of Four, Te Wei reassumed his position as studio head and put the former staff together. Thus began the second prosperous period of Chinese animation, which lasted until 1986. More than ten animation studios were established.

⇒ The Films ⇐

1973

Little 8th Route Army/Xiaobalu

Synopsis: A boy takes revenge against the Imperial Japanese Army.

Little Sentinel of East China Sea

Synopsis: A young girl named Jiedaling follows three chemical warfare workers in disguise and calls upon the People's Liberation Army to wipe out the enemy.

Comment: The last of the genuinely revolutionary Maoist entries in Chinese animation.

Little Trumpeter/Xiaohaomao

Directors: Wang Shuchen, Yan Dingxian

Synopsis: Hsiao Yung, a shepherd boy, becomes a bugler in the Red Army during the days of the civil war and joins the fight against the Nationalists.

Comment: According to Giannalberto Bendazzi, "In the film, Chiang Kai-shek's soldiers resemble demons, while the Red Army soldiers jump magically from mountain to mountain. The historical theme becomes a fight between the old and the new, with images echoing the magniloquence of Mao's Red Guards."[1]

1976

The Fox and the Hunter/The Fox Hunts the Hunter/Huli Dalieren

Director: Hu Xionghua

Synopsis: A smart fox, using a wolf's skin, is scaring a young hunter, cheating and hunting him. Finally, an old hunter recognizes the scheme and shoots the fox.

Comment: Paper-cut animation.

Award: Prize, Fourth Zagreb International Animated Film Festival, June 1980.

1978

One Night in an Art Gallery

Directors: Xu Jingda (A Da), Lin Wenxiao

Synopsis: Makes fun of the Gang of Four: caricatures of the Gang leaders censor and turn upside down the most innocent of paintings. In the end, children drive them off.

1978–1979

Nezha Conquers the Dragon King/ Nezha Nao Hai

70 Minutes
Directors: Wang Shuchen, Yan Ding Xian, Xu Jingda [A Da]
Co-director: Lin Wenxiao
Chief Animator: Chang Guangxi
Voice Actor: Ke Bi (Li Jing)

Synopsis: Nezha, a mythological boy hero of Taoist origin (also known as Na-zha or Nata) who has a universe ring around his body, a fire-tipped spear in his right hand, fiery wind wheels under his feet, and the red armillary sash around his shoulders, fights four evil dragons, the Dragon King himself and his trio of brothers, which could be seen as a symbol for the Gang of Four. (They demand children to be sacrificed and have to be punished.)

In turn the adversaries don't give up but flood Chentangguan, Nezha's birthplace in the region of Chentang Pass, and ask for Nezha's life. Nezha commits suicide in defense of all residents in Chentangguan but is revived from death by having his body rebuilt with fresh lotus roots and lotus flowers. The resurrected Nezha, a divine warrior with three heads and six arms and the ability to spit fire, destroys the dragon palace and defeats the Dragon King.

Comment: Based on a segment from the *Investiture of the Gods (Fengshen Yanyi)*, "Apotheosis of Heroes." China's first widescreen animated feature film. Preproduction was begun before the Cultural Revolution but was suspended for almost ten years.

Co-director Wang Shuchen was born in Dandong City, Liaoning Province, and studied art for a brief time. He was one of the group that started to do animation in the Northeast Film Studio in Changchun and eventually would go to Shanghai.

Awards: Best Film Award, Ministry of Culture, 1979.

Best Animation First Prize, Third Hundred Flower Awards (Bai Hua Prize), 1980.

Special Prize, Second Manila International Film Festival, Philippines, 1981.

Award, Bourg en Breese Youth Fairytale Film Festival, France, 1988.

Screened to great critical acclaim at Cannes Film Festival.

1979

Cat Mimi

Director: He Yumen

Synopsis: When the mice find out that Mimi is a lazy cat, they get more and more audacious.

Award: Excellent Film Award issued by the Ministry of Culture, 1979.

Eight Hundred Whips

Comment: Paper-cut film.

A Fool Bought Shoes

9:32 Minutes
Directors: Fang Runnan, You Lei

Synopsis: The story of a bookworm who, while absorbed in reading, accidentally burns his shoes and needs to find new ones. He goes out to buy some, but the shoes he tries on are too small and only would fit children's feet.

Comment: Puppet animation.

Hedgehog Carries Watermelon

10 Minutes
Directors: Wang Borong, Qian Jiaxing

Synopsis: A little hedgehog is out with his mother. After a while they find a huge watermelon. Mother tries to push it but is unable to do so and eventually is buried inside the heavy fruit. The little one has to free his mother and asks a white rabbit for help. When they push it, it rolls away together with his mother. Finally the little one asks a woodpecker who frees the mother with his beak.

Comment: Cut-paper animation.

Pandas' Department Store/Panda Store

6:14 Minutes
Directors: Shen Zuwei, Zhou Keqin

Synopsis: Senior panda and junior panda open a department store in the bamboo grove.

Comment: Simple, very limited Chinese animation starring old-fashioned animal characters such as hippo, elephant and giraffe, who as customers have their dreams

Panda's Department Store (1979).

fulfilled. The squirrel receives new shoes, the monkey a drum.

Songs Out of Five-Fingers Mountain

30 Minutes
Director: Fang Runnan
   Synopsis: A Mei, a girl of Li Minority, proves her gratitude to the Communist Party by singing songs.

CHAPTER 7

The 1980s: Reform Period, Transitional Stage and Decline

According to Justin Sevakis:

China has had a strange history of producing interesting animation, but that history is not exactly a glorious one. The Cultural Revolution of the late 60's and 70's resulted in much of the country's artistic talent being forced to do farm work in the countryside, accept re-education, or even be thrown in jail. After a brief recovery in the 80's, China's new economic open-ness with Japan and America meant that their market was flooded with those countries' respective top-quality productions, and the unprofessional backwater of the Chinese industry, having lost all of the talent that knew what they were doing, just couldn't compete. Even fill-in work for Japanese and American producers often came back late and shoddy. Young new artists, increasingly influenced by anime, found funding from the government, who started new initiatives to try to get their industry back on track.

But neither the technical knowledge nor the storytelling background was there. Chinese animators were essentially starting over.[1]

Liu Qing Fang writes,

These imported animation works have changed the desires and tendencies of Chinese audiences. Following the popularity of televisions in the late 80's, more and more foreign-styled entertainments have emerged into China. When imported animation characters and plot styles are deeply engraved on Chinese audiences' memories, they unconsciously change the aesthetic standards among audiences. In turn they become the referential standards for audiences to judge the quality of animations and guide them to consume in the future. In China, many adults still narrow mindedly consider animation as an entertainment for children. However, they neglect the impact of imported animations on the younger generations. By consuming imported animations, children and young people will unconsciously accept the value and life styles that foreign animations present to them. In the long term, the values of foreign cultures and life styles from imported animations may play a dominant role and further replace the original cultural values among Chinese youth.[2]

⇒ The Films ⇐

If not indicated otherwise, all productions are by Shanghai Animation Film Studio.

1980

The Adventures of Jiaojiao
20 Minutes
Director: Jiao Yesong
   Synopsis: The girl Jiaojiao is fastidious about her food and as a result doesn't grow. In a dream she is taken away by a dragonfly into the world of insects. There she becomes aware of her faults. She will certainly change her habits in the future and be less picky.

The Beauty of a Peacock
20 Minutes
Director: Lu Heng
   Synopsis: Beauty contest between three peacocks.

The Black Rooster/The Black Chicken/ The Black Cock

10:12 Minutes
Director: Pu Ka-Cheung

Synopsis: "Our hero is a very unusual chicken. First, it is unable to lay eggs! Second, it is unable to crow! Also, it has been painted on paper!" It is a little girl who paints the chick with a big brush.

A wild goose arrives delivering a message.

"Congratulations, black rooster," the goose greets the drawing. "Because you were the prettiest entry in the children's painting contest, you get a gold medal."

Suddenly, at night when the stars shine, the rooster realizes that he can move and proudly produces the gold medal, claiming it for himself. A cricket appears at the window and applauds the rooster for his beauty.

The sweet words of the little katydid immediately go to the rooster's head. "Okay," the rooster decides. "I will go out and let everyone know that I am the most beautiful rooster in the world!" He leaves the room and shows other animals his gold medal: "Hey, do you have one of these? Of course, I know you don't."

The rooster becomes more and more arrogant and aloof. He comes to a beautiful place, but for him it is not beautiful enough: "Ha! Even something this pretty cannot compare to the attractive colors of my body!" A bird lands on a branch. It is beautiful. The rooster has to admit it. However, he says: "You are beautiful, but do you have a big gold medal?" "That medal was not given to you. It was given to the young painter. You don't even exist in the real world." The rooster feels offended by that kind of criticism: "It IS mine! It really IS mine!" he snaps back. "You have no humility, none at all! This medal is mine. MINE!" Outraged, he lands on the water, and the paper he is painted on gets soaked.

He has to expose it to the sun, losing all beauty. Bees surround him. What are they doing? They tell him that they are working. "Ha, I've never done work in my life. And look, I got a gold medal!" "Wrong, that reward is for the young artist who worked hard to paint you! The paper and pigment she used also helped you."

Now the black rooster is throwing a tantrum. "Just watch! I don't need to depend on paper and pigments! Red comb, you get out of here! But without me, you won't be beautiful!" The paper rooster parts from his colors to prove that it's only his personality that wins. "Hm, you nasty black pigments also need to get out of here!" Now he is completely colorless. The birds and insects around are laughing. The rooster wants to know what's so funny about him: "Without colors I am much more attractive!" The rooster, feather-light now, is doing a funny dance. The birds warn: "Hey, be careful! Don't fall down!" The rooster pirouettes. "Remember," a bird tells him, "you are still reliant on the paper!" "Paper? Paper, you get out of here!" He parts from the paper. "Hey, now the rooster is transparent!" While he is just an outline, insects stretch him and change his form. "You are still dependent on the outline," the bird tells the rooster. "Outline?" The rooster is upset. "I don't need the..." The outline disappears and with it the image of the rooster: "I'm finished!" One bee suggests that it's time now to help the poor guy and do him some good. The bee approaches the finished rooster: "Do you see where you went wrong?" "Yes, I was wrong," the rooster croaks. He asks a goose to take him home. The goose agrees and puts the outline back onto the paper. All of a sudden the colors return and complete the image of the rueful rooster: "I suppose the children who will come and look at me today wouldn't like me if I was such an arrogant rooster!"

The Little Duck/Duckling Yaya

Synopsis: A little duck is being chased by a fox, but with the help of other animals the adversary is drowned in the lake.

Comment: Folded paper animation.

My Friend Little Dolphin/Wo De Pengyou Xiao Haitun

20 Minutes
Director: Dai Tielang
Synopsis: A Po, a little boy, befriends a young dolphin and explores the beauty of the underwater world, riding on his friend's back. Finally the dolphin disappears mysteriously, but A Po is going to save the friend from a shark attack.

Comment: May have been inspired by Ivan Tors series *Flipper*.

Award: Italian International Children and Youth Film Festival, 1982.

My Friend Little Dolphin (1980).

Snow Kid/Xue Haizi
20:24 Minutes
Director: Lin Wenxiao
Chief Animator: Chang Guangxi

Snow Kid (1980).

Synopsis: A young rabbit makes a snowman that comes to life, to the amazement of mother and child. The snowman and the kid have lots of fun on the frozen lake and in the winter forest. Finally the snowman sacrifices his own life to save his little creator from the flames when the rabbit's log cabin is burning. After the rabbit's rescue the snowman is melting. There is only some water left, out of which the spirit of the snowman rises to heavens.

Comment: Similar to a German wartime cartoon, *Der Schneemann,* made by Fischerkoesen Studio (1943).[3]

Award: Excellent Film Award issued by the Ministry of Culture, 1980.

Snow Kid (1980).

Three Monks/San Ge He Shang

20 Minutes
Directors: A Da, Lin Wenxiao
Screenplay: Pao Lei
Photography: You Yong
Animation: Han Yu, Ma Kexuan, Fan Madi

Synopsis: The daily duties of a little monk who lives in a small temple on a mountain are adding water to the holy water bottle on the table honoring the Goddess of Mercy, and keeping the mice from stealing food at night. Soon after, a tall monk arrives and drinks half of the jar's water. The little monk asks him to fetch water. Thinking it unfair to fetch water alone, the tall one suggests that they both go and do the job together. Using a pole, instead of two buckets they can carry only one bucket. Finally, a fat monk turns up and wants to drink, but the others are short of water and ask him to go himself and fetch

Original designs for *Three Monks*.

***Three Monks* (1980).**

some water. The fat one carries a bucket but empties it immediately. From then on, no-body will go. At night, a mouse knocks over a candleholder and causes a fire. Now the three monks are forced to join and make a concerted effort to put out the fire. With the monks having learned the lesson, the temple will never lack water again.

Comment: According to David Erlich,

The original [folk] proverb that is the basis of the film's narrative tells us that when there

Three Monks (1980).

is only one monk, he alone carries the water (in two pails); when there are two monks, they carry the water together in one pail; when there are three monks, no-one has water to drink.... The film that follows the title, however, ends in an entirely different manner, with the three monks learning that they must work together to survive. It was also A Da's special cry that the split in China caused by the Cultural Revolution, the split that turned one family member against another, would result only in destruction and should never be repeated.[4]

A Da was born in 1934 as Xu Jingda. His father graduated from the University of Michigan and returned to Shanghai in 1928 to become a banker. He and Lili, Xu Jingda's mother, married in 1932. The father would have liked to turn him into a banker too but finally permitted him to enter Soochow Art Institute. Later, in 1953, Xu Jingda graduated from Beijing Film Academy and returned to Shanghai to join Shanghai Animation Film Studio. Aged 53, A Da, chosen to start a new animation department at Beijing Film Institute, died in 1987 in a Beijing hospital from a cerebral hemorrhage.

Awards: Award for Excellent Animation Film issued by the Ministry of Culture, 1980.

Best Animated Film Prize at the First Chinese Film "Golden Rooster" Competition.

Silver Prize at the Fourth Odense International Fairytale Film Festival in Denmark.

Silver Bear for Short Film at the Thirty-second Berlin International Film Festival, 1982.

Best Film Award, Portugal International Film Festival.

Special Prize, Second Manila International Film Festival, Philippines, 1983.

Zhang Fei Interrogates Watermelon

Directors: Qian Yunda, Ge Guiyun

Synopsis: Zhang Fei judges the theft of a watermelon.

Comment: Cut-paper animation. This tale of Chinese wisdom uses the example of a character from the classic *Chronicles of the Three Kingdoms.*

1981

Ginseng Fruit/The Monkey King and the Fruit of Immortality

Director: Yan Dingxian

Comment: Water-ink cartoon based on an episode from *Journey to the West* recruiting all popular heroes again.

Award: Special Prize, Second Manila International Film Festival, Philippines, 1983.

Lao Mountain Taoist/Nao Shan Dao Shi

Synopsis: When he reads about the immortals in Lao Mountain, a young man named

Wang Qi goes there and becomes one of the pupils of a Taoist who is very old and is said to possess magical skills.

Wang Qi, of course, is only interested in the secrets of magic. During the first month, however, he is ordered to the hills to chop wood with others every day. Result: "My hands are covered with callosities—but I still haven't learned any magic."

In the second month, he feels that he cannot stand the hard and tiring life, but he still waits for the master to teach him magic. In the third month, he cannot bear the suffering any longer. He goes to see the teacher and says, "I've been working hard for so many days. Now would you please teach me some skills, or it'll be a waste of time for me to be here. I want to learn a supernormal ability before I leave."

"What do you want to learn?"

"I would like to learn how to go through a wall."

"Then I'll teach you." The Taoist tells Wang Qi the specific incantations. After reciting the words of magic that enable him to pass through a solid mural, Wang Qi thanks him and is ready to return to his family.

"But remember," the master reminds him. "You must have a high moral value! If you are going to abuse this power it will vanish."

Back home, Wang Qi tells his wife that he has met with an immortal and learned how to go through a wall. He sings: "Some families are wealthy, some families are rich. I will go through their walls, take their treasures and run."

His wife is aghast: "What? You want to use what you have learned to become a thief?"

Wang Qi remembers what the master has told him: that he would lose his magic skill if he left the path of right. "Ah ... nonsense. The power already is mine!" To demonstrate it Wang Qi recites the incantations and runs towards a wall. However, his head hits the wall with a bang, and he is knocked heavily.

"Are you crazy?" his wife asks.

He tries again and fails a second time. His wife helps him to his feet and finds a large bump on his forehead.

Comment: Puppet film: Stop motion and ink and paint.

Monkeys Fish for the Moon/Monkeys Fish Up the Moon/Hou Zi Lao Yue

10:29 Minutes

Director: Zhou Keqin

Animation: A Da and others

Synopsis: A group of greedy little monkeys literally chase and vainly try to catch the moon, which seems to have fallen into a lake.

Comment: Illustrates the proverb: "The monkeys fish for the moon but do not catch anything."

Director Zhou Keqin was director-general of Shanghai Animation Studio. This lovely cut-out animation short, although quite simple, remains his most famous work.

Awards: Award for Best Cartoon, Third Magic Festival, China, 1983.

Award for Best Short, Fourth Kablov International Comic Film Festival, Bulgaria, 1987.

Group Prize, First China International Animation Film Festival, 1988.

Mr. Nan Guo

Director: Qian Jaxin

Synopsis: A musically ignorant man is employed as a court musician.

The Nine-Color Deer/The Deer of Nine Colors/A Deer of Nine Colors/Pinyin: Jiu Se Lu/ Laoshan Daoshi

24:17 Minutes

Directors: Qian Jiajun, Dai Tielang

Synopsis: "Dunhuang Cave is like an oasis in the desert. It is a treasure trove of ancient cultural relics. Mogao Grotto is undoubtedly the greatest treasure in this trove as it has preserved many hand-painted images from unknown artists. Here is an ancient story from one of those beautiful paintings."

In the beginning a Persian merchant and his caravan get lost in a windstorm. Suddenly, a spiritual deer of nine colors appears and talks to them: "Have you lost your way, O travelers from afar? Shall I show you the way?" The travelers bow and thank the animal. The animal stomps with its feet and the mountains open up a route: "This way. Please follow me." So it guides the caravan out of the danger: "May you return safely."

The deer also protects animals, ants and other insects in need and makes the flowers bloom, asking the others if they enjoy the flowers. All like it very much.

"When you meet the magic deer, you will be granted health and happiness! You will be blessed with good luck when you meet the magic deer!" A bird comes to warn the holy deer: "I saw a group of people with weapons chanting something about you. Perhaps you saved them once. If anyone else finds out, a great misfortune may befall you." "Thank you for your advice, White-Throat. But human beings are usually conscientious. I don't think they will be ungrateful." "We should be very careful anyway. They have weapons," replies the bird.

One day a snake charmer comes to the water to look for bigger snakes and herbs as well and drowns accidentally. While the bird is still warning, nine-color deer hears the man screaming: "Someone's in trouble!" "No, dont go," the bird warns. But the deer rescues the man from drowning by magically parting the water: "Who are you? How did you fall into the water?" "I am a merchant. I came here to find medicinal herbs. I slipped and fell into the water by accident. Thank you for

The Nine-Color Deer **(1981).**

The Nine-Color Deer **(1981).**

saving me. I will never forget your kindness." "Life is valuable. I wouldn't have let you die. But please don't tell anyone else about this incident." "I swear I will never speak of it," the rescued man assures. "May the gods strike me down if I break my promise!"

The man bows three times but in the end proves ungrateful. In the meantime the Persian merchant has arrived at the king's court: "Your majesty, we lost our way because of a storm. We were able to survive because a magical deer helped us. This deer can talk, and it has a glistening coat with nine different colors. Our country will be blessed with happiness because of this magical deer." "Oh," the empress says, "it sounds like a beautiful deer." She goes to sleep and dreams about the magic. In the morning the emperor stands at her bed: "Empress, my Empress!" "Your majesty! I want that nine-colored deer. Please grant me this wish!" "No one knows where the deer is. Besides, we can't hurt a magical creature that brings us happiness. You had better not cause any trouble." The empress reacts furiously and complains bitterly: "Why can't the deer be caught? Do you not care about me? I want a cloak made from its skin!"

"The deer simply cannot be found." "Although I am an empress, I am not as important as the deer? I don't want to live if you care about that thing more than me!" She confronts her husband and threatens: "I will commit suicide in three days." The emperor tries to console her: "I'll issue a proclamation to find the nine-colored deer."

Of course the snake charmer hears about it and hopes to gain the reward: "This is like a gift from heaven. It must be my lucky day. I will tell the king about the deer right now." For a moment he hesitates: "No, I can't. I swore to the gods. I can't break my promise. How could I even think of it?" Then he hears again about the reward: "If anyone catches the deer, that person will be appointed a county commissioner." So he thinks to himself: "It's not my fault if I break my promise. It will just be the nine-colored deer's bad luck. Since you already saved me once, why not save me again? I'll trade your life for great wealth and luxury. I'm very fortunate to have a chance like this. I'm going to be a county commissioner. I'm going to be rich."

So, mounting a donkey, he leads the emperor's hunters to find his lifesaver. The bird tries to warn the deer: "Hey, nine-colored deer. You have to wake up. The king has sent soldiers to capture you." "Relax, they won't be able to find me," the deer says.

In the meantime the hunting party has reached the water where the man drowned: "This was where I found the nine-colored deer." But the deer doesn't show up. So the man is going to slip into the water again: "I will ask the nine-colored deer to come out." He enters the water and pretends to drown, crying for help. Despite the bird's warnings the deer rushes for help: "I can't just leave him to die." Bowmen have hidden around, and the king spots the deer arriving at the lake.

"Why are you trying to capture me?" the deer asks the man. "The queen wants your skin," the traitor tells quite frankly. "Aim at the deer!" the king commands. The archers do but the arrows are ineffective, as the animal is protected by its strong nine-colored energy field. The men are shocked.

The deer proceeds to unmask the backstabber in front of the king: "Now listen, all of you. I am the queen among the deer of this country. I have saved many lives. The other day, I saved a man from drowning. That man is now standing right in front of me. How heartless of him to break his promise and repay me with such ingratitude!" The shivering and sweating man tries to escape but gets his deserved punishment and drowns with the bird picking on his head: "Evil will be paid back with evil! That man has lost his life. Although life is valuable, evil will be punished eventually."

All the others bow to the sacred animal, which is riding up to the sky and becoming a star.

Comment: The narrative is based on Buddhist Jataka tale of same title; its artwork is preserved as one of the famous Dunhuang Cave frescoes. One of the strongest works of classic Chinese animation.

1981–1983

Old Master Q (1981)/Lao Fu Zi/Old Master Cute

Hong Kong Film Services Ltd.
Executive Producer: Wu Sau-Yee
Directors: Wu Sau-Yee, Tsai Chih-Chung, Hsieh Chin-Tul

Old Master Q, Part II (1982)
Directors: Wu Sau-Yee, Tsai Chih-Chung, Hsieh Chin-Tul

Old Master Q, Part III (1983)
Directors: Honda Toshiyuki, Choi Ming-Yum
Animation Supervisor: Tsai Chih-Chung
Screenplay: Alfonso Wong, Fung Yuen-Chee

Synopsis: In the first part of the trilogy Old Master Q, who often faces street bullies, decides to take self-defense lessons from a Bruce Lee look-alike (who for the first time is transformed into a comic personality).

In part 2 Master Q and his friends, Big Potato and Mr. Chun, use a time machine to travel back to Sung Dynasty to support the heroes of the Water Margin with modern technology in their fight against a corrupt government. They find out that the "heroes" of the marsh are actually cowards.

In part 3, released shortly after Spielberg's *E.T.*, Old Master Q encounters a little alien. Ruthless developers try to get their hands on the amusement park where Master Q works. With the alien's help their business scheme is stopped.

Comment: Wu Sau-Yee turned a popular comic strip (*manhua*) created by Alfonso Wong that first appeared in Hong Kong magazines and papers in 1962 into a series of three cartoon films featuring Old Master Cute and his friends, Mr. Chin, Miss Chan and Mr. Chiu. In the different episodes they change professions in various time periods, encounter aliens and sight ghosts.

Award: Taiwan Golden Horse Award for Best Animation (part 1).

1981–1988

Story of Effendi/Afanti De Gushi

Conceived by Jin Xi

Directors: Qi Jianfang, Cai Yunlan
Synopsis: Effendi, meaning "sir" and "teacher" in Turkish, is a respectful name and title for a person of wisdom. The protagonist's real name is Nasreddin. He is a witty character, riding a donkey and always helping the poor to resist exploitation, particularly by Lord Bayi.

Comment: Stop-motion puppet series begun by Jin Xi, one of the two original leaders of the Shanghai studio, and continued by Qu Jianfang. The stories are based on Uigur (not Turkish) folklore.

Story of Effendi puppet series (1981–88).

Story of Effendi (1981–88).

1982

The Deer's Bell/Lu Ling

20 Minutes
Directors: Cheng Tang, Wu Qiang
Chief Animator: Chang Guangxi
Screenplay: Hu Sang

Synopsis: A girl living with her grandfather in the mountains cares for a young deer that got lost. To call the animal the girl uses a bell that she wears on a chain round her neck. She also takes the animal down to the village to see the market so that it can bring goods when sent. Eventually, the deer's parents find it, and the girl, sad to no end, has to let it return to its family but gives it the bell.

Comment: Ink-and-wash animated, "brush painting"–style film in the tradition of Te Wei.

Award: Golden Rooster Award, 1982.
Hundred Flowers Award, 1982.
Excellent Animation, Moscow International Film Festival Award, 1983.

If I Were Wu Song

30 Minutes
Director: Zhan Tong

Synopsis: The boy Wu Song, who wears a cap that sports a fish hook, is a boaster. He claims, "If I were Wu Song, I could also kill a tiger." When a real tiger turns up, Bigmouth is frightened to death, but finally both, tiger and Wu Song, enjoy playing hide-and-seek until the tiger is captured and Wu Song hailed as sort of Brave Little Tailor. But the tiger gets free and Wu Song's position becomes weak again. The boy has to relearn. The tiger even tests him in arithmetic. In the end everything turns out to have been a dream and the tiger a toy. Wu Song rolls his eyes.

Comment: Puppet animation. The animation can be compared in style to George Pal's old *Puppetoons*.

The Red-Faced and the Blue-Faced

10 Minutes
Director: Dai Tielang

Synopsis: Dental care: Two disruptive dental bacteria, identified with red and blue faces, are defeated by dental hygiene.

Award: "Xiao Bai Hua" Best Animated Film Award, 1982.

Weighing the Elephant

Comment: According to the Anipages Web site,

> a good example of what makes me admire the studio's films—daring and bold use of materials to achieve strong visual impact. In this case they've used what would appear to be some sort of traditional handcrafted wooden doll, looking like nothing so much as oriental Lego figures. But they're magnificently gorgeous, carved and painted with painstaking precision and detail, and they feel alive on the screen. The movement and camerawork is spare to provide ample time to appreciate the beautiful figurines. Watching the film surprisingly evoked a strange sensation in me, as if I was a child again watching the film in the genuine belief that those wooden blocks were really alive and moving around. The studio's films are full of that kind of magic.[5]

1983

Butterfly Spring/Hu Die Quan

24 Minutes
Director: A Da

Synopsis: A classic love story. A woman is trying to save a wounded fawn from a falcon's grip when a young man comes to her rescue. They also escape a hunting party and fall in love with each other. But the noble hunters don't give up, and kidnap the woman. The young man has to save his beloved again, but when they are trapped by the pursuers they commit suicide and transform into a flower.

Comment: The first Chinese animation aimed at adults, it tells a myth about the origin of Butterfly Spring. The Butterfly Spring is located at the foot of Mount Shenmo. The pool is some fifty square meters, and above it is an ancient tree, the famous Butterfly Tree that in summertime attracts thousands of butterflies. The film opens with a live prologue of people visiting the famous site, then turns into images of animated butterflies and a cartoon story.

The Fight Between the Snipe and the Clam/Yubangxiangzheng

Director: Hu Jinqing

Synopsis: In the fight between the snipe and the clam, the fisherman has the best of it. Or, as we would say: While two dogs fight for a bone, the third runs away with it.

Comment: Cut-paper animation.

Hairdresser Squirrel

10 Minutes
Director: Pu Jaziang

Synopsis: A squirrel offers the same haircut to different animals.

Comment: Modern-style drawing in vivid colors.

Legend of Sealed Book/Das Himmelsbuch/Tianshu Qitan

Manfred Durniok Produktion für Film und Fernsehen, Berlin/Shanghai Animation Film Studio
90 Minutes
Directors: Wang Shuchen, Qian Yunda

Synopsis: Dansheng, a boy born from an egg, is given a holy book by the Deacon of Heaven to help human beings. Female fox spirits, however, who are in league with venal officials, steal the precious book.

Comment: This work started the cooperation of Shanghai Animation Film Studio with a Berlin-based filmmaker. Manfred Durniok was mainly known for his live-action features and for his work with Hungarian director István Szábó but, as his long-time cinematographer Herbert Schramm revealed, his secret ambition was to become a producer of great animation, the German Walt Disney. At the same time he was attracted to Asia: "Manfred Durniok was always drawn to distant places. A traveler in many continents, it was specially Asia which attracted him most. As one of the pioneers who brought Asian films to the attention of Western audiences, he promoted at the same time through co-productions the cultural encounters between East and West in films." He worked in Japan, Thailand and eventually China: "Manfred Durniok's first visit to China was in 1971. Shortly after, he made his first documentary for German television there in the People's Republic of China, followed by many other documentaries. It was during this time, in the beginning of the 70s, when Chinese films were nearly unknown outside China, that Manfred Durniok began to screen and select

Chinese films in order to introduce them to German audiences."[6]

The Mouse Gets Married/The Mouse Daughter's Wedding

9:38 Minutes

Synopsis: To celebrate the wedding properly, they try to get the wedding cake out of a mousetrap, which turns out a bad idea.

Comment: Paper-cut animation.

1984

Fire Boy/Huotong

30 Minutes

Director: Wang Borong
Synopsis: At the cost of his life, a boy named Mingzha returns a sacred tinder that was stolen from the Hani people by the Devil.

Comment: Paper-cut animation.

The Plank Bridge

8:05 Minutes
Director: Wang Shuchen

Both photographs: *Legend of Sealed Book* **(1983).**

Synopsis: There is a lot of traffic around a particular log bridge. Two pandas want to cross it. They do so one after the other. Then two bulls appear, a brown one and a red one, and fight for who is going to cross it first. Fighting, they both end up in the water. Then a bear and a wild boar turn up. The bear has to use a trick to overcome the fierce pig. A monkey and a baboon cross imaginatively. The wolf has no chance against the elephant. A dog carries a bone onto the log when father and son approach. The dog marks the tree, then leaves, while a girl comes from the other side. Then a red-haired lady who has bought a chicken, and a man carrying a bicycle. The woman asks the man to let her through, and they have a shouting fight as neither of them wants to give in. The woman loses a shoe, which falls into the water. The man laughs. The man loses his false teeth, to the amusement of the woman. Furiously, the man stomps on the tree trunk until it breaks and both fall into the water. All others come to see the result of failed cooperation. Two water buffaloes save the two people.

Comment: Another lecture in cooperation.

Story of Lunar New Year's Eve

18 Minutes
Director: Qian Jiaxing
Comment: Paper-cut animation.

Wanderings of Sanmao

Director: A Da
Synopsis: During an air raid by Japanese invaders, Sanmao's home is destroyed and his mother killed. An old fisherman takes the poor boy in, but when he also dies Sanmao escapes to Shanghai, where a foster family takes care of the orphan.

Comment: Tragic sepia-toned cartoon starring Zhang Leping's famous comic character who had been an icon in director A Da's youth. The creator even appears in the prologue drawing his famous, three-haired character.

By the way, in 1949 a live-action version of the comic strip was the first feature film released to the public in Shanghai since the foundation of the People's Re-public of China. Sanmao was played by Wang Longji.

36 Characters

10:31 Minutes
Director: A Da
Synopsis: A son (live action) asks his father: "Dad, do you recognize the characters in this book?" "Ah, pictographs. There used to be many pictographs." The father teaches his son to read by illustrating Chinese calligraphy through pictographic characters: the sun, a mountain, water (with the images starting to move)."Tree... Oh, woods! Oh, I get it! Many trees together make a forest!" "Right, right!" Father continues to sketch: "Look here." Birds flying through the forest. "Chirp chirp! Chirp chirp chirp chirp chirp!" Then an elephant. "Hey... How did you recognize it?" "Um, it has a long nose and four legs." "That's right. That is how our ancestors created pictographs. What does this look like?" "Grass." "Let me write." New pictographs: "Doesn't this look like the fields that farmers grow?" "It does." Pictographs be-

36 Characters (1984) by A Da.

come words: "This word reads zhú. The zhú in zhúzi [bamboo]." "These are ... um ... horse, man, child." "Let's use the pictographs to tell a story, shall we?" "Okay." "There is a man riding the pictograph horse. When he comes to the water he wants to cross the river of course but there's no boat. Then what should we do?" Father paints a knife. "Man uses it to cut trees and make a boat." "Chuán." "No, it reads zhou. Back then, boats were called zhou." The elephant places the man inside the boat.

"Moon." "Okay, this story is finished." "Hey Dad, this story should be called *Adventures of the Groom*. (This is a play on the words "horse" and "man," which, when put together, mean "groom.")" "Silly child, this is so you can recognize characters. There are many, many more ancient Chinese pictographs. Do you remember these characters now?" "I remember! Thirty-six characters!"

Comment: An intelligent graphic comedy.

Award: Education Film Award, Seventh Zagreb International Film Festival, 1986.

36 Characters (1984).

1984–1985

The Monkey King Conquers the Demon/ Jinhou Xiangyao

90 Minutes
Supervising Director/Producer: Te Wei

Animation Directors: Yan Dingxian, Lin Wenxiao

Synopsis: Sun Wukong, the Monkey King, has been punished by Heaven and was trapped beneath the Five-Finger Mountain by Buddha Rulai. Five hundred years later, while on the way to the Western Heaven to obtain precious Buddhist scriptures, Tang priest Xuanzang releases the Money King from his stone prison and accepts him as his disciple. As discipline is not one of Wukong's strengths, the monk has him wear a golden headband. Whenever the monk recites an incantation, Wukong will have a serious headache. Nevertheless, Wukong loyally protects his new master. On the road, Monk Tang accepts two more disciples, Zhu Bajie (Pigsy) and Sha Tseng (Friar Sandy). As the four of them head west, they encounter treacherous roads and difficulties that become part of mythology.

One day, the monk and his group pass by the White Bone Cave. This is reported by a bat creature to the reigning sorceress, Lady White Bone, who wants to capture the pious monk. By sounding the drums she wakes up the grotto creatures and demons. If they eat the monk's flesh, they believe, they will become immortal; but the Monkey King renders their nefarious plan void.

Comment: Another episode adapted from *Journey to the West:* Following the popularity of *Havoc in Heaven,* the studio decided to revive the character in its fourth feature-length entry. The Monkey King returns and is his true self, designed the same as in previous entries, a clear signal that the Cultural Revolution was over. The witch opponent is reminiscent of Disney's Maleficent of *Sleeping Beauty* fame, and her beastly but inept cohorts are a slight nod to Jiang Qing, Mao's widow, and the Gang of Four. The monk character, by the way, refers to Xuanzang, a famous priest of the Tang Dynasty and great translator of Buddhist scriptures, born in 600 AD. When he was 28 years old he departed from Chang'an to India to fetch scriptures and bring them back home.

Inspector Black Cat (1984–87).

1984–1987

Inspector Black Cat/Black Cat Detective/Marshall the Black Cat/ Heimao Jingzhang
TV Cartoon Series
Directors: Dai Tielang, Fan Madi

Inspector Black Cat (1984–87).

Synopsis: Law and order enforcement: A black cat policeman fights a nasty gang of rats and other misfits that are after the grain.

Comment: The cat character from the 1950 *Thank You, Kitty* becomes a policeman. The hero cat was revived in 2006.

Award: Excellent Film Award issued by the State Administration of Radio, Film and Television.

"Xiao Baihua" Best Animated Film Award, 1984.

Episode One, First Calf Award.

Episode Four, National Oil Doll Award.

1985

Goddess Nuwa Patches Up the Sky
Director: Qian Yunda

Synopsis: Nv Wa, a character from Chinese mythology, is said to have created humans with mud and to have used a multi-colored stone to fix a hole in the sky.

Award: Special Prize, St. Rome International Children's Film Festival, France, 1986.

The Straw Man/The Grass Man
10:38 Minutes
Director: Hu Jingqing

Synopsis: The straw man who wears a straw cape and a straw hat tries to chase away two nasty waterfowls that feed on the fish, but it is no easy task. The birds always return. To hold them away he builds a scarecrow out of straw with some moving parts he manipulates from afar. The birds, however, do not fall for the trick and take it apart. The man is upset when he realizes what's going on. Eventually he hides himself in a straw-man disguise and waits for the feathered troublemakers. When he sees them fish he gets nearer in the disguise and tries to catch them. Finally they rest on the man-turned-scarecrow.

Comment: Cut-paper animation.

1986–1987

Calabash Brothers/Gourd Brothers/ Hulu Brothers/Seven Brothers/ Pumpkin Brothers/Hulu Xiongdi

Directors: Hu Jinqing, Ge Guiyun, Zhou Keqin

Synopsis: Two demon ogres, a male scorpion spirit who likes to drink and a female snake spirit, are jailed in the Calabash Mountains, but they escape and cause grave harm to the residents. An old man who has learned that only by growing calabashes in seven colors can he annihilate the evil spirits spares no time in growing seven calabashes in red, orange, yellow, green, cyan, blue and purple. One after the other, the calabashes become ripe and fall off their stems to the ground, becoming seven boys dressed in suits of different colors who fight the evil one by one, finally in a concerted effort and a united mind. During the climactic fight, the wonder boys save the old man's life, spit water, grow

Calabash Brothers (1986–87).

to gigantic proportions and throw rocks until they finally become a huge, seven-colored mountain that buries the evil-doers.

Comment: Paper-cut animation.

Later transformed into a thirteen-part TV series.

Award: Third Place Prize, Cairo International Children's Film Festival, Egypt.

Best Film of 1988, CPC Tibet Autonomous Regional Committee.

1987

The Adventures of Floppy King/Lata Dawang Lixianji

130 Minutes
Directors: Qian Yuanda, Yan Shanchun

Synopsis: A boy nicknamed "Floppy King" is cheated by a mouse spy into an ancient kingdom because he doesn't have manners and always is naughty.

Comment: Thirteen-part TV series.

The Fox's Gift

Director: Hu Jinhua
Chief Animator: Chang Guangxi

Synopsis: In exchange for a big rooster that he has eaten, a sly fox gives an old man a bunch of grapes that he has stolen elsewhere. As he sees that the old man seems to appreciate the deal, the fox continues to trade all the animals the old man has by wheedling. At last, the old man understands that grapes offered by a fox are not for free.

Comment: Paper-cut animation.

Award: Golden Elephant Award for Best Short Film, Indian International Children's Film Festival, 1987.

The Nightingale

Atkinson Film Arts/Animated Investments/ CTV Television Network/The Ontario Development Corporation/Téléfilm Canada/ Hi-Tops Video in association with Shanghai Animation Film Studio
TV Special
30 Minutes
Director: Rick Morrison
Voice Actors: Christopher Plummer (Narrator), Polly Jones, Terrence Scammell, John Tarzwell, Noel Counsin, Barry Edward Blake
Screenplay: Mary Crawford, from an Original by Hans Christian Andersen

Synopsis: The famous tale of an emperor who prefers a mechanical bird to the real thing.

Comment: Canadian fairy-tale animation outsourced to China.

Selecting a Beauty/Beauty Selection/ The Emperor Selects a Beauty
9:51 Minutes
Director: Wang Shuchen

Synopsis: The film opens with a singing announcer with a gong: "Come here, take a look! I have a movie to show today! It's about a king, who was riding around in his sedan chair. What was he doing? He was looking for beauties. Why was he doing that? Because he was still a bachelor at the time. He wanted to have a beautiful wife to accompany him."

Servants who carry the king's sedan shout: "The king would like to select a beauty! Ladies, come out! Have a look! Come, be interviewed by the king!" The king in his sedan watches a number of women, but in the village they pass there are none he would like to marry.

"There are so many women here," the king complains. "Some are like phoenixes, some are like hens. How could the king possibly decide on a wife?" Suddenly he has an idea when he spots a painter: "You, painter, will make portraits of beauties so that the king can choose a wife." The artist agrees. Many women come to have themselves painted by the artist.

This painter, however, is quite special.

They all would pay him well, hoping they will be the future queen sitting next to the king. "If you were rich, an ugly woman could become beautiful. If not, a beautiful woman could become as ugly as a pig!"

Finally he hands the king the finished paintings. The king wonders about an ugly one: "Even a beggar wouldn't want her as a wife!"

After a while they pass a conjuror who is demonstrating his tricks for a small audience. The king asks for one of the conjuror's objects, a pot, and in return would like to give him a wife: "How about that?" He shows the conjuror the ugly one's painting. "But this is just a picture," the magician frowns. "Not at all. She is Number 6, and she is yours!"

Finally, the king has the ladies come in and compares them with the paintings, but to his disappointment they all look different and not as beautiful as he had imagined from the paintings. None of the five ones he invited equals the respective painting. The king is furious, upset and snorting with rage. "Go, catch that painter," he commands. The painter, realizing what's going on, tries to escape.

Finally the conjuror arrives to thank the king for the sixth lady, who doesn't resemble the ugly painting at all. She is the only beauty. The king rolls his eyes and can't believe what he sees: "How did the ugly woman become the beauty? Hey, you can keep the pot! I want *her* as my wife!" He sends his servants after the conjuror and his beautiful wife, but the only thing left is the ugly painting.

Super Soap/Chaoji Feizao
Synopsis: A canny businessman plays on people's desire for fashions and fads and sells what he claims to be a super soap that makes everything brilliantly white. Word of mouth spreads and creates demand. Lines peak up at the salesman's stand. Even A Da's Three Monks wash themselves white. While everything turns white, a girl in colorful dress appears and changes the demand of the masses. Actually the girl is the daughter of the salesman, who in the meantime has founded his Supercolor Company and started a new business offering new soaps that re-color every dress and gown.

Comment: Chinese satire, Zagreb-like in style and score. A variation of Hans Christian Andersen's *The Emperor's New Clothes* and a lecture in capitalist sales methods.

Award: Award for Best Animation Film, Seventh Chinese "Golden Rooster" Competition, 1987.

Second Prize, Second Hiroshima International Animation Film Festival, 1987.

1988

Clever Silly Piggy/Lonely Pig
10 Minutes
Directors: Qu Jianfang, Cai Yunlan

Synopsis: A little pig that lives in a log refuses to help a hedgehog, a goat and a rabbit. In turn, the three ignore piggy for its selfishness; but when the pig is being seized by a jackal all three rush to the rescue.

Comment: Paper-cut animation.

Feeling from Mountain and Water/ Shan Shui Qing
19 Minutes
Supervising Director: Te Wei
Associate Directors: Yan Shanchun, Ma Kexuan

Te Wei (gesturing) and members of his staff planning the director's farewell: *Feeling from Mountain and Water* **(1988).**

Screenplay: Shuchen Wang
Photography: Duan Xuao Xuan

Synopsis: A young girl, ferrying an aging musician across a river, nurses him to better health after witnessing him collapse on the shoreline.

Comment: Watercolor-and-ink animation.

One of the later works of Te Wei, who says farewell in the animated part of an old artist-musician. After this film he retired. Shanghai Animation Film Studio never has been the same since. Te Wei died on February 4, 2010, in Shanghai.

Awards: Award, First Shanghai International Film Festival, 1988.

Best Animated Film Award, Ninth Chinese Film "Golden Rooster" Festival, 1989.

Excellent Film Award issued by the State Broadcast, Film and TV Department, 1988.

Prize, First Film, TV and Animation Program Exhibition.

Courage and Beauty Prize, First Moscow International Film Festival for Children and Youth.

Excellent Film Award, Sixth Varna International Animated Film Festival of Bulgaria.

Best short Film Award, Fourteenth Mon-

Te Wei in his later years.

《三个和尚》获金鸡奖特别奖
（文化部奖）
1981年 春

Staff members of the Shanghai Animation Film Studio with their Golden Rooster Award, 1981.

treal International Film Festival of Canada, 1990.

Best Film, Bombay International Short Film, Documentary and Animation Film India Festival, 1992.

Fushanosha

25 Minutes
Director: Kihachiro Kawamoto

Comment: Designed by famed Japanese puppet-film master Kawamoto Kihachiro (1925–2010) and made in Shanghai with a Chinese team. *Fushanosha* is a zenlike phrase and means "shooting without shooting."

Mantis Stalks Cicada/Tang Lang Bu Chan

Director: Hu Jinqing

Synopsis: A Chinese idiom, meaning to covet gains ahead without being aware of danger behind:

There is a cicada resting high on a tree. It is chirping for all it's worth and drinking in the dew, oblivious of a mantis appearing behind. The mantis, bending over and arching up its front leg, is going to catch the cicada but does not know that there is an oriole beside it. The bird has stretched out its neck, ready to peck at the mantis, which is after the cicada. Similarly, the oriole is unaware that it is also under threat down below.

Comment: Paper-cut animation.

1989

Adventures of Shuke and Beita/ Luxixi's General Mobilization/ Luxixi's Adventure

Directors: Yan Dingxian, Lin Wenxiao

Synopsis: The twins Pi Pi Lu, a naughty but kind-hearted boy, and his little sister Luxixi have two unusual friends, the rats Shuke and

Beita, who are extremely smart and know human language.

Comment: Thirteen-episode TV series based on the work of Zheng Yuanjie, titled *King of the Fairytales.* Zheng spent thirteen years finishing this popular children's stories. All in all, he has written seventy stories spanning nine series, totaling twenty million copies in print.

Pi Pi Lu's series is an essential part of these stories. Pi Pi Lu and Luxixi are twin brother and sister, known to children all over China. Over the course of the years, many of her adventures have been adapted from books to TV, such as *Pi Pi Lu and Lilliputians in a Tin* and *Magic Cube Mansion.*

Award: Outstanding Animation, Golden Calf Awards, 1991.

Fishdish

Director: Fang Runnan

Comment: Cel and object animation: A painted fish swims off a real three-dimensional dish.

Reineke Fuchs/Reynard the Fox

Manfred Durniok Produktion für Film und Fernsehen, Berlin/Zweites Deutsches Fernsehen (ZDF), Mainz/Oriental Communications/Shanghai Animation Film Studio
80 Minutes
Producers: Manfred Durniok, Markus Schächter (ZDF)

Directors: He Yumen, Zhuang Minjin
Associate Director: Manfred Durniok
Production Managers: Zhang Hefen, Gao Huifa, Rainer Schulte
Animation Artists: Jin Dewu, Xin Guizhen, Li Meijuan, Dong Peizhen, Gu Wenqin
Voice Actors: Tobias Meister (Reineke Fuchs), Julia Biedermann (Ermelyn), Heinz Theo Branding (King Nobel), Andreas Mannkopff (Isegrim, the Wolf), Helmut Krauss (Braun), Friedrich W. Bauschulte (Bellyn), Andreas Fröhlich (Lampe the Rabbit), Wilfried Herbst (Hinze), Uwe Paulsen (Wackerlos), Santiago Ziesmer (Grimbart), Susanna Bonasewicz (Narrator)
Screenplay: Fu Bing, Zhongli Yao, Michael Kerwer, from a Poem by Johann Wolfgang Von Goethe
Musical Score: Fang Zheng
Conductor: Chen Chuanxi
Photography: Yichu Tang
Associate Photographer: Herbert Schramm
Art Director: Yan Ding Xian
Editors: Mo Pu Zhong, Barbara Hiltmann

Comment: Johann Wolfgang von Goethe's poem (1793/94) in 2D animation. Manfred Durniok (1934–2003), the Berlin-based producer of István Szabó's *Mephisto* and *Oberst Redl,* had not only the dream to become a German Walt Disney, but also a second ambition: to produce animation cheaply. Durniok was an honorary citizen of Beijing and is fondly remembered by old members of the Chinese animation community.

CHAPTER 8

The 1990s:
The End of Shanghai
Animation Studio's Monopoly

Shanghai Animation looked for partners abroad and subcontracted outside work from France, Germany, the United States, Japan, Canada and Australia, including Fox Linea, specials such as *Noah's Ark, Merlin and the Dragons* and *Frere Jacques*, feature films such as *Around the World in 80 Days*, series such as *Baby Follies, Toothbrush Family, Miss Mallard Mystery* and *Tracey McBean*.

Suddenly there was competition for the once-prestigious Shanghai Animation Studio. Two decades later, it wasn't releasing new films anymore but was trying to protect its past. In 2013, unable to cope with cross-media, the prominent studio filed a lawsuit against Apple and a Chinese subsidiary claiming 110 of its productions had been illegally sold on iTunes, including *Calabash Brothers* and *Black Cat Detective*, and sought $500,000 in monetary damages.

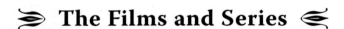

The Films and Series

1990

Fantastic Mongolia Horse
Shanghai Animation Film Studio
Director: Chang Guangxi
  Comment: Shanghai Animation Film Studio begins to give TV series a try. Production on this one started in 1989.

1990–1991

Robinson et Compagnie/Robinson ja Perjantai
Bat Productions/Belstar Productions/Films A2/Institut National de l'Audiovisuel (INA)/Parmentier Productions/Ministère de la Culture et de la Communication/Centre National de la Cinématographie (CNC)/Sacem/Revcom Télévision in association with Shanghai Animation Film Studio
70 Minutes
Director: Jacques Colombat

Voice Actors: Jacques François (Robinson Crusoe), Rolando Faria (Vendredi), Julien Guiomar (Bougainville), Gérard Hernandez (L'oiseau Dodo), Benoit Allemane, Nanette Corey, Isabelle de Botton, Joel Demarty, Lucie Dissouva, Jean-Claude Donda, Guy Grosso, Claude Guyonnet, Didier Hervé, Lorraine-Soeni Heymes
Screenplay: Jacques Colombat, from the Novel by Daniel Defoe
Synopsis: The classic survival story of shipwrecked Robinson Crusoe on a deserted island.
  Comment: French production with animation outsourced to China.

1991

Merlin and the Dragons
Lightyear Entertainment/Hi-Tops Video in association with Shanghai Animation Film Studio

37 Minutes
Directors: Dennis Woodyard, Hu Yihong
Story Written by Jane Yolen
Narrator: Kevin Kline
   Comment: Fantasy TV special.

1991–1992

Deer and Bull

9:56 Minutes
Director: Zou Qin
   Synopsis: A deer and a bull are at a water hole. Suddenly a lion attacks, but the deer and the bull unite to defend themselves and put the lion to rout. Then they turn again to the water, but there isn't enough for both of them. The bull empties almost everything by himself. Suddenly they are engaged in a fight between themselves. That is the moment the lion was waiting for. When the two animals part the lion attacks the deer, then turns to the bull. At the end only the skulls of the animals remain.
   Comment: Sophisticated stop-motion project outlining a metaphor for war. Deer and buffalo puppets were made from bamboo. This is apparently the only movie using this special technique of moving articulated bamboo figures. Director Zou Qin, who devoted a whole year to finishing this film, began his career at the Shanghai Animation Film Studio but found the situation gradually depressing: "When I started working in the studio, everybody liked to devote their lives to animation, to do the best work they could for China. Since 1986, with the 'open door,' everyone has come only to think of how best to make as much money as they could on their own.... Many Chinese animators are just copying the west now."[1]

1992

Fox Dividing Flapjack

10 Minutes
Director: Jin Xilin
   Synopsis: While dividing a flapjack for the Bear Brothers, Little Fox eats it up and pretends to be ill. The Bear Brothers bring Little Fox to a hospital but on the way fall into a trap. Little Fox, hearing their cries for help, compensates and rescues them.

1993

Hulu Xiao Jingang

   Comment: Thirteen-part TV series adapted from *Calabash Brothers.* Planning began in 1989.

1995

Big Head Son, Small Head Father

TV Series
   Synopsis: The daily life of a two parents–one child family.

Cyber Weapon Z

Creator: Chris Lau
Illustrator: Andy Seto
   Synopsis: While Park Iro and Anling, two newcomers with Southern Shaolin, arrive at the monastery of Shaolin, Molitofu, a demon, locked up ten years before, is awakened by an unknown force.
   Comment: Ten-volume *Manhua* series started in 1993 and adapted into a 3D-CG Chinese animation TV series produced in Hong Kong.

Little Heroes

Shanghai Animation Film Studio
   Comment: For the first time, Shanghai Animation Film Studio invested private money to run a TV series.

1995–2000

The Blue Mouse and the Big Faced Cat

CCTV
2D TV Series
30 × 10 Minutes (1995, Part I)
39 × 12 Minutes (2000, Part II)
   Synopsis: The adventures of a clever, always-helpful mouse and a greedy, lazy cat who are joined by two beetles, Jin Doudou and Lu Fanfang.

1996

The Adventures of Panda Jing Jing

Director: Wang Borong
Supervisor: Zhang Songlin
   Comment: Shelved project.
   When we talked to Wang Borong, former deputy of Shanghai Animation Film Studio,

and asked him why Chinese animation hadn't come up with anything like *Kung Fu Panda*, an enormous success in China too, he told us about *Panda Jing Jing*, a project about a panda who had escaped from an American zoo and crossed the Pacific Ocean on board a freighter to return to his beloved bamboo home. The concept had apparently been in the planning stages since the late 1980s.

While Mr. Wang wanted to show the ancient evolutionary power of a heroic animal character, co-producers in the United States asked for a Disney-like pet whereas partners in Hong Kong voted for a Kung Fu hero. As the Chinese backed out for some political reason, the project mutated, via Saban, into *The Adventures of Kung Fu Panda* and eventually transformed into DreamWorks' acclaimed *Kung Fu Panda*.

Panda JinJin, the blueprint for *Kung Fu Panda* (courtesy JAI).

Schneewittchen und die Sieben Zwerge/ Snow White and the Seven Dwarfs

Manfred Durniok Produktion für Film und Fernsehen, Berlin/Shanghai Animation Film Studio

Director: Qian Yunda

   Comment: A Grimm Brothers story filmed in China.

1996–1997

Kerabans Phantastische Reise/Jue Jiang Kailaban

Manfred Durniok Produktion für Film und Fernsehen, Berlin/Shanghai Animation Film Studio

90 Minutes

Directors: Manfred Durniok, Hong Hu Zhao

   Screenplay: Günter and Sibille Rätz, Manfred Durniok, Chen Gui Bao, Wang Da Wei, Hong Hu Zhao

   Synopsis: Keraban, a Turk, whom they call Die-Hard, doesn't want to pay the new taxes for passing the Bosporus from Constantinople to Skutari. Instead he travels round the Black Sea and has many adventures.

   Comment: A Jules Verne puppet animation adventure.

1997

A Chinese Ghost Story: The Tsui Hark Animation/Xiao Xian

Film Workshop Co., Ltd./PolyGram K.K./Win's Entertainment Ltd./ Cathay Asia Films Pte Ltd.

84 Minutes

Executive Producers: Nansun Shi, Meileen Choo, Charles Heung, Tsuneo Leo Sato

Producer: Tsui Hark

Director: Andrew Chan

Supervision: Tsui Hark

Production Managers: Bill Kong, Pui-Ki Chan, Raymond Fung

Animation Artists: Justo D. Cascante III, Bart Wong

Original Story: Tsui Hark

Screenplay: Songling Pu, Tsui Hark

Original Music: Ricky Ho

Editor: Tsui Hark

Character Design: Frankie Chung
Character Animation Director: Tetsuya Endo
Background Design: Caspar Schmidlin
   Comment: The animated version of the famous trilogy of live-action films supervised by the creator of the original tale, Tsui Hark, but with an animation director borrowed from Japan (Tetsuya Endo). A bizarre mix of manga and 3D animation effects. The hero, Siu Sin, looks rather Japanese-anime style next to the Taoist priest, Red Beard, and his opponents, the Buddhist priest White Cloud and his disciple, Ten Miles.
   On July 1, 1997, 156 years of British colonial rule in Hong Kong ended and the former Crown Colony became China's first special administrative region. The production itself, however, was begun much earlier. It was in 1991 that Tsui Hark came up with the idea of an animated version of *A Chinese Ghost Story*. He found partners in Taiwan (Cuckoo's Nest Studio), and secured some investment from Japan and the support of mainland animation processing factories. So it took five years to finish the project.

1998

Learned Cat Teaches Chinese Characters

Director: Wu Guanying
TV Series
72 Episodes
   Comment: Another attempt to teach kids Chinese writing by using a popular animal character.
   Award: Golden Award, Children's Programs of Federation of Asian Radio and Television, 1998.

Die Reise um die Erde in 80 Tagen

Manfred Durniok Produktion für Film und Fernsehen, Berlin/Mitteldeutscher Rundfunk (MDR)/Oriental Communications/ Shanghai Animation Film Studio
80 Minutes
Directors: Hu Zhao Hong
Associate Director: Manfred Durniok
Stop-Motion Animation: Zhu Bing, Shang Ning Hua
Screenplay: Günter and Sibille Rätz, Manfred Durniok, Hu Zhao Hong
Photography: Hu Zhao Hong, Lin Jide
   Synopsis: Phileas Fogg, member of the very British Reform Club, starts a journey round the world in eighty days to win a bet of 20,000 pounds.

   Comment: Puppet animation version of the Jules Verne novel.
   Award: Chinese State Prize for Best Animation.

1998–1999

Von der Erde zum Mond/Die Reise um den Mond

Manfred Durniok Produktion für Film und Fernsehen/Mitteldeutscher Rundfunk (MDR)/ Oriental Communications/Shanghai Animation Film Studio.
80 Minutes
Directors: Hu Zhao Hong
Associate Director: Manfred Durniok
Stop-Motion Animation: Zhu Bing, Shang Ning Hua
Screenplay: Günter Rätz, Manfred Durniok, Hu Zhao Hong
Photography: Hu Zhao Hong, Lin Jide
   Synopsis: Barbicane, a member of the Cannon Club of Baltimore, is obsessed by the idea of using a giant projectile to go to the moon.
   Comment: Another German-funded puppet animation version of Jules Verne's novel. Conservative in concept and execution.

Lotus Lantern/Bao Lian Deng

94 (85) Minutes
Producer: Chongqing Sheng
Director: Chang Guangxi
Voice Actors: Wen Jiang (Er Lang), Fan Xiu (Sanshengmu), Jing Ning (Gamei), Peisi Chen (Monkey King), Jie Cui (Tudi Ye), Jiali Ding (Mai Bing Fu), Ping Jiang (Qin Yong Yi), Kesheng Lei (Tai Wei Jia), Tian Liang (Jia Dao Shi), Jingwu Ma (Wu Shi), Ling Ma (Lao Yao Po), Xiaoqing Ma (Bu Luo Nv), Shuo Yang (Chen Xiang), Erga Yao (Guan Jia), Pengfei Yu (Young Chen Xiang), Shimao Zhu (Mei Shan Xiongdi), Xu Zhu (Qin Yong Jia)
Screenplay: Wang Dawei
Design: Wu Yigong
Editor: Liming Gong
Musical Score: Jin Fuazi
   Synopsis: A fairy who has fallen in love with a mortal is imprisoned by Erlang Shen for violating the divine laws. Her son Chenxiang, guided by Su Wukong, is going to free and rehabilitate her.
   Comment: Traditional Chinese folklore. Four years in production with a budget of 21 million RMB, a lot for Chinese animation

back then, but only 2.6 million in U.S. dollars. Director Chang Guangxi, who was the chief animator on a number of projects including *Nezha,* a member of the studio since 1962 and vice production head since 1987, created his best work.

Awards: Award for Excellent Animation Film, Nineteenth Chinese Film "Golden Rooster" Competition, 1999.

Award for Excellent Animation Film, Chinese Film "Bai Hua Prize" Competition, 2000.

Award for Excellent Animation Film, Ninth Chinese Children's Film "Calf Prize" Competition, 2001.

Golden Film Prize, First China Animation Achievements Competition, 2003.

Special Prize, First Mal del Plata Children and Teenage Film Festival—Sweet Dream Category, Argentina, 2003.

1999–2000

Journey to the West: Legends of the Monkey King

CCTV

TV Series

Comment: Fifty-two-episode cartoon series.

Director Chang Guangxi.

Shadow play character.

The Proud General.

Little Carp Jumps Over the Dragon Gate.

Chuang Tapestry.

Poster art, *Havoc in Heaven.*

Little Sisters on the Grassland.

Nezha Conquers the Dragon King.

Nezha Conquers the Dragon King.

Three Monks.

Monkeys Fishing for the Moon.

C5

Nine-Color Deer.

The Monkey King Conquers the Demon.

Havoc in Heaven.

Xi Yang Yang.

Little Trumpeter.

Lotus Lantern (1998–99).

CHAPTER 9

2000 and On: Relaunching Animation in China

Re-emerging after the Cultural Revolution, Chinese animation, in the long run, never really recovered from the wounds. Veteran animator Qu Jianfang explained why:

> We got pushed back 20 years in terms of television and the international market. In the 1980s, foreign companies rushed here to have work done. We were not creating then; we had to learn mass production, mass consumption. But, no creativity as we had to face the challenges of the market. Sure, we had a glorious past in animation, but we have to change. But we don't have to change our culture to have a market economy.[1]

Throughout the 1990s, the Chinese government modified the animation industry in a number of ways to bring it from a planned to a market economy. As studios had to scramble to support themselves, they sped up production (at Shanghai Animation Film Studio, from 500 minutes annually in 1995 to 5,000 in 2000), primarily to satisfy CCTV and the television market; served as work stations for overseas clients; sought global markets for their own works (but failed sadly); and increasingly entered the digital world.

In the meantime, the government had begun to take more notice of animation in a manner similar to that of the South Korean authorities a decade before—singling out nine cities as animation industrial bases, supporting animation and cartoon festivals, and encouraging the development of four national animation teaching and research bases: Beijing Film Academy, Chinese Arts University, Jilin College of the Arts, and Communication University of China.

At an animation festival in Changzhou in 2005, Liu Yuzhu, director of Culture Market Department, Ministry of Culture, said the central government

1. would increase investments and set up a special fund for animation. The government would help build a base for folk art, help in giving awards to artistic animation works.

2. would improve enterprise competitiveness, providing substantial support for enterprises doing research and development. In addition to this financial support, the government would give favorable help to the software industry, such as software industrial parks.

3. would support animation bases integrating the industry and academic research. The industry is in great need of high-end technical talents and more professionals would be cultivated. Institutes of higher learning and research institutes would be involved in training to provide high-level, high-end creative and marketable talents. Youngsters would be encouraged to enter animation through competitions and interest groups.

4. would implement a complete industrial changeover for the animation industry. Production takes a critical position. The government would encourage separation of production and the broadcasting of animation and make full use of derivative products, such as toys, apparel, etc.

5. would improve efforts in copyright regulation and crack down on piracy, and would also increase self-regulation in the animation industry.

Liu said Chinese federal and state governments had instituted policy statements because of a number of obstacles to growth that the animation industry faced. Among these were a public mentality concerned with children's addiction to animation, the loss of the adult market for which animation is not geared, low-level quality and quantity of domestic animation, a lack of Chinese stories and propensity to copy and imitate, an immature industrial base with insufficient markets and loss of part of the local market to cheaper foreign animation, a non-integrated administrative structure of the industry, and a lack of sufficient professionals, especially screenwriters and market personnel with creative ideas.[2]

Audiences by then still preferred foreign animation. A 2004 survey issued by China Mainland Marketing Research Co. found that of the top ten cartoon shows broadcast in China six were Japanese and two were American and two Chinese. According to Qu Jianfang, "Children here like Japanese animation, because it has no limitations. And, the Japanese do series of 26 or 54 episodes, while the Americans do 13. Japanese animation teaches children who the good and the bad guys are; children in the U.S. develop this concept themselves. Asians want big episodes, more episodes like the Japanese give."[3]

Afraid that foreign shows might have negative impacts on children's values and morals and on the creation of a national identity, the Chinese government clamped down in 2005–2006, limiting the amount of foreign cartoons on television to 40 percent, barring foreign channels such as Disney, banning TV shows and movies that blend animated elements with live-action performers, and eliminating foreign cartoons from the 5–8 p.m. prime time slot. These rulings by the State Administration of Radio, Film and Television (SARFT) were designed to nurture local animators who had no chance to compete with foreign product. A poll conducted in August 2006 proved that 80 percent of Chinese schoolchildren preferred foreign animation to domestic products. Two years later SARFT announced that it had added another hour to the "foreign cartoon-free zone" on domestic children's and cartoon channels, extending the zone from 5 p.m. to 9 p.m. SARFT also decreed that the ratio of domestic product to foreign shows on China's television channels should be increased. Under the new regulations, seven out of ten shows on Chinese television must be produced in China.

⋟ The Animated Series ⋞

1999–Present
(First broadcast in 2001)

3000 Whys of Blue Cat/Naughty Blue Cat 3000 Questions/Blue Cat/Lan Mao

Conceived by Sunchime Cartoon Group, Ltd. (Sunchime Film Studio Development Corp., aka Sunchime Digital Cartoon Development Co., Ltd.), Changsha, Hunan/Beijing Sunchime Happy Culture Company

Comment: With almost three thousand episodes, this series was unsurpassed in terms of quantity for a long time. It is mainly science fiction. The cat's blue color symbolizes a dream world between ocean, dinosaurs, or outer space. Blue Cat's friends include a spectrum of colors: Feifei, an orange fox; Taoqi, a turquoise mouse; Ms. Gali, a pink mouse, Feizai or Fatty, a yellow mouse, Sweet Sister Tianniu, a red pig.

In January 2001, when fifteen television stations began to broadcast *Blue Cat*, Sunchime Group, the producers, almost went broke. As cartoons, both foreign and domestic, were broadcast free on Chinese television and profits only came from the products derived from the cartoons, the producers got next to nothing even though *Blue Cat* was broadcast on one hundred TV channels nine months later. But in June 2002, when Sunchime signed a contract with Hong Kong–listed sports- and casual-apparel maker Tack Fat International Group, which secured an exclusive license for the cartoon character, the group began making money and the series continued.

Since then, Sunchime has taken advantage of the series' success to build a network with more than two thousand Blue Cat Chain Stores and to merchandise a collection of featured products. Currently, there are more than three thousand derivative products and licensed items that include video CDs, books, stationery, toys, teaching instruments, learning tools, food, apparel, cosmetics, and kids' bicycles.

Today Sunchime employs more than eight hundred talented and well-trained artists. Their philosophy:

- educate kids and transfer knowledge of science and technology;
- turn learning practice into entertainment;
- simplify social knowledge as common sense;
- internationalize Chinese national culture; and
- express philosophical ideas and turn them into ordinary language.

The series has included a number of themes:

- 424 episodes of *Classical Blue Cat* (Humors Stage Series)
- 384 episodes of *Star Wars*
- 257 episodes of *Living Olympics* (Sports Competition Series)
- 400 episodes of *Adventure in Space* (Space Series)

Blue Cat

- 108 episodes of *Safe Driving*
- 119 episodes of *The Team 119*
- 365 episodes of *Incredible Adventures of Blue Cat*
- 180 episodes of stories devoted to basic science and technology based on the best-selling textbook for elementary and primary pupils
- 130 episodes of *Green Glove* environmental series
- 365 episodes devoted to five thousand years of Chinese history
- 264 episodes of *Dinosaur Times* or *The Age of Dinosaurs*. Here is a synopsis:

When Earth suffers an incidence of surprise dinosaur attacks, Blue Cat and Taoqi, the green mouse, whom they also call Naughty, take a time machine back to the age of dinosaurs. They experience innumerable trials and hardships while they pass through space-time and return to prehistoric times. They undertake important missions, even forming profound friendships with dinosaurs. Reluctantly they part with their newly won friends, but just as they are preparing to return to their time, disaster strikes: a volcano erupts! In the disaster, the characters disperse and are divided into two groups: Dr. Sheep and Feifei, the orange fox, escape in a flurry along with the Dinosaur Chief, while Blue Cat, Naughty, and Ms. Gali run away with Edmontosaurus. The volcanic eruption not only destroys the dinosaurs' homes, but also disrupts the peace and order of their daily lives. Dr. Sheep and the Dinosaur Chief guide a group of dragons out of danger, arriving at what at first glimpse seems to be heaven, only to find much to their chagrin that it's nothing but wasteland.

When everyone is feeling low, Tyrannosaurus takes advantage of the situation to raise a disturbance, hoping to worsen conditions, kill the Dinosaur Chief, and reassume his lost status of being a tyrant. Faced with these incessant troubles, the Dinosaur Chief along with the other dinosaurs opts for lenience, pardoning and accepting Tyrannosaurus back into the fold. Yet this action has only buried a hidden danger. Tyrannosaurus camouflages himself by correcting his past aggressive behavior, but meanwhile he stealthily works to disintegrate the group of dinosaurs and rope in supporters. It is his latent animal nature emerging. Blue Cat and Naughty also experience repeated disasters, such as magma eruptions and forest fires, every so often landing them in difficult straights. While fleeing from the calamities, Dr. Sheep begins to feel more and more somber, for the disasters are not regional; the degeneration of the environment is reaching far beyond what anyone could have imagined. There are so many latent problems within the group of dinosaurs (the rise of the vicious power represented by Tyrannosaurus, the friction between dinosaurs when confronted with matters of food and water, and so on). If things escalate any farther, they will soon become unmanageable. Even so, Dr. Sheep does her utmost to help the group of dinosaurs overcome their difficulties, keeping her eyes on the future. She manages to contact Blue Cat, and prepares to guide the dinosaurs to a safe place where they all can converge.

The two groups experience many hardships until they finally get together. But crisis strikes again: volcanic eruptions, earthquakes and tremors.... The group of dinosaurs becomes restless, filled with fear and beginning to lose their reason, some even devolving into a state of half-madness. Using this for an opening, Tyrannosaurus starts a revolt. The Edmontosaurus hatches a deformed offspring, seemingly an ill omen. Faced with the incessant deaths of friends buried in a sea of flames, the friends resolve on delaying their return to Earth and decide to stay to rescue the prehistoric animals and guide them to a more promising place.

Blue Cat and Naughty, along with the Dinosaur Chief and Edmontosaurus, try their best to placate the unruly dinosaurs. Ultimately, the Dinosaur Chief uses his status as king to keep the dinosaurs in line. Tyrannosaurus, realizing his opportunity is gone, turns his evil efforts towards manipulating the dinosaurs.

At this time, Dr. Sheep learns from a high-tech scan that the Earth is completely covered by a "red zone," with only one remaining "green area." It is an extremely urgent situation. Thus the Dinosaur Chief, Blue Cat, Feifei and Ms. Gali lead the way, and Dr. Sheep and Naughty bring up the rear, guiding the group of dinosaurs. They form a long, snake-like caravan, like Mao's famed Long March, on a vast and endless search for morning, on their way to the "Land of Promise."

While progressing, they meet even greater resistance: poisonous gas in the woods, unusual shifts in climate, and more. Dinosaurs are continuously losing their lives. Even more terrible is the absence of food and water, as the deterioration of the environment grows increasingly grave. Although Blue Cat and Dr. Sheep go through immeasurable difficulties to find food and water for the dinosaurs, this does little to solve the problem. The dinosaurs' hearts are filled with fear.

Seizing the opportunity, Tyrannosaurus lures other dinosaurs with food, the evil forces around him gradually expanding. He also uses food to rekindle old conflicts between the dinosaurs. The road to the land of promise seems desolate indeed. With the help of Tyrannosaurus, some carnivorous dinosaurs begin to massacre the other dinosaurs, not even hesitating to devour their own children. Some begin to lose all hope, and are just waiting for death. Even worse, the dinosaurs' love and care has become nothing more than a tool for Tyrannosaurus. Family, friendship and love all become means of bartering for food. Ultimately, his own mother—the Edmontosaurus—dies as a result of his evil schemes. The group of dinosaurs begins to disperse as "humanism" and emotion are twisted, presenting a bizarre spectacle of the struggle between life and death.

The death of Edmontosaurus is a major blow for Blue Cat, who loses faith and becomes extremely negative. But Dr. Sheep and the others earnestly believe that as long as they refuse to give up, they can continue in their hope of saving the dinosaurs. Even in the face of ugly and evil farces, goodness and beauty still manage to radiate from the Dinosaur Chief and others. They have an incomparable love and devotion to life, and have never given up hope. With comfort and encouragement from Dr. Sheep and Feifei, Blue Cat finally overcomes his dejection. With a renewed sense of responsibility and reignited confidence, he works with every-one to help the dinosaurs move towards the land of promise.

At this time, the forces of evil led by Tyrannosaurus take advantage of the right-eousness of the Dinosaur Chief. While Tyrannosaurus is bursting with pride at his successful comeback, a natural disaster occurs. The meaningless fight for power has become a double-edged sword, leading the challenger himself into a fatal position. Before he dies, Tyrannosaur suddenly comes to his senses, using the flesh and blood of his body to provide a means of survival for oth-ers. The remaining dinosaurs come to understand that only united can they make it to the promised land. Under the leadership of Blue Cat and his friends, they finally accomplish the goal.

Waking up one night, they suddenly dis-cover that the Land of Promise has sepa-rated from mainland. Looking out across the sea, they see erupting volcanoes, continual earthquakes, and dinosaurs dying one by one. It is clear that Earth is in the grips of death, and so is their lone island. There is no way back.

Blue Cat and friends still try to rescue the dinosaurs, but they only wail in desperation and refuse any help, urging Blue Cat and friends to leave. As comets strike the Earth, in the last moments before all is about to explode, the doomed dinosaurs force Blue Cat and party to board their space and time shuttle. The Dinosaur Chief collapses hero-ically in a wall of flames. An entire age passes into extinction.

• 312 episodes of *Ocean World*:

Owing to excessive human exploitation of the Earth's natural resources, the environ-ment deteriorates to the point of disaster. Finally, although the deterioration has been temporarily contained, a report by Aunt Chicken and some environmental protection and population experts reveals that thanks to population growth, the whole of the Earth's energy sources are already insuffi-cient. Environmental problems could flare up at any moment, and unless human beings find a better and broader living space, the consequences will be inconceivable.

Thus, humanity scrambles to turn its attention to a second living space—namely the sea and its abundant natural resources. But humanity actually knows very little of the sea, especially of the marvelous and vast world of the ocean floor. Therefore head-quarters decides to establish an ocean floor

resources investigation team. The clever Naughty is appointed leader of the group, with Blue Cat, Feifei and Sweet Sister Tian-niu as part of his team. Together they start onto the ocean floor to carry out their mis-sion and start investigation.

Their first task is to look for a site that is geologically stable, suitable for establishing a city where humans can live and also rich in sufficient natural resources for those remain-ing on land. Dr. Sheep and Feizai, the yellow mouse, are in charge of monitoring, super-vising and organizing the challenging project from the earth's surface. As Naughty is already experienced in dinosaur research, he gets on well with sea animals too. He man-ages to collect many materials from sea plants and animals, information on the dis-tribution and reserves of the ocean's resources, materials from the environment of the ocean floor, and more. The process is fraught with dangers and difficulties, yet reveals the beautiful and mystical side of the sea.

Based on the materials provided by the brave investigation team, earth headquarters' operations progress smoothly. For instance, seaweed and fish are captured and killed in great numbers, the ocean floor's oil and nat-ural gas are mined, nuclear power is used in the sea, and a city above the sea as well as ocean floor homes are under construction. The human crises are alleviated one step at a time. Everyone on the investigation team is filled with joy at their success.

However, while continuing investigation, observing certain phenomena and guided by intuition, Blue Cat comes to believe that the world of the ocean floor is in fact different from the age of the dinosaurs. The presence of seawater makes the ocean a more complex ecosystem. Invariably, striving to meet the current demands without systematically investigating further will mean that develop-ment operations will remain shrouded in ignorance. It could cause even bigger disas-ters for the earth and sea.

Blue Cat lets his perspective be known. However, the disaster has yet to occur, and Blue Cat is unable to produce any strong evi-dence. Naughty and the others try to con-firm Blue Cat's theory to no avail, while Aunt Chicken and the other experts at head-quarters tenaciously hold to their belief that the present development is faultless. They cease to pay any attention to Blue Cat, who is nonetheless convinced he is right. Seeing that Naughty and the others no longer take any notice of him, Blue Cat believes that they are intentionally defying him, and decides to go back in search of support.

Back at headquarters, Blue Cat turns to Dr. Sheep and Feizai for help. Seeing the earth in crisis, they feel it likely that Blue Cat might be right, and so assist him in adjusting their plans for investigation. However, a series of overt mistakes causes the investigation to be delayed time and again, and the crisis that had been somewhat mitigated veers once more towards danger. In addition, Aunt Chicken and others, after hearing that Blue Cat wants to adjust the plan, oppose him vigorously. At headquarters, Dr. Sheep also begins to hesitate. Under these circumstances, it is only Feizai, with his scientific outlook, who believes that Blue Cat may be right. He finds an excuse to leave his post and enters the sea with Blue Cat to do research on their own.

Thus operations are once again divided into two: The developments carried out by Naughty and Dr. Sheep continue on a grand and spectacular scale, as Blue Cat and Feizai start a deep and specialized exploration of the relations within the ocean's ecosystem. Although their exploration is difficult, they acquire a lot of information. However, as there are always setbacks on the way to success, Feizai goes missing at the critical moment. After headquarters and the investigation team get the news that Feizai is missing, they all blame Blue Cat. Further development, along with the entire project, is now blocked because Feizai while serving at headquarters was in control of certain vital information. Losing contact at this point means that resolution of the earth's crisis must be delayed.

Blue Cat lapses into a deep self-condemnation: On the one hand, he has lost his good friend Feizai; on the other, the danger he was so anxious to apprehend has yet to appear, whereas he has managed to aggravate the earth's crisis time and time again. Although he still believes that he's right he asks himself if the hazard is really as large as he thinks. Isn't it as delusional as fearing that the sky might fall in? Blue Cat again lapses into deep self-condemnation.

Right then, the consequences of ignorant human exploitation materialize one after another; petroleum blowouts, a "new Bermuda triangle," a red tide, the extinction of sea animals, a fever in the sea, and the nuclear threat; even the El Niño phenomenon intensifies, bringing huge disasters to earth. Human beings feel helpless, unable to find either reasons or solutions, and just as

expected are in the position of facing ever bigger earth and sea disasters.

When a series of sea disasters strike, Blue Cat realizes that they really were caused by ignorant human exploitation; it proves that he was right all along. He gradually recovers from his self-condemnation, and is also cheered by something that Feizai once told him. Headquarters are at a complete loss, repeatedly receiving contradictory reports. The experts, including Aunt Chicken, refuse to take the information seriously, and instead it is Dr. Sheep who discovers what information is key to solving their present problems. She argues with Aunt Chicken, who stubbornly won't listen. Dr. Sheep has no alternative but to use this information in secret to help everybody alleviate the crisis.

Everybody begins to realize that Blue Cat was right, and begin to cooperate with him. Humanity's destiny is bound up in Blue Cat, and with this series of events he has grown stronger and braver. He leads others in a systematic investigation of the ocean's ecosystem, the results of the former investigation also advancing the progress of this one. At length they make concerted efforts to get to the bottom of each disaster, its causes and patterns, learning how to effectively control and avoid more and bigger disasters. Luckily, Feizai turns up as they are working on the last great crisis, and he assists in solving the problem. Originally, after Feizai got lost, he arrived on an island, with no means of returning. All along he has been studying the origin of each disaster, and at the critical moment it was he who managed to restore communications and send another set of information to headquarters.

Thanks to Dr. Sheep's efforts, Aunt Chicken and the experts finally realize their errors and agree to support Blue Cat's vision. Humanity eventually achieves an understanding of the sea and how to make a reasonable use of it. The crisis is cleared up, and as the burden on the earth lightens, it is restored by degrees to ecological health.

2000

Little Monk

Shanghai Animation Film Studio
Totaling 572 Minutes
Director: Zeng Weijing

Synopsis: The film shows differences between an old and a young monk who live together in a small temple.

Comment: Inspired by A Da's *Three Monks.*

2001

Big-Ear Tutu
Shanghai Animation Film Studio
Totaling 312 Minutes
Director: Su Da

Synopsis: The joyous growth of a three-year-old boy.

Comment: Each episode runs eleven minutes.

Music Up
CCTV
2D Animation
52 × 22 Minutes

Synopsis: Four teenage boys form a band, which causes all sort of personal, family and emotional problems.

Comment: First Chinese animation series to focus on pop stars, in style close to Japanese anime series. The budget is estimated to have been RMB 18 million. Not as successful on TV, more so on the merchandising front (CDs, books, video game).

Shaolin Soccer
Star Overseas, Ltd. and Universe Entertainment, Ltd. (Hong Kong)
Producer: Yeung Kwok Fai
Creator: Stephen Chow

Synopsis: A former Shaolin monk reunites his five brothers to use their superhuman martial arts skills to play soccer.

Comment: Animation series based on a Hong Kong comedy film co-written by, directed by and starring Stephen Chow.

2001–2002

Zentrix
Imagi Animation Studios, Hong Kong
Directors: Tony Tong, Felix Ip
Creators: Tony Tong, Benny Chow, Felix Ip, Francis Kao
Voice Talents: Michelle Ruff, Steven Blum, Stephen Prince, Richard Cansino, Bob Papenbrook, Brianne Siddall, Melissa Fahn, Ezra Weisz, Mona Marshall, Lia Sargent, Ardwright Chamberlain, Michael McConnohie
3D CG-Action Adventure

Synopsis: Like the masters of Fritz Lang's *Metropolis* who turned to robotics, Emperor Jarad, a respected scientist, has created an all-powerful computer called OmnicronPsy, which controls Zentrix City's daily affairs, machines and robots. Eventually, the computer system decides that it can do better without Master Jarad. When they realize the revolt, Jarad and fellow scientist Dr. Roark travel back in time to stop it before it happens.

Awards: Nominated, "Best Series for Children of the Year," Pulcinella Awards 2002, Positano, Italy.

"Gold Camera" Award, Thirty-fifth U.S. International Film and Video Festival, Los Angeles, 2002.

2002–Present

CG Bond Warrior in Future World/ Piggie Hero
Guang Dong Winsing Company Limited
Totaling 160 Episodes
Created by Zhibin Gu
3D Animation

Synopsis: A naughty, orphan boy pig born with superpowers is raised under the custody of Dr. Mihu, an inventive supplier of gadgets.

Comment: In a way, China's comedy answer to *Astro Boy*, the perennial nemesis from Japan.

Awards: Domestic Animation Golden Award, Seventeenth Shanghai TV Festival.

Nominated, Best Domestic Animation, Shanghai TV Festival, 2009.

Annual Best Animated Series 2009, sponsored by KAKU at Aniwow! Festival, CUC Beijing.

2003–2004

The Legend of Nezha
CCTV
2D Animation

Synopsis: To fight Shi Ji, the representative of the Devil's school, the Goddess of Creation selects Ne Zha and arms him with two mighty weapons, a Silk Ribbon and the Ring of Universe.

Comment: Fifty-two episodes on a ten-million-Yuan budget. The boy hero's design equals that of the fabulous feature, *Nezha Conquers the Dragon King*.

2004

Shaolin Kids/Shaolin Wuzang

Shanghai Fantasia Animation Co., Ltd.
26 × 26 Minutes
Producer: Zhang Tianxiao
2D Animation

Synopsis: In ancient times, a reign of terror swept the central area of China. A malicious demon by the name of Heihu has escaped from his magic prison, where he was locked away for a thousand years. Obsessed with vengeance, and more powerful than ever, he brings misery and destruction on a mission to conquer the world.

To stop him Sanzang, the great Shaolin master, communicates with the divine spirits of his ancestors for advice. They suggest he should search for the current reincarnations of the three Shaolin heroes who had captured Heihu in the past.

But when Sanzang finally finds them, he is in for a surprise: The three heroes—Cheng, Tang and Hua—are practically children, two boys and a girl, who have to start from scratch again. They are just kids who must be taught the art of Kung Fu to become veritable masters again before they can confront the fearsome demon.

Comment: Producer Zhang Tianxiao is a member of the Cartoon Arts Committee of China TV Artist Association, as well as the Cartoon Society of China, and graduate supervisor at the Animation College of Chinese Media University. In 1998 he founded Fantasia Animation.

Over the course of years, Fantasia Animation has taken on a leading position in the Chinese animation industry and also has earned a high reputation in overseas mainstream media cooperating with Disney Channel, ZDF (Second Channel German Television), France Television, TF 1, M6, and SMG as well as domestic CCTV. Well-known companies they are cooperating closely with include Moonscoop, Futurikon, Marathon, Dupuis, Ellipse and others.

2004–Present

Pleasant Goat and Big Big Wolf/Xi Yang Yang Yu Huitai Lang

Creative Power Entertaining
2D Animation

Synopsis: The perennial but vain attempt of a grey, loser wolf (Hui Tai Lang or Wolffy), who lives with his narcissistic tyrant wife queen, who wears a battered crown and is known as Hong Tai Lang, Red Wolf or Wolnie, in the ruin of an old castle tower, to catch the cute sheep that happily live in their village on pastoral Greengrass Land. Besides the hero goat Xi Yang Yang (Pleasant Goat, Happy or Weslie) who wears a small bell on its neck, there are Man Yang Yang (Slow Goat/Slowy), the mayor of the village, who also is the local teacher; Mei Yang Yang (Tibbie), Lan Yang Yang (Paddi) and Fei Yang Yang (Jonie).

Comment: A Chinese animation series created somewhat in the tradition of *Coyote and Road Runner* by Huang Weiming, Lin Yuting and Luo Yinggeng.

With a twenty-million-yuan investment, the series got very soon to the market value of more than one billion and became China's most successful cartoon series so far, with initial audience ratings up to 17.3 percent.

The Wolf Queen, who constantly commands her husband to go and catch some

Pleasant Goat and Big Big Wolf.

Xi Yang Yang.

lovely goats, resembles Chinese wives and therefore always gets some laughs. She certainly is over-demanding and abusive.

2005

Chinese Chess Master/Hong Ying

2D Animation

Comment: China's first completely homemade anime series. Previously, all anime series produced in China were funded, guided and directed by Japanese companies. Due to a strict policy in monitoring animated series in China, it was not immediately broadcast when finished but was shown some years later. Patterned after a Japanese series, *Hikaru No Go.*

The Dreaming Girl

CCTV
26 Episodes
2D Animation

Synopsis: A thirteen-year-old schoolgirl and her friends experience all kind of teenage problems. Fantasy and dream elements.

Comment: Anime-style. In planning since 2001.

2005–Present

Sky Eye/Eye of Heaven

CCTV Animation
500 × 7 Minutes
2D/3D Animation

Synopsis: A boy with a magical eye in the sky institutes justice and honesty.

Comment: Produced with a budget of RMB twenty-four million (according to other sources, RMB forty-eight million).

2006

The Adventures of Little Carp/Xiao Li Yu Li Xian Ji

52 × 30 Minutes
CCTV Animation, Inc.

Synopsis: Grandmother carp tells Bubbles, a curious fish with the ability to blow bubbles, about the Dragon, the ruler of rivers and seas, who she says has become dormant after stopping a volcanic eruption. In order to stop a thorny weed, which spreads throughout the lake and turns his grandmother into a bubble, Bubbles is going to summon the legendary Dragon King but only finds an imposter, anthropomorphic Evil Snake, who claims to be the legitimate Dragon King.

Comment: Loosely based on the Chinese folktale "Little Carp Jumps Over the Dragon Gate."

When *Adventures of Little Carp* was broadcast on Nickelodeon Asia Channel, it received the highest viewer ratings in animation category. It was released worldwide to nearly sixty countries and regions.

Blazing Teens

Alpha Animation, Guangzhou
Comment: One season of this series, season four, was done in animation.

2006–Present

Century Sonny: The Adventure of the Extra-Galactic Prince

Lonma Company
104 × 18 Minutes

Synopsis: Set in Numen Kingdom far away on an extragalactic planet. The Source of Life, the protector of Numina and human beings, has been safeguarded in the Numen Kingdom for centuries.

Comment: The first large-scale Chinese animation TV series. RMB 1.5 billion were invested in 104 episodes.

Tortoise Hanba's Stories/Hanbagui

Shenzhen Toonring Animation for CCTV
52 Episodes
Synopsis: After he fell on Earth, the cosmic turtle Hanbagui befriends teenagers Abu, Annie, and Siaomei and looks for his lost fellows.

Comment: Comedy series produced with an estimated budget of RMB thirty million. A mix of *E.T.* and *Alf.*

The Wanderings of Sanmao/Story of Sanmao's Vagrant Life/New Adventures of Sanmao

CCTV

Synopsis: The adventures of a poor orphan boy wandering in Shanghai of the 1930s. Together with his baldheaded friend Xiao Laizi, Sanmao unexpectedly receives grain from entrepreneur Wu Zifu but later falls into a coma. Hou Yiwen, a reporter, tries to investigate the relationship between Wu Zifu and Sanmao.

Comment: Remade as a tribute to the seventieth birthday of one of China's most famous cartoon characters in 2005.

2006–2008

Naughty Boy Ma Xiaotiao

104 × 22 Minutes
China Film Animation

Synopsis: Once upon a time, there was a strange boy who wanted to stay in his mother's body forever because it was the softest, safest and most comfortable place in the world. And when the boy, whom they named Ma Xiaotiao, finally appeared, he surprised everybody with his ability to jump. His father, Ma Tianxiao, was a famous toy designer, and he immediately designed a "Jumping Baby" for sale that became a quite successful item. Gradually Ma Xiaotiao grew up to become the naughty boy of the title and went to school, where he met a number of colorful schoolmates.

Comment: Sounds like a story conceived by Dr. Seuss. Made into a feature film in 2009.

2007–2008

The Olympic Adventures of Fuwa/ Hanyu Pinyin: Fuwa Aoyun Manyouji

Kaku TV/China Beijing TV Station
100 × 11 Minutes
2D Animation
Characters Designed by Wu Guanying

Voice Actors: Tao Hong, Mei Ting, Jin Haixin, Jane Zhang, Cao Ying, Pan Yueming, Gong Nagel, Lu Jianyi, Zeng Weijing, Zhang Zhen, Zhang Guoli

Comment: Chinese animation series portraying the *Fuwa*, the 2008 Summer Olympics mascots, the so-called Friendlies.

Episodes include: "Sprint Crazy," "Boxing World," "Target Shooting," "The Beach and the Volleyball," "Sword Skills," "Tennis Is Fun," "Missing Marathon Man," "The Different Medal," and "Hockey in the Tang Dynasty."

No. 1 Happy Street

Jilin Animation Institute for CCTV
26 Episodes
2D Animation
Producer: Zheng Liguo

Synopsis: The series' heroine, Xiao Jia, and the other protagonists are children who live in a remote, old district of town.

Comment: The series' funny stories reflect the imaginary worlds of children and how they pursue paths that will lead them to a hopefully bright future. The cartoon series was broadcast during the Beijing Olympic Games to favorable reviews.

2007–2010

Qin's Moon/The Bright Moon of Chin Time/Qin Shi Ming Yue

ZN Animation/Hangzhou StarQ
99 × 11 Minutes (4 Seasons)
3D Animation
Executive Producer: Shen Leping
Producers: Chen Qianyuan, Shen Leping
Directors: Wu Yun, Shen Leping
Voice Actors: Feng Junhua, Shen Dawei, Shen Lei, Huang Yiqing, Sun Ye, Zhai We, Hong Haitian
Screenplay: Shen Leping
Musical Score: Westlife

Synopsis: In the Qin Dynasty, more than two thousand years ago, a brave assassin-warrior wants to save his homeland and tries to kill the emperor but fails. In turn the emperor is going to kill his eight-year-old son, Jing Tianming, who is rescued by a swordsman. Together they have many adventures.

Comment: The Wuxia martial arts novels were created by Taiwanese writer Wen Shiren (born in 1948 in Taipei), who combined past and present methods of animation, including traditional Chinese ink painting.

ZN Animation is part of Zhongnan Group of Companies, whose core business is in construction. It is one of the biggest production companies in China. With production studios in Hangzhou, Shanghai and Beijing, as well as a full-time strength of five hundred animators, it has produced 2D and 3D animation of more than ten thousand minutes. Apart from its commitment to animation production, it is also very active in video program distribution, audio and video book marketing, online gaming and related product merchandising.

2008

Little Fox Inventing Stories/Fox's Experience

52 × 22 Minutes
Director: Ge Shuiying

Synopsis: Living in Rabbit Town, which is located near a forest, an active, highly inventive fox joins forces with a smart spider. Little Fox is willing to help everybody around, using his knowledge to change life in town for the better.

Magic Wonderland/Magic Xianzong

Zhejiang Zhongnan Group Cartoon Film/ CCTV Animation Inc.

Comment: First original, fully 3D, animated TV series of China, budgeted at 60 million Yuan. Exported to more than 30 countries and regions. Also played on Nickelodeon. There is a musical version as well as a feature film finished in 2012.

2008–2009 (?)

Changbai Wizard/Changbai Mountain Spirit

Jilin Animation College, broadcast on CCTV and Jilin Satellite Channel
104 × 22 Minutes
2D Animation
Producer: Zheng Liguo

Synopsis: The Changbai Mountains area is located in the northeast of China, on the border between China and North Korea. Most peaks exceed two thousand meters in height, with the highest being Changbai Mountain, where we encounter the spirit of a boyish Ginseng Prince.

Comment: The series uses the legendary

Ginseng Prince as hero and focuses on harmony, environmental protection, integrity, honesty, courage and similar virtues to advocate the harmonious development of humans, animals and plants. We follow the adventure story of Brave Little Ginseng Prince, White Eye Wolf, Monster Race and Plant Race. Every animal, plant and monster has its own character. They all have their own pursuits and individual goals with the ideal of respecting each other and expressing their and the Jilin people's love of Changbai Mountains.

2009

Intelligent Lun Wenxu

Totaling 676 Minutes
Director: Liang Wanlin
    Synopsis: Guangdong's best national scholar in the Ming Dynasty, Lun Xuwen, uses his intelligence to punish evil and helps the ones who deserve aid.
    Comment: Chinese poems are added to the little stories for educational value and to promote Chinese culture.

The Romance of Three Kingdoms

Beijing Huihuang Animation Company/Beijing Glorious Animation Co./Future Planet Studio Co., Tokyo/Brilliant Animation Company, Beijing
52 × 25 Minutes
Historical
Producers: Zhou Feng Ying, Ishihata Shunzaburo
Director: Zhao Huayong
Inspired by "Romance of Three Kingdoms," written in the 14th century by Luo Guanzhong
    Synopsis: Set in the turbulent years near the end of the Han Dynasty and the Three Kingdoms era, this story is part historical, part legend, part martial arts myth. Plots, personal and army battles, intrigues, and struggles take place between the three states of Wei, Shu, and Wu, which emerged from the remnants of the dwindling Han Dynasty.
    Comment: First official animation co-production between China and Japan that was approved by the State Administration of Radio, Film and Television, totaling 1,300 minutes of TV (25 minutes per episode) with a budget of RMB 30 million. An adaptation of *The Romance of Three Kingdoms.*
    According to Asahi Shimbun,

The novel depicts the tumultuous warring period of second-century China and the political intrigue between the different factions.... The Beijing Glorious Animation Co., an affiliate state-owned CCTV broadcaster, is producing on the Chinese side. The company's managing director Zhou Feng Ying noted that the novel is one of China's Four Great Classical Novels (along with *Journey to the West, Dream of the Red Chamber,* and *Water Margin/Suikoden*) that has been popular in Japan. She also said that the company is ensuring that the new *Three Kingdoms* anime retains the 'essence of Chinese history and culture' while the Japanese anime industry is bringing the project to fruition....
    On the Japanese side, Future Planet Co. is producing. Future Planet President Shunzaburo Ishihata said that the bilateral cooperation extends beyond anime production and into the development of related products.[4]

This series returned one of China's great novels to the television screen, true to the words of Premier Wen Jiabao, who asked for uprising of Chinese culture in animation. The myths from Three Kingdoms existed as oral traditions before they were compiled in writing. One of these compilation writers was Luo Guanzhong.

The derivative products for this HD animation maxi-series included audio-visual products (CITVC Books), books (Children's Publishing House), costumes, stationery, toys (Tomy Company), cards, online games, and WAP products. The total value is over RMB 70 million.

In October 2010 it was reported that the Japanese co-producer, Future Planet Studios Co., had filed for bankruptcy at the Tokyo District Court on August 26 and that the bankruptcy procedure had been approved on September 29. The company was founded in 1999 and incurred 1.026 billion yen (about U.S. $12.34 million) in debt to 160 creditors. After several delays, *The Romance of Three Kingdoms* premiered under the title *Saikyo Busho-den Sangoku Engi* in Japan in April 2010. According to animeanime.biz the overall production budget for 52 episodes, split between the co-producers, was 650 million yen (U.S. $7.8 million). Another Sino-Japanese co-production was already in the planning: another one of China's four great classical novels, *Water Margin.*

Soul's Window
Lanhai for CCTV
52 Episodes

Comment: As opposed to the *Romance of Three Kingdoms,* this is no Sino-Japanese joint venture but, at least aesthetically, sort of a rip-off:

On August 22, Chinese broadcaster CCTV released "Soul's Window," a much-trumpeted "original production" aimed at a child audience. But Web users haven't fallen for it.

Same set, same features, same hairstyles—manga fans were not fooled. Several scenes from the 52-episode cartoon were copied directly from "Byousoku" (Five Centimetres per Second), a popular Japanese animated film by Makoto Shinkai released in 2007.

CCTV, China's state-owned television network, says it was not aware that the production violated copyright. China's propaganda department, which co-produced the cartoon, had billed it as an educational program. "Soul's Window" was supposed to teach children a lesson in ethics.

Replying to the accusations, the cartoon's producer, Lanhai, recognized that roughly 1 percent of the 2,500 scenes mirrored parts of "Byouskou" and offered an apology. The company said it would launch an inquiry in order to "identify those responsible and draw lessons from this case."[5]

The correct title of the Japanese production is *Byosoku Go Senchimetoru.*

2009–2010

Astro Plan
Released in Japan as Star Field Record Astro Plan
Golden Eagle Channel, Hunan

Synopsis: Forced by global warming and the bombardment of asteroids, a Space Migration Fleet leaves Earth and encounters an alien race that originates from Planet Iccus. The heroes are six teenagers who are recruited into the Sky Arrow Flight Team.

Comment: Apparently modeled after *Battlestar Galactica,* also borrowing from similar sci-fi series.

Go! Calf
Ordos Dongsheng Skywind Animation Film Co., Ltd./CCTV Animation Co., Ltd.
52 × 22 Minutes
2D and 3D

Supervising Director: Cai Zhijun
Written by Yuan Zhifa

Synopsis: The location is Calf City. To protect his homeland, a cute bighorn calf fights the monstrous Evil Bat who was accidentally released by Ox Demon.

Comment: Capitalizing on its animated star, the series was launched to celebrate the Chinese zodiac animal of the year 2009, which was the ox.

Go! Calf promotes the "spirit of the calf," which overcomes all difficulties and setbacks, making unremitting efforts to move forward.

Zhifa Yuan, former chief editor of *Guangming Daily* and dean of the Communication and Animation Academy of Qingdao University of Science and Technology, served as principal writer. Cai Zhijun, at that time director of CCTV Animation Department, was selected as supervising director.

"The story is inspiring," says Wang Ying, back then general manager of CCTV Animation. "The role we designed is an ordinary one, unlike the usual on-screen heroes who are out of reach for children. The big-horn calf is just like a friend of yours." It is famous throughout China and Asia, so it was a likely choice.

The series had an investment of more than RMB 50 million and totaled 1,144 minutes in length.

Merchandising items and derivatives included toys, books, stationery, shirts and games.

2010

Blue Cat Dragon Riding Team
60 × 17 Minutes
Director: He Mengfan

Synopsis: In the year 2300, Earth civilization enters an age in which everything is being developed at high speed. At the same time, however, all kind of evil forces and antagonists begin to grow. In order to protect world peace, scientist Lala from Planet OZMA comes to Earth and helps humans to set up the best defense system, personified by the Dragon Riding Team. The main representative of the evil forces, one Dr. Vikey, who hides just inside the Dragon Riding Research Center, attempts to rob the miraculous bracelets that contain OZMA power in order to perfect his evil weapon, the "Beast Master," and conquer the world. Lala and Blue Cat, leading the others to repel the Beast

Master and get back the bracelets, find out about the enemy's plan, but all the robotic dragons that correspond to the respective bracelets have defects. The only way is to go back to the Dyna Gear to find corresponding dinosaur genes and then return and beat the Beast Master.

Bug's Plan

13-Minute Episodes
Screenplay: Du Yanhua

Synopsis: In the vast universe there is a tiny planet called Village Sweet. There lives a special breed of bugs, extremely clean and always afraid of getting infected by dust and pollen that might threaten their lives. So they hide and don't dare to go out. Thousands of years pass and one day peace is broken. Human rubbish (such as paper clips, buttons, needle tubes and toothbrushes) falls from the sky and hits the small planet. Bugs begin to complain and quarrel. But while one side of them strongly objects to all rubbish, the other part is willing to accept it and adapt to it to make ordinary life more interesting.

Gog Dibby

Totaling 650 Minutes
Director: Wang Wei

Synopsis: Di and his companions live in the happy environment of Planet Dibby. Here many mysterious guests from other planets gather such as magicians, popular rock stars, romantic adventurers, and elegant Queen Cat. All are attracted by this charming planet but everybody has his/her/its own secret. Why are they coming to Planet Dibby? Di will lead us to find the truth.

Kaka Dragon in Steel Armor

52 × 22 Episodes
Screenplay: Yan Jiang

Synopsis: In the year 3000 human beings live in an age ruled by machines. All their activities are controlled by those machines. Old Dr. Charley, a devoted robotics researcher, realizes that while machines can bring people convenience, they also can cause dangers. By accident, Dr. Charley finds the ancient records of Zodiac elves, which enables him to invent Chinese Zodiac robots, hoping his mechanical creatures will find the original Stone and protect Earth.

Kung Fu Masters of the Zodiac

52 × 22 Minutes
Fantawild Animation Inc., Shenzhen

Synopsis: The powerful Nian has evil designs on the world. With the blessing of the Kitchen God, Little Hoffen, the earthly incarnation of Polaris, sets out with Rascal the Rat—an unlikely master in the Circle of Twelve—in search of the other eleven animals of the Chinese zodiac to support him in the final confrontation with Nian. The Sacred Animals represent the full twelve-month period in the twelve-year lunar cycle.

Comment: Fantawild Animation Inc. is a professional company engaged in original animation design and production under Fantawild Holdings, one of the largest groups in China's cultural industry. In 2011, their annual output got top ranking and was widely broadcast by CCTV, Beijing's cartoon channel Kaku and Guangdong Jiajia.

Loving Theatre of Baby Luo

52 Episodes Totaling 780 Minutes
Screenplay: Zhang Siwei

Synopsis: School is holding the Chinese "traditional culture broadcast activity." Proposed by Baby Luo, pupils establish a loving theatre, work together and do their best, performing many vivid and interesting plays, telling audiences fifty-two warm and inspiring traditional Chinese love tales.

Comment: There is love for the nation and love for people. There is Yu, who prevents floods. There is moving family love and touching friendship. There is a chapter devoted to Huatuo, who cures sickness to help his suffering patients, and the classic tale of Mulan, who joins the army.

Lucky Star Bajie

52 × 13 Minutes
2D
Director: Wu Minghong

Synopsis: Bajie and his animal friends live in a modern tree city.

Comment: There are lots of modern tools around that are familiar to children. The animation absorbs Chinese characteristics in its style and mixes the national element with internationally fashionable concepts.

Nuonuo Forest the Second

Totaling 707 Minutes
Director: Wu Kun

Synopsis: Bu and his friends are primitive men who live in the jungle. They hunt, pick fruit and gradually get to know nature. They work together and help each other to overcome various difficulties, obtaining lots of information closely related to their daily life. They also learn to peacefully live together with animals and build a family in harmony with nature.

Rainbow Cat and Blue Cat Come Back

34 Minutes per Episode
Director: He Mengfan

Synopsis: Seven swordsmen and Little Fox chase Little Black and, in doing so, enter a mysterious forest. Here Blue Cat loses his Kung Fu skills and disappears, while the swordsmen turn into babies. Fortunately, before turning into an infant, Doudou leaves a message that the Pure Yuan Pearl stored in the Hangzhou Three Court Pavilion is the purest item in the world and as such will heal and restore everything. However, the pearl is born by a ten-thousand-year-old tree only every ten years. Whoever will overcome the students enrolled to protect the tree will get the pearl. To master the task, Rainbow Cat and Little Fox travel overseas to Phoenix Island to join the Phoenix Martial Club and learn Kung Fu from scratch again.

Rubi and Yoyo: Education Series

ZN Animation
312 × 8 Minutes
52 × 6 Minutes (Sequel)
Flash Animation
Screenplay: Xu Hui

Synopsis: Rubi, her magical pet Yoyo and their friends play together, learn from each other and spend their days happily. While they are growing up, they learn to distinguish various shapes and colors. What's more astonishing is the experience of meeting Numeral Baby when learning the twenty-six English letters.

Comment: Targeted at preschoolers. Meant to help kids learn simple life truths. Every episode carries messages that propagate prosocial and educational values such as personal responsibility, care and concern for others, creativity, making friends, safety at home, and a clean environment.

Sergeant Biscuit

52 × 13 Minutes
Screenplay: Ma Hua

Synopsis: In Cookie City, which belongs to Queen Dessert, the various cookie people live happily and peacefully. Sergeant Biscuit and his assistant Cookie are the only policemen in town. However, on distant Moldy Planet, greedy Dr. Mildew and his stupid brothers, Moldy Head and Moldy Mind, board Spittoon Spaceship to invade Cookie Town and rob all precious flour resources.

Swallow Tail Man

26 × 11 Minutes
Director: Wu Jun

Synopsis: During summer vacation in the twenty-first century, twelve-year-old brother and sister Leilei and Xinxin are sent to KaiYuan Temple to participate in Hardships Summer Campaign but mistakenly enter a mysterious base, actually an interstellar spaceship manned by space traveler Tangtian. Their bodies adapt to the new situation and so the kids become Swallow Tail Men. During this they learn about a plan created on Planet × to destroy Earth. Alien forces are under the command of Iron Arrow. To prevent disaster the Swallow Tail Men cross time and space.

Tiny Bugs with Big Wisdom

14 Minutes
Directors: Wu Bin, Hou Zhe

Synopsis: In Bug Village lives a group of cute bugs that are curious and eager to seek for answers to all questions and overcome all problems.

2010–2011

Moon Circus

CCTV Animation Inc.
52 × 12 Minutes
3D Animation
Director: Cao Liang

Synopsis: Moon Circus is the children's favorite place. From the giant sky wheel they can view the whole beautiful scene of the city, have the feeling of flying by riding on wooden horses, and watch fantastic circus performances and conjuring tricks.

The leading characters of Moon Circus include Bamboo Baby, a panda who is good at conjuring; Fei Fei, a naughty, smart monkey; Lu Lu, a little rhinoceros, lovely but a little bossy; Da Guo, a timid tiger; and Ban Ban, a penguin who likes to play jokes on others.

They perform their tricks with pleasure and live a happy life. But just like common people, they have their own strong points and shortcomings.

2011

Adventure in Jungle

26 × 11 Minutes
Screenplay: Liu Sheng

Synopsis: In the jungle there live five good friends headed by Deer. In order to realize their wishes, they search for the magic mirror. Unexpectedly, the mirror has already been obtained by Fox and Tiger, who have bad intentions towards the five friends. The rivals try their best to cause trouble, but Deer, together with his friends, fearlessly solves all conspiracies and tricks and pursues his dreams.

Animen

26 × 14 Minutes
Director: Xu Ke

Synopsis: Gangshou, Kang, Beck and Cannon meet in Mecha Army College and soon become good friends. They participate in a supply task undertaken by both Fengyan and Captain Ming, but are attacked by Ti people under the command of Wu Emperor and Lipton. The Second Fleet is almost destroyed except for Shixi and Jiangmai. Leaders in the Frog Family are not pleased with the loss, and Captain Ming takes all responsibilities. The leaders plan to reorganize the Second Fleet. Gangshou and the other cadets join Captain Ming.

The Big Horn Dream Works

Ordos Dongsheng Skywind Animation Film Co., Ltd./CCTV Animation Inc.
150 × 12 Minutes
2D/3D Animation

Comment: Repackaging the main characters of *Go! Calf.*

Boonie Bears/Boonie Bears or Bust (Sequel)

Fantawild Animation, Inc., Shenzhen
104 × 13 Minutes
208 × 13 Minutes (Sequel)
3D Animation
Director: Leon Ding

Synopsis: Set in a lovely forest. Bear brothers Briar and Bramble constantly rally their nefarious nemesis, diminutive logger Vic.

Comment: Fast-paced comedy, almost American-style.

The Happy Baby

156 × 15 Minutes
Screenplay: Huang Weiming

Synopsis: Somewhere in universe there is a place called Star Planet where humans, robots and aliens live together. One day a Universe Developing Company from Grey-Hearted Planet sends two King Warriors, tentatively named General Big and General Small, to occupy Star Planet by using their top weapon—the five-color magic stone that can give machines life and wisdom. When they enter the atmosphere, however, an accident occurs. Excepting the black gem, the red, pink, green and blue ones scatter on Star Planet. A talented mechanic by the name of Dr. Zhai, who repairs the machines, finds these parts and activates them. Out of it, Happy Superman, Sweet Superman, Love-fickle Superman, Careless Superman and Careful Superman are born, and under the leadership of Dr. Zhai they beat General Big again and again, protecting the world of Star Planet.

Huoxing 500

104 × 22 Minutes
Comment: Series celebrating Chinese space travel.

Little Freckles and Natural Curls

42 × 11 Minutes
Director: Yang Aihua

Synopsis: Five children in kindergarten learn from everyday troubles.

Comment: The little worries of preschool children.

Little Rui and Big Devil Lord

Xiamen Domoko Animation Co., Ltd.
60 × 15 Minutes

Synopsis: The adventures of five children led by Little Rui and Big Devil Lord, a weird inventor, in Village Luo Keke at Song Forest.

Magic Teenager Group of Magic Game

26 × 14 Minutes
Director: Dai Yan

Synopsis: A group of children mistakenly enters a magician's secret room. The magician attempts to keep the kids confined in the game world forever. The children, however, work together and manage to return to the real world.

Qi and Her Friends Beauty and Happy

Totaling 312 Minutes
Directors: Shui Jing, Zhang Mingxin
Synopsis: Qi and her friends fight with Yaya Wu, who destroys the environment.
Comment: Topic: environmental protection.

Three Strong Agents

13 Minutes per Episode
Screenplay: Fu Yan
Synopsis: Three agents—Little Bei, Little Yu and Little Fei—leave Heaven to find Sister Flower Goddess, who is missed. Thanks to their braveness, they go through many hardships, overcome various difficulties, and cooperate with other gods from Heaven. They defeat monsters, make extraordinary achievements and finally complete their tough mission by saving Sister Flower Goddess.
Comment: A comedy series.

Traveler Cool Doggy

26 × 9 Minutes
3D Animation
Screenplay: Wang Liping, Guo Guannan
Synopsis: Cool Doggy travels around the world in a hot balloon and gets a book titled *The Legend of Dragon.* With the help of this book he discovers Kowloon Island and on the way makes friends with Milk and Doudou. Meanwhile the evil Dr. Bala on Kaka Planet also searches for the precious book to find the trace of the dragon who protects the Luminous Pearl. Dr. Bala arrives on Earth and inspires Evil Dog Gang to help him steal the book. Finally Dr. Bala challenges Old Dragon and threatens to destroy the forest. Cool Doggy wakes up Old Dragon and finally defeats Dr. Bala.

2011–2012

Monkey King/Mei Hou Wang

CCTV Animation Inc.
52 × 22 Minutes
2D/3D Animation
Synopsis: Long ago, there was a monkey-shaped stone filled with superior spirituality. After adopting the essence of nature, a monkey bursts out of the stone and starts his legendary life. Once he joins a local monkey tribe, he is declared the new king. In order to protect the tribe, his newly won family, he leaves his friends, Jade Rabbit, Six Ear Monkey and Ginseng Fruit, and travels far away to learn magical skills and Kung Fu from the patriarch of Daoist Mountain. Thus he gets his name, Sun Wukong.

After gaining great magic power, Sun Wukong defeats a demon, breaks through Hell, and gets the As-You-Will Gold-Banded Cudgel as his weapon from the Dragon King of the Eastern Sea. For comforting Sun Wukong, the Jade Emperor asks him to become the Protector of the Horses in Heaven. Doing so, however, he brings Heaven into trouble. After realizing his hasty behaviors, Sun Wukong accepts the punishment and eventually passes the final test to finish his mental and physical growth. Then he becomes the real Monkey King.

When returning to the Mountain of Flower and Fruit, he finds that another Monkey King is ruling the tribe who actually was his childhood friend, Six Ear Monkey. For ruling the universe, Elder White Deer (Nine Soul Saint) releases his powerful but evil soul by capitalizing on the desire of Six Ear Monkey—to become king of the monkeys. However, Elder White Deer is finally defeated by Sun Wukong and his faithful compatriots. The handsome Monkey King saves his friend, Six Ear Monkey, and resumes his position as the legitimate king of the Mountain of Flower and Fruit.

Comment: Monkey King is the fourth epic animation project developed and produced by CCTV. The creative team consisted of many top Chinese animators and directors.

CCTV Animation Inc., an animation company fully invested by CCTV, was founded on March 18, 2007, and reformed by the former animation department of CCTV Programs Center for Youths and Children. Right after the transfer, it was rated as one of the "70 Representative Cases of the Cultural System Reform."

Relying on its first-rate animation, creation, production and maintenance and logistics talents as well as excellent animation equipment, software and management, CCTV Animation Inc. has developed various projects of different genres (such as fairy tales, education, science fiction, fantasy, and adventure) and different techniques (2D, 3D, stop-motion animation, motion capture, etc.).

CCTV Animation Inc. has done more than two hundred TV animation series. The annual output of original animation is up to more than eight thousand minutes.

2012

Adventures on Island of Gigantic Insects

CCTV Animation Inc.
52 × 22 Minutes
2D Animation

Synopsis: Three children who are not acquainted with each other go on board a vessel for their summer camp at sea. At the beginning of the journey, they are attacked and brought to a mystic island of giant insects by some unidentified organism. Those gigantic insects have multiplied from generation to generation. They occupy the island and threaten the lives of the three kids. The kids fight for survival in gruesome nature and overcome all dangers. Meanwhile, they meet an aborigine girl named Chacha, who appears occasionally but cannot be called an ally. Little by little, the secrets hidden in the jungle of the solitary island for centuries are revealed.

Baiji Academy/Lucky Town

CCTV Animation Inc.
52 × 15 Minutes
2D Animation

Synopsis: A group of children lives happily in a beautiful town called Baiji. They are Xia Xiaozhi, a dinosaur expert, Lee Xiaoxue, a gentle and lovely girl, Zhao Zilong, a hunter, Ren Manman, an authoritative spokesperson, Li Taibai, a foreigner who is interested in Chinese culture, and an alien with eight fingers.

Xia Xiaozhi's abundant imagination makes his simple life interesting and colorful. Actually, Xia Xiaozhi, a fourth-grade student at Baiji Academy, is naughty, dynamic, lively, and cheerful. Sometimes he makes mistakes, but generally he is kind and sweet by nature. When he learns that other kids learn many skills through extracurricular activities, Xia Xiaozhi gets the idea of becoming an "all-round talent." His grandfather and mother support him unanimously. Through the joint efforts of the whole family, although he doesn't achieve his dream of being an "all-round talent," he truly begins to understand what "hard work" means. Eventually he earns high praise for his creative dinosaur products.

Beanie's Secret World

CCTV Animation Inc.
13 × 13 Minutes
2D Animation

Synopsis: Beanie is a little girl who has the special ability of talking to animals, even communicating with them from a distance.

One day, Beanie happens to meet and become friends with Paul the Octopus, who has just become world famous for his foretelling concerning soccer games.

By helping Paul to rescue his family members who were captured by humans, Beanie discovers her own courage and determination to do whatever she can to help animals and the environment. Since then, more and more animals look for her and seek her help. As she discovers more miracles and secrets of the animal kingdom, she also finds out about her own mission of coming to planet Earth.

Cat-Eyed Boy Bao Dada

26 × 22 Minutes
2D Animation

Synopsis: Bao Dada, an ordinary-looking pupil, is fond of looking for the truth and curious about everything. One day, a stream of unknown energy from one thousand years ago transforms Bao Dada into a mysterious cat-eyed boy, a fancy detective genius, for Bao Dada can keenly observe like a cat, sophisticatedly analyze like a computer, and closely reason like Sherlock Holmes himself. However, his talent causes the jealousy of Black Wizard, who is a sinister and crafty thief. He also wants to adopt the mysterious energy from ancient times and completely defeat the hated Bao Dada. For this purpose, Black Wizard sets up a series of mazes and creates havoc everywhere, making the genius boy-detective face great dangers and challenges. The boy has only one aim: Let the cat eyes see through to the truth!

The Cloud Baby

Tsanghao Animation and CCTV Animation Inc.
39 × 20 Minutes
2D Animation

Comment: Fairy-tale series for 3- to 6-year-old children.

Dream Adventure

CCTV Animation Inc.
26 × 22 Minutes
2D Animation

Synopsis: Qingfeng (Breeze) and Mingyue (Moon), two little night-angel novices, are responsible for managing kids' dreams to guarantee that every child has sweet dreams. With the strong desire to become a dominant god, Baoyu (Storm) targets a group of summer camp children on a cruise and tries to control their dreams. During the fight, children overcome their weaknesses. Meanwhile, Qingfeng and Mingyue learn a lot and gradually become mature.

Comment: As a fairy-tale cartoon series, it aims to help children develop healthy life attitudes and habits. By amplifying children's shortcomings in their dreams, it doesn't use the traditional boring and didactic description, and it makes it easier to accept the truths conveyed from the story.[6]

Happy Town

CCTV Animation, Inc.
52 × 13 Minutes

Synopsis: Xiao Mi, the main character, is a folded-paper boy who together with his friends lives on Origami Street.

Comment: Origami World is a fairy land made of origami models. Classical Chinese visual elements and modern lifestyle blend in this world. Animals, plants, the sun, the moon, vehicles and houses, even the residents, all things are made by paper-folding.

Hi! Myself!

Guangdong Benko Cartoon Group Limited
Co-Presented by CCTV Animation Inc. and
    Guangdong Benko Cartoon Group Limited
312 × 11 Minutes
2D Flash Animation, HD

Synopsis: If magic can make your dreams come true in an instant, will growing up be less troublesome?

In a magical town called "Oohope" a tiny magician named Benko, a toy-shop owner named Sanzi, a cartoon artist called Pochy, a salesgirl named Fenko and a physician by the name of Fengo live happily together in mutual friendship. They also consider growing up a terrible, troublesome issue. They ask such questions as, Why can't I meet my fairy-tale prince? Why can't I sleep all day and night? Why is there never enough pocket money to buy toys? Why do I have to go to work? Why can't I fly?

When such troublesome questions come along, Benko the little magician summons his powers to make all wishes come true. Let the printer print out your fairy-tale prince! Make the sun go away so that you can be lazy and sleep all day! Let potato chips become flakes of real gold!

But the truth is, Benko's magic always leads to hilarious problems. Eventually, everyone realizes that true magic isn't about transforming the world, but transforming your inner self.

At the end of each episode, all the friends come together, and with their hearts and will united create their own miracles.

Comment: With headquarters located in Jiangmen City, Guangdong Benko Cartoon Group Limited has branches all around China and the world. Their operation center is in Guangzhou, creation center in Dalian, game center in Chengdu, animation center in Vancouver, and product R&D centers in Guangzhou, Jiangmen, Seoul, and Paris. Their sales channel is varied and widespread around the domestic market, and it includes supermarkets, department stores, and e-commerce.

The Legend of Huainanzi

CCTV Animation Inc.
52 × 22 Minutes
2D Animation

Synopsis: During the time of ancient Western Han Dynasty (206 BC–AD 9), a series of disasters caused by occult phenomena swept across the entire world. Huainanzi, the mysterious Chinese book bound in bamboo, was ripped apart and sent through time to different historical junctures. The pieces of the book were transformed into various objects, waiting to be rediscovered.

A hundred years later, a young man named Hong Lie takes up the burden of collecting the missing pieces of the ancient bamboo book. With the help of Ba Gong and his friends, going through the Gate of twenty-four Solar Terms, Hong Lie travels through dynasties to search for the lost pieces.

In his adventure, Hong Lie and his loyal friends, Ji Ming and Gou Tiao, together experience the greatness of the ancient legends, appreciate the wisdom of the ancestors from

Chun Qiu Period, and witness all the weird things happening among ordinary people. Stories of warmth and coldness, sadness and happiness, separation and reunion lead them to the great universe that is opened in the pages of the book Huainanzi, and through exciting adventures he makes lifelong friends. In this special way, Hong Lie communicates with the ancestors and begins to recognize the principles of the world, realizing that obeying the laws of nature and being in harmony with the environment is the right thing to do. A simple collecting journey slowly becomes a trip that challenges him to go on with his family mission and inherit the ancestors' spirit.

One Hundred and Eight Heroes

Beijing Glorious Animation Company
108 × 22 Minutes
3D Animation
Producer: Zhou Feng Ying

Synopsis: During the period of the Song Dynasty, AD 960–1279 in Chinese history, the government was corrupt and people lived in bad conditions. A girl named Jin was detained by a bully and then saved by Lu Da. When the government was looking for him, Lu had to become a monk and named himself Zhishen to elude the search. Eventually he joins forces with Kung Fu instructor and nobleman Lin Chong, who felt the responsibility of taking revenge for his family. At that time there were four treacherous court officials in central government who often would have conflicts with each other. One day they entered a competition and assigned their henchmen to participate, but Lin Chong had the upper hand and defeated all rivals. Gao Qiu, one of the Gang of Four, was very upset that Lin Chong had damaged his plan, so he ordered Lin Chong to calumniate Lin and exiled him to the border, hoping to kill him on the way. Finally, on a fodder farm, Lin learned of Lu's betrayal and killed him. After that, Li went to Liangshan Mountain overnight. At almost the same time, Senior Grand Tutor Cai was going to celebrate his birthday. Cai's son-in-law sent lots of treasures as a present to Cai and assigned Yang Zhi to transport them. However, the treasure was stolen by Chao Gai, Wu Yong, three brothers surnamed Luan, and others. Wu Song, after killing the tiger, became an officer, but he also went to Liangshan Mountain, as he killed the ones who had plotted to assassinate his brother and hit a bully who colluded with a governor. Song Jiang had been sentenced to death because he had written a poem that contained offensive content, but he was lucky to be saved by the heroes of Liangshan Mountain, and so he joined the group of freedom fighters.

Steel Team

CCTV Animation Inc.
100 × 12 Minutes
3D Animation

Synopsis: Residents live a peaceful life on Machine Planet. Li Gangzai and his uncle, Da Tie, run a small fast-food restaurant. Gangzai, a naughty boy by nature, is always very reckless and causes trouble almost every day. His imprudence and impetuousness accidentally help the Black King's man rob a King Stone. As long as he absorbs the energy of another two King Stones, he can break the ice of the Milky Way and create havoc on Machine Planet.

Dr. Fa Tiao, commander of the Steel Team, comes to Da Tie's fast-food restaurant and reveals the truth that Gangzai, Lei Bing and A Ya are descendants of the Seven Warriors. Gangzai's father left a King Stone in Gangzai's body. In order to fight the Black King, the descendants of the Seven Warriors must reorganize as the Steel Team.

The new Steel Team experiences many dangers but finally overcomes all difficulties in friendship and trust. Gangzai, Lei Bing and A Ya gradually grow up and fill the shoes of their ancestors. With the support of Queen Sun, Dr. Fa Tiao, Uncle Da Tie, and Hunter, they eventually defeat the evil and greedy Black King, and compel him out of Machine Planet for good. Laughter and cheers resound in the sky of Machine Planet again.

To the Galaxies

CCTV Animation Inc.
26 × 11 Minutes
2D Animation

Synopsis: Lei Lei and Jing Jing, two juveniles from Earth, save a homeless dog they name Tuo Tuo and adopt it. However, a strange blinking necklace on the neck of Tuo Tuo catches their attention. One day, Tuo Tuo disappears. While trying to find him, Lei Lei and Jing Jing encounter a great number of other animals with blinking necklaces like Tuo Tuo that seem to be hypnotized and run towards a spaceship hidden in the forest.

In order to rescue Tuo Tuo, Lei Lei and Jing Jing decide to take a risk and enter the spaceship. They find that the spacecraft's mission is to hypnotize Earth animals and smuggle them to a strange planet called Tiezha Star. Trying to stop it, Lei Lei and Jing Jing learn the basic skills to operate and fly the spaceship, with the help of Mr. Green, a mechanic who doesn't want to be a smuggler. After a fierce fight with Ahuo, the head of Tiezha Star, the kids from Earth return the animals to their home planet. However, the emperor of Tiezha has built a huge fleet and is racing towards them.

The Wisdom Forest
Beijing Glorious Animation Company
365 × 9 Minutes
2D Flash Animation
Producer: Zhou Feng Ying

Synopsis: In the Wisdom Forest lives a group of cute animals who engage in all kind of activities, such as distributing presents, organizing a Love Parade, and venturing into Mushroom Valley. A little puppy gets its first tooth, the calf elephant becomes stronger every day, and the young tiger often bullies others.

Zheng He's Voyages to the West Seas
ZN Animation
52 × 22 Minutes
2D Animation with 3D Elements

Synopsis: Six hundred years ago, before Christopher Columbus or Ferdinand Magellan, Chinese emperor Yongle (Zhu Di) of Ming Dynasty fame approved Admiral Zheng He's project to set sail to the Western Seas (now known as the Indian Ocean) to spread his Imperial influence.

The first voyage of Zheng He (1371–1433) consisted of three hundred gigantic, six-masted ships holding twenty-eight thousand crewmen: sailors, soldiers, workers, navigators, explorers and physicians. This unprecedented event impressed all of China and the sight of the vessels off a foreign shore would have been a majestic and awesome spectacle.

With his trusted companions, Commander Wu Baisheng and footman He Bi, tens of thousands of crewmen, countless cattle, sheep and poultry, and bearing stores of rice, gifts and treasures, Admiral Zheng He embarked on a mission that would take him to the far-flung corners of the world and distant islands, navigating treacherous waters and stormy seas, fighting vicious pirates and dealing with unfriendly rulers.

Comment: Targeted at the ages 7–14. Two stowaways were added as identification figures: a young boy and his pet monkey.

Undated Series

Abu, the Little Dinosaur
ZN Animation
26 × 24 Minutes
3D Animation

Synopsis: A long time ago there reigned a virtuous dinosaur king. Everything was good—until a power-hungry courtier, the diabolical sorcerer-fox, cast a spell upon the poor king that turned his heart from good to evil. A sense of foreboding, a portent of doom, swept over the kingdom. On the night of the lunar eclipse, the spellbound ruler shall draw the life force away from his subjects, the unfortunate forest animals.

Luckily, a baby dinosaur turns up, Abu, son of the feared dinosaur king. Taken under the tutelage of an old and wise lemur, the hatchling grows in strength and skills, desperate to save his father and the fellow forest dwellers from the spell.

Comment: Targeted at 5–8 years of age.

The Configurators
ZN Animation
26 × 22 Minutes
3D Animation

Synopsis: A long time ago our prehistoric ancestors roamed Earth. The apeman is thought to have been a primitive human species, but truth be told, they were not hunter-gatherers—they were masters of technology; for they had invented the dinosaur attack transformer, a rugged vehicle wielding fearsome weapons. And they needed these machines, as hostile jellyfish-like aliens were invading Earth. Their swarms blotted out the sun as they massed to conquer the planet. But the apemen in their dino-transformers waged a heroic war and defeated the Jellies. They saved the world and fulfilled their destiny—to become modern man.

Thousands of years later the Jellies try again but are defeated by a new Super Force consisting of three friends: Andy, Toothy and Hero.

Comment: Targeted at 8–14 years of age.

Dream Town

ZN Animation
104 × 12 Minutes
3D Animation

Synopsis: Dreamtown is a community of animals: Princess Mimi and Dou-Dou are the nice mice. There are Mr. Frog, Miss Toad, Dragon Fan-Fan, Big-Mouth Duck and baddie Ata, another mouse.

Comment: Targeted at 5–9 years of age.

Dreamy Kitty House

Hangzhou StarQ Xunaji Science and Technology Information Technology Co., Ltd.
26 × 12 Minutes
2D Animation

Synopsis: In a city there is a busy Happiness Avenue and in it a special toy store they call Dreamy Kitty House. The proprietor has collected many cat dolls from all over the world for the kitty house. The main characters are the cute cat doll Lin Li and her friends who watch the people walking by in Happiness Avenue through the small window of the toy shop. From the angle of the cat dolls, the spectators get to know the life stories of the passers-by.

Comment: The fairy tale shows the ups and downs of the dolls as well as the humans they watch so intensely.

The production company, Hangzhou StarQ, was established in 2005. The company was one of the first entrants into the National Cartoon Industry Base in Hangzhou (West Lake) as well as one of the original cartoon and comics enterprises highly supported by Hangzhou Binjiang Hi/New-Tech Zone and respective government authorities in Zheijiang Province, Hangzhou City and Binjiang District.

Equipped with a multi-channel platform for publicity, plus sound channels for circulating products domestically and internationally, the company is dedicated to the exploration and operation of the industrialized Chinese cartoon.

Electro Boy

Alpha Animation and Culture Co., Ltd., Guangzhou
52 × 24 Minutes

Synopsis: Capri is a robot coming from the future to accomplish a secret but important mission. Capri comes across Scott and gives him a magic watch that transforms him into Electro Boy—a superhero with strong powers and great combat skills. To save today's world and the future, Scott and Capri must defeat Ropri, the evil robot.

Comment: Targeted at ages 4–12.

The production company, Guangdong-based Alpha Animation and Culture Co. (motto: "Bringing joy, wisdom and dreams to the world!") is one of the most powerful animation and culture industrial-group corporations in China. It integrates cartoon program production; the toy industry; comic magazine creation and distribution; and licensing and merchandising with the objective to establish a "one-source multi-use" business pattern.

In 2011, it was rated as one of the "Top 30 Cultural Enterprises in China." Ever since its establishment in 1993, Alpha Animation has followed the principle of development based on innovation and has created the unique and new pattern of "interactive growth of culture and industry."[7] As the only animation enterprise that has an "omni-media industrial chain in operation in China, Alpha Animation has extended its business to the fields of creation of animation, media disseminating, image authorization, product manufacture and marketing."[8]

Alpha's animation studio has one hundred staff members, the comics department twenty, license and merchandising fifteen, the toy sales department one hundred, and the toy manufacture department two thousand.

On October 11, 2012, Alpha Animation announced a strategic co-development partnership with Hasbro, an American multinational toy and board game company.

Fruity Robo

Alpha Animation and Culture Co., Ltd., Guangzhou
52 × 24 Minutes

Synopsis: One day the mysterious Lotus Flower on top of the Fruit Mountain, which protects all fruit, disappears without trace. Without protection, however, the Fiend leads Four Villains to occupy Fruit Mountain and set up a huge fruit factory. They keep looting every fruit village and grabbing fruit to produce juice for sales. At this critical juncture, three students of Jelly Academy, who have the ability to summon the skill of the Fruit Robot, stand up to save their families, friends and the whole mountain. They discover that the real intention of the Fiend is to protect the Fruit Mountain in his own way, since he knows that without the Lotus Flower, the hearts of fruit villagers will gradually weaken and Fruit Mountain will be destroyed. To suppress the deterioration, the Fiend dedicates himself to reviving the Lotus Flower.

Comment: Targeted at ages 4–10.

Galaxy Racers

ZN Animation
52 × 22 Minutes
2D/3D Animation

Synopsis: Set in the future on the Yellow River Planet, where the realm of car racing has advanced far beyond Formula One—into the domain of Galaxy Racers. Riders steer their simulator-racers, which remotely control the actual customized speedsters hurtling around a track. The hero, a teenager named Roy, was born to race and aspires to be the King of Galaxy Racers. But his guardian, his grandfather, sees a threat from the evil and greedy Taz, the CEO of the Titan Space Navigation Auto Group, which seeks to swallow or destroy all competitors. Their Mosha Racing Team crushes everything ruthlessly under its thundering wheels. So Grandpa arranges for Roy to join the good guys of the Matela Racing Team.

Comment: Targeted at 8–12 years of age.

Go for Speed

Alpha Animation and Culture Co., Ltd., Guangzhou
64 × 24 Minutes
2D/3D Animation

Synopsis: In Mini 4D racing world, only one thing matters—the national championship. To fulfill the dream of his father and his missing brother, Dragon, the young Mini 4WD enthusiast, is striving for the ultimate success. Meanwhile, for personal reasons, Black Devil, Dragon's evil counterpart, tries to prevent him from winning. Dragon has to strengthen his skill and face the challenges. Whenever there is a problem, a mystery man appears to help him. To defeat Black Devil and find his brother, Dragon must disclose all mysteries. There only is one truth.

Comment: Targeted at 5–14 years of age.

The Grimoire of Future

Producer: Zheng Min
Director: Lin Guan Ming

Comment: One who criticized the situation of Chinese education in animation was producer Zheng Min, president of Zhejiang Pro and High Culture Industry Co., Ltd.: "We are facing a situation in which many graduates cannot find a job. On the other hand, cartoon and animation companies complain it is hard to find the right talented people."[9]

Keke's Story

ZN Animation
104 × 12 Minutes
2D Animation

Synopsis: The grownups call him naughty, but Keke feels he is just being curious like any other boy—with a nagging mother who loves her family dearly, a father who is a philosopher-inventor, a mischievous puppy, Pippi—and a cute, smart, pocket-sized alien companion, Meme, who dropped in one day and decided to stay with Keke.

Comment: Targeted at 7–12 years of age.

The Legend of Qin: The Great Wall

Hangzhou StarQ Xunaji Science and Technology Information Technology Co., Ltd.
40 × 22 Minutes
3D Animation

Synopsis: After the Mech-Fort had been destroyed, the Mohist rebellion was almost eliminated. The Qin Empire seemed to return to its peaceful heyday illusion.

The emperor, Yin-Zheng, commandeered thousands of laborers to build the Great Wall.

There also was a huge ship named *Mirage* built by the Yin-Yang School, ready for sail, its enormous body floating on the sea.

Magic Eye

ZN Animation
156 × 22 Minutes
2D Animation

Synopsis: Magic Eye, a boy from outer space, decides to come to Earth for summer vacation and makes friends with Lina and her pals. His special ability: to grant wishes. But eventually they all learn that magic does not solve any problems.

Comment: Targeted at 6–12 years of age.

Magic Tiger

ZN Animation
52 × 22 Minutes
2D Animation

Synopsis: Linked to the series *Magic Eye*. Like his master, the Wonder Boy from Outer Space, Candy Stripe, a playful tiger, has magical skills, can transform himself, and can change into other animals.

Comment: Targeted at 6–12 years of age.

The Mechnimals

Alpha Animation and Culture Co., Ltd., Guangzhou
52 × 24 Minutes
2D/3D Animation

Synopsis: One day, in a future world, three mysterious aerolith pieces fall from the sky. Dr. Yan, father of the hero, finds out that the aerolith contains huge power. It can integrate with an organism and metalize the organism into a mechanical tank. Upon this great discovery, a criminal organization kidnaps Dr. Yan, intending to use aerolith power to control the world. When the hero, Neo, learns this, he and his friends wish to use the result of Dr. Yan's research, the Beckoning Device, to save his father and his discovery, the organism.

Comment: Targeted at 4–12 years of age.

Mini Gongfu

Fantasia Animation
100 × 2 Minutes
Theatrical Release: 90 Minutes
2D Flash Online Animation

Comment: Q-version animation based on Fantasia Animation's *Shaolin Wuzang*, released both conventionally as the theatrical version and as online clips.

Panda Fanfare

ZN Animation
256 × 22 Minutes
2D Animation

Synopsis: Deep in the forest lies the peaceful Dragon Valley. At its head, a spring gushes from the ground. It is a magical fountain that can grant one's wishes and is a gift to the pandas for their loving care and concern for plants and nature. Not far away from the peaceful community, there is a mountain lair, home of a female leopard and a male tiger who try to take over. Panda Big Wei and his son, Small Wei, have to defend the valley and fight for justice.

Comment: Targeted at 7–14 years of age.

Race-Tin Flash and Dash

Alpha Animation and Culture Co., Ltd.,
  Guangzhou
26 × 24 Minutes
2D Animation

Synopsis: Frank and Karl are twin brothers proficient in all games and sports except for remote-control car racing (R/C car). They become interested in R/C car and join the R/C car club run by Sally's father. By practicing with Sally, Mike and Don, they make great progress. Soon they team up to participate in an R/C racing competition. They overcome many difficulties and finally encounter an R/C car expert known as "Sword." Instead of defeating Sword, they show him the true spirit of R/C racing and change his life attitude. R/C car is not only an arena of speed and skill, but also a game to make friends and have fun.

Comment: Targeted at 4–12 years of age.

Super Buffalo

ZN Animation
52 × 22 Minutes
2D Animation

Synopsis: The buffalo's magic comes from his horns. He can travel in time and comes from the same planet as Magic Eye and Magic Tiger.

Comment: Targeted at 6–12 years of age.

Swirl Fighter

ZN Animation
39 × 22 Minutes
2D Animation

Synopsis: Spinning tops is no fun, but pitching specially made spinners forcefully into an arena to challenge and fight one another—to swirl, whirl and twist into spirals, whorls, curls and coils; careering and careering; smashing and crashing top on top, and knocking losers down or out—this is the world of the Swirl Fighter. It is where our hero, Tiger, aspires to be champion, but first, the kid has to learn to spin a top and to be humble—no fun at all.

Comment: Targeted at 8–12 years of age.

Zobotz

ZN Animation
52 × 22 Minutes
2D Animation

Synopsis: At the dawn of the Age of Darkness, the mysterious Dark Lord falls upon Earth and destroys everything in his path. A supreme hero rises to battle him, harnessing the power of the twelve Zodiac Stones to vanquish and imprison the evil marauder. But the Stones go missing—scattered at Oolala Mountain.

A thousand years later the planet has transformed into a world where man co-exists with robots—where ingenious humans make clever machines in their image. In the mountain district of Oolala City two robotics engineers, Charles and Grey, discover a manuscript that chronicles the ancient epic battle on the mountain and warns that the Dark Lord's incarceration will last a millennium only—meaning he will be out soon!

To find the Stones they design and build twelve Zodiac Robots or Zobotz, each representing an animal in the ancient Chinese horoscope and each endowed with its respective qualities and powers.

Comment: Targeted at 7–14 years of age.

The Animated Feature Films

2000

Magic Umbrella/Coco's Magic Umbrella

Shanghai Arts Studio

Comment: First Chinese feature film to combine live action elements with a cartoon.

2000–2001

Fünf Wochen im Ballon

Manfred Durniok Produktion für Film und Fernsehen, Berlin/Shanghai Animation Film Studio
85 Minutes
Director: Hong Hu Zhao
Associate Director: Manfred Durniok
Screenplay: Manfred Durniok, Günter and Sibille Rätz, Hong Hu Zhao

Synopsis: Fergusson and Kennedy, two friends, take an adventurous balloon trip to Africa. One wants to explore the continent for scientific reasons, the other only has a "Magic Stone" in mind.

Comment: Puppet film inspired by Jules Verne's novel.

2001

Master Q 2001

Tsui Hark's Film Workshop
Executive Producer: Tsui Hark
Director: Herman Yau
Screenplay: Tsui Hark, Roy Szeto, Herman Yau

Synopsis: Cartoon characters Master Q, Big Potato and Mr. Chun meet pop idols Nicholas Tse and Cecilia Cheung.

Comment: Tsui Hark invited Alfonso Wong, the creator of the original character, to appear in the film as himself. Computer animation was composited with live action.

My Life as McDull/Mak Dau Goo Si

Bliss Pictures Ltd.
A Lunchtime Production, Hong Kong
76 Minutes
Executive Producer: Brian Tse
Director: Toe Yuen
Assistant Production Manager: Ho-Kuen Wong
Animation: Kwong-Kuen Chueng, Chung-Tak Wong
Voice Actors (English Version): Lee Chun-Wai (McDull), Jan Lamb (McDull/Adult), Sandra Ng Kwan Yue (Mrs. McDull), Anthony Wong Chau-Sang (School Principal/Doctor/News Reporter/Restaurant Owner/Logan)
Screenplay: Brian Tse, Alice Mak
Sound Effects Editor: Charlie Lo
Sound: May Mok
Music: The Pancakes

Synopsis: Piglet McDull, as a kid, observes and reacts to the absurdities of Hong Kong's adult world.

Comment: First animated feature film made entirely in Hong Kong.

McDull, the popular Hong Kong cartoon character on which the film is based, was created by the husband-and-wife team of Alice Mak and Brian Tse.

According to William Chung,

McDull is an anthropomorphised piglet. He has a big nose and a small mouth, with a birthmark on one eye and another eye as small as a dot, as well as a pink complexion. This gives the impression of a somewhat "dull" kid. Mrs Mc is like an ordinary Hong Kong middle-aged woman, with a perm hairdo and button earrings. Her eyes and eyebrows move up and down while scolding her son. She is presented as an astute and bossy mother....

Alice Mak created the family of McDull based on piglets not only because she wanted to add interest and humour by using animals, but because she conceived the story as a "fairytale for adults," something she and

Brian Tse have always stressed. McDull has evolved into a silly but likeable character. The characters of *McDull* enact a typical Hong Kong story about ordinary people. Instead of striving for realism in her drawing, Mak tries to make the characters and settings close to life.[10]

Bringing it to animation was another thing. Animator-turned-director Toe Yuen remembers:

The first time we met, Tse asked whether I was interested in helping him on McMug. Knowing that I had never read McMug, he gave me a whole series of the cartoon. At that time, I was engrossed in writing a violent novel. The warm and sentimental McMug was simply not my cup of tea. So I told him I would give it some thought only after I finished the novel.

But after a while, the novel was going nowhere. I was in a daze. Then, Tse called me again.

"All right, I'll do it. But just to warn you, I don't know how to do it, and have never done it before."

"You'll be fine."

Thanks to his trust, so began the incredible journey of McMug animation.

We began recruiting the production crew in the spring of 1997....

As for animation style, Tse and the team stood on the same ground: we should not imitate Japanese anime or Disney (not that we could, anyway). Take McMug for example. He was supposed to be a porker and Mrs. Mc was "a fat woman with a deep voice."[11]

The little episodes are simple but charming.

Awards: Grand Prix at the Annecy International Animated Film Festival, 2003.

Seventh Chinese Language Films Bauhinia Award.

2004

Kung Fu Hustle

Hong Kong
Director: Stephen Chow
Screenplay: Man Keung Chan, Stephen Chow, Xin Huo, Kan-Cheung Tsang

Comment: According to Stephen Chow, computer effects are inseparable from space and action: "*Kung Fu Hustle* is enjoyable because we spent a lot of time getting the timing right. The key to creating a seamless interface between the real and the fake lies in the right timing."[12]

McDull, Prince de la Bun/Mai Dou Bo Luo You Wang Zi

Bliss Picture Ltd., Hong Kong
73 Minutes
Director: Toe Yuen
Animation: En-Kai Chen, Siu-Ling Shi, Si-Yong Tong, Mokana Wong, Chi-Cu Yeung, Ming Jan-Yip
Computer Animation: Kwong-Kuen Cheung, Jan-Min Lee, Chung-Tak Wong, Toe Yuen
Voice Actors: Chet Lam, Jan Lamb, Andy Lau, Sandra Ng Kwan Yue, Anthony Wong Chau-Sang
Screenplay: Alice Mak, Brian Tse
Sound: Charlie Lo, May Mok

Synopsis: Mrs. Mc tries her hand at writing. Her son would prefer not to listen to her poetry but rather to that of her inspiration, J. K. Rowling: Harry Potter.

Comment: Second *McDull* feature.

2004–2005

Dragonblade: The Legend of Lang

DCDC and China Film Company, Hong Kong
Distributed by ERA Company/Kantana Animation
85 Minutes
Producers: Stanley Tong, Wendy Choi
Director: Antony Szeto
Voice Actors (original was recorded in English language): Karen Mok (Ying Ying), Daniel Wu, Stephen Fung (Hung Lang), Sandra Ng (Cantonese), Ruby Lin (Mandarin) (Bali-Ba), Jim Chim (Master Wu), Doug Baker (Lord Ko), Sam Bobertz (Mr. Hung and Guardian Spirit), Simon Broad (Sifu), Anna May Chan, Anson Chan
Screenplay: Trevor Morris

Synopsis: A deadly creature attacks a town. Only DragonBlade, a legendary weapon, can stop the danger, but first it must be found.

Comment: First 3D-CG movie fully rendered in Hong Kong, and the first 3D-rendered martial arts film made for $10,000,000. Research for the kung fu scenes was done in Shandong, where director and animators flew to meet the reigning all–China *wushu* champions.

2005

Children of Captain Grant

Manfred Durniok Produktion für Film und Fernsehen, Berlin/Shanghai Animation Film Studio

Comment: The final entry in Manfred Durniok's co-produced Jules Verne puppet series. Released after Durniok's death.

Little Soldier Zhang Ga/Zhang Ga, the Soldier Boy

Produced by Sun Lijun, Animation School of BFA (Beijing Film Academy) in association with Ai Yi Mei Xun Animation Production Company/BTV/Youth Film Production Unit

Producer: Sun Lijun

Synopsis: Zhang Ga, a boy soldier, fights Japanese invaders. Based on the actual life story of Yan Xiufeng (Gazi) who was born in Baiyangdian in Hebei Province.

Comment: Propaganda with ethnic stereotypes. Made for a budget of 12 million RMB and shown on the occasion of the sixtieth anniversary of China's war of resistance against the Japanese.

Thru the Moebius Strip/Pinyin: Mobisi Huan

87 Minutes

Producers: Raymond Neoh, David Kirschner, Jun Aida

Directors: Glenn Chaika, Kelvin Lee

Screenplay: Jim Cox

Editors: Bob Bender, Lois Freeman-Cox

Comment: Hong Kong–produced CGI feature film (budget: 156 million RMB = U.S. $20 million). An aesthetically and economically failed attempt to cash in on sci-fi and 3D animation. Even the DVD jacket (www.kochvision.com) had doubts about the quality and quoted criticism to sell it as trash:

This is a CG film that makes Final Fantasy seem like a brilliant epic by comparison. The direction is sub-par, the story run-of-the-mill, the design unappealing, and the "animation" (if you could call it "animation") just revolting. Just because things move doesn't mean they're animated. It doesn't appear that anyone involved with this production has any concept of communicating an idea to an audience. But to do that, of course, you'd have to have an idea, which this film has not one.

Awards: Second Annual Hong Kong Digital Entertainment Excellence Award.

2005–2007

Warrior/Brave Warrior/Guan Gong

Shanghai Animation Film Studio

Released by Shanghai Film Group Corporation

84 (80) Minutes

Director: Chang Guangxi

Synopsis: Coming to Balin grassland and Bahraini steppe, Bateer, a young warrior, rescues a girl from a herd of running horses. She turns out to be Wurihan, the daughter of the wrestling coach, Buheh, who works for the grassland lord. Bateer begins to work for him too as a coolie while learning wrestling, for he has fallen in love with beautiful Wurihan. There are more heroic deeds in between, such as killing a huge bear that attacks his beloved. But his secret mission is to look for the murderer of his father. This enemy, he finds out, is none other than Buheh himself.

Comment: Wide grasslands, race horses and wrestlers. Four years in production, *Warrior,* in style a mix of American TV animation and anime, marked the fiftieth anniversary of Shanghai Animation Film Studio and is based on a folk legend set in the Keerqin grassland in Inner Mongolia. The production costs were RMB 15 million (U.S. $2 million), nothing to compare to U.S. budgets. Not to be confused with Tsui Hark's *Warrior* project. French director Luc Besson was given a preview of the movie. He praised the unique depiction of Chinese national characters.

In a new move for the Shanghai Animation Studio, the film is targeted at adults instead of children.

2006

McDull, the Alumni/Chun Tian Hua Hua Tong Xue Hui

Hong Kong

95 Minutes

Director: Leung Chun "Samson" Chiu

Screenplay: Brian Tse

Comment: Only one third of the movie is animation; the rest is live action. The real people are supposed to represent McDull's ordinary life.

Saving Mother

85 Minutes

Director: Hu Zhao Hong

Synopsis: Chenxiang learns that his mother was a fairy and is imprisoned beneath Mount

Hua. With the help of the God of Thunder, the smart boy finds the divine axe to save his mother.

Comment: Puppet film version of *Lotus Lantern*.

The Warrior

Hong Kong
Distributed by Kam and Ronson
88 Minutes
Director: Tsui Hark

Synopsis: After a war, four treasures are created to seal the mystic power of the sacred stone. Yuan Boo and kung fu master Wong Hei Hung are the ones to protect and save it from any harm.

2006–2007

Monkey King vs. Er Lang Shen/The Big Fight Between Wukong and God Erlang/Wu Kong Da Zhan Er Lang Shen

Producers: Shen Yuang, Zhou Meiling, Liang Hansen
Director: Liang Hansen

Synopsis: As he was causing so much trouble in the Jade Emperor's heavenly mansion, Wukong, the Monkey King, is given the task of running the peach orchard. But after he has spoiled the Mother Queen's peach party and stolen the Golden Elixir, Mother Queen sends Heavenly King Lee with one hundred thousand heavenly soldiers to capture the rebel. Wukong defeats them all. Finally, God Er Lang Shen, the nephew of the Jade Emperor, is sent to fight him, and after three hundred rounds Wukong is eventually captured. But as he possesses the Golden Elixir, the Jade Emperor has no other choice than to turn to Rulai Buddha, who has boundless supernatural power.

Comment: Another episode of *Journey to the West.* Mix of puppet live action and 3D animation, budgeted at $1 million. In the English version, Erlang Shen was dubbed by Jason Tolhurst.

Award: Nominated Best Animated Feature Film, First Asia Pacific Screen Awards.

2006–2008 (2009)

Storm Rider Clash of the Evils/The Clash of Storm Rider/Feng Yun Jue

Puzzle Animation Studio Limited
Distributed by Asia Animation Ltd., Hong Kong, and Shanghai Media Group
Director: Dante Lam
Story: Ma Wing-Shing
Voice Actors: Nicholas Tse (Striding Cloud), Richie Ren (Whispering Wind)

Synopsis: Ngou Kuet, the young master of Sword-Worshipping Manor, is the only survivor of a brutal massacre of the best swordsmiths. He vows to finish the family task of forging the Kuet Sword, then attacks Tin Ha Wui and battles with Wind and Cloud to obtain the blood of the Fire Kirin that will unleash the power of the sword.

2007

The Secret of the Magic Gourd/ The Magic Gourd/Bao Hulu De Mi Mi

Centro Digital Pictures Ltd. in cooperation with China Film Group and Walt Disney Studios
Producer: Jon M. (Jonathan Murray) Chu
Production Management: Vivian Cheuk, Wai Luen Pang
Director: Jon M. Chu, Frankie Chung
Actors: Chen Peisi (Bao Hu Lu), Ching Wan Lau (Voice of Magic Gourd), Gigi Leung (Miss Liu), Qilong Zhu (Wang Bao)
Story: Zhang Tianyi
First Assistant Director and Second Unit: Lanbo Cheuk

The Secret of the Magic Gourd (2007).

Cinematographer: Chi Ying Chan
Production Design: Chung Man Yee
Art Director: Pater Wong
Costume Design: Dora Ng
Visual Effects: Henry Kwok Ho Chan, Cecil Man Ching Cheng, Dy Choi Ying Chung, Ralph Chun Ho Poon
Computer Graphics Supervisor: Harry Ching Wei Hung
Effects Supervisor: Centro Digital, Don Wong
Editor: Angie Lam
Dialogue Editor: Boom Suvagondha
Sound Re-Recording Mixers: Ben Wilkins, Traithep Wongpaiboon
Original Score: Peter Kam

Synopsis: A boy befriends a magic gourd that grants him any wish until he learns the meaning of work.
Comment: Live-action and 3D animation. Premiered at Children's Film Festival in Ningbo.

Tonki Bear

Innotion Studio Ltd., Hong Kong
85 Minutes
Producer: Tony Tang
Comment: Touted as the world's first CGI bear movie.

2007–2009

Laura's Star and the Mysterious Dragon Nian/Laura's Star in China

Rothkirch Cartoon-Film Berlin/Warner Bros. Germany/MaBo Investment/Shanghai Media Group with 3DAnimagics Entertainment Co., Ltd., Beijing

71 Minutes
Producers: Thilo Rothkirch, Maya Rothkirch, Jakob Bosch, Willi Geike, Jung Chi Gwang
Production Manager: Beate Andorff
Directors: Piet de Rycker, Thilo Rothkirch
Animation Directors: Kris Van Alphen, Alberto Campos
Art Directors: Alexander Lindner, Anne Domberg, Ralph Niemeyer, Gabor Steisinger, Sabine Weisser
Original Art Concept: Manuel Arenas
Animation: Christian Bahr, Tobias Gembalski, Alexa Müller-Heyn, Oliver Stephan
Character and Prop Design: Anette Hoffmann
Layout/Blocking Artist: Markus Hund
Stage Design: Matthias Lechner
Screenplay: Rolf Giesen, Piet de Rycker, Thilo Rothkirch, Alexander Lindner
Additional Material: Ma Hua, Li Wei Si
From the children's books by Klaus Baumgart
Musical Score: Guy Cuyvers, Henning Lohner
Pianist: Lang Lang
Sound Design: Jan Petzold
3D Supervisor: Markus Wagenführ
Photography: Ralph Niemeyer
Visual Effects: Ronney Afortu, Daniel Beckmann, Michael Best
Postproduction Supervisor/Editor: Erik Stappenbeck

Synopsis: Set against the background of a rural Mongolian area and the Chinese capital, and offering awesome sights of past, present and future at the time of New Year's Spring Festival. Two girls, Laura, born in the West (Germany), and Ling-Ling, raised in the East (China), master their initial misunderstandings and with the help of a tiny, miracle-working star become close friends.
The family of a little German girl, Laura,

Laura's Star and the Mysterious Dragon Nian (2009) (courtesy Cartoon Film).

is going to China. Laura's mother, a cello player, is scheduled to appear in concert with a *pipa* player on stage at the New Year's concert at the opera. A faithful friend, a living tiny star that has befriended Laura, is following the plane like a guardian angel. Hitting turbulence, however, the star gets lost somewhere over Inner Mongolia.

Laura feels totally alien in the big Chinese city Beijing after she has lost the star, while Ling-Ling misses her father, a renowned yak-researcher, who very often is out in the countryside and not at home. It is Ling-Ling, on one of her rare trips to visit her father at a field of yaks located in a national park, who finds what she thinks is a sparkling glass object. Actually it is Laura's star, which she brings to Beijing.

Meanwhile Laura and her family are shown around the huge concert hall where mom will appear. This also marks Laura's first encounter with Ling-Ling, who has been pulled to the hall by the star's power. Ling-Ling's aunt, by the way, is the *pipa* player who will be on stage with Laura's mother. Fighting over the glowing gem, the star, the girls realize that they have much in common and that they only have to share the sense of wonder that the star opens up for them.

But before that can happen there are trials and tribulations to test the seriousness of their friendship. On the darkest night of the year, a whole twilight world of imagination materializes. Although Laura is worried about her star, assuming that it might be blackened, the girls dare to face all dangers and, illuminated by the star's magic and with the support of a makeshift Nian, overcome their fears to emerge as twin sisters.

Nian, a creature that is half dog, half lion, has been awakened by the girls' initial dispute over the ownership of the miraculous star, although this Nian was only a costume appearing on stage with the musicians at New Year's eve. Some stardust has fallen onto a Nian costume prepared for the New Year's concert and made it come alive. According to legend, Nian's mission is to scare people in the darkness of the last night of the old year. To their great surprise Laura and Ling-Ling find out that the creature that once had been a costume is unaware of its menacing role and even is too scared himself to scare others.

Riding on the back of the Nian creature, tamed by cookies, the girls travel high above Beijing to defeat the Cloud of Darkness and save the star from being blackened.

A giant firework celebrating New Year causes the Black Cloud to retreat and brings the girls back to the reality of their families and to a springtime of star-blessed friendship.

On stage, Laura's mother and Ling-Ling's aunt have come to the finale. They end nicely, holding one last tone, and look happily at each other and to their families sitting in the first row. The delighted audience applauds frenetically. Overjoyed, the two girls hug.

Through their mutual care, the girls will grow to the understanding that a shared life is a prosperous life.

Comment: First Sino-German co-production in 3D (more than 50 percent of the movie was produced in Beijing, a small percentage in India, and the rest in Berlin, Germany). A sequel to *Laura's Star* (2004), which told how Laura and the star became friends. The famous Chinese pianist Lang Lang was delighted to take part in the production, as he had seen a Tom and Jerry cartoon, *Cat Concerto,* at a young age.

This writer, who participated in the making of the film, still thinks that the first outline discussed at the beginning of the production would have been better. In this version the tiny Miracle Star didn't "crash" over Inner Mongolia but over the Forbidden City in Beijing. On the roofs of the ancient buildings there are nine little stone dragons, and one of them is brought to life by the power of stardust. This little creature befriends Ling-Ling, a little girl who attends a kung fu school. The climax was supposed to happen not in Beijing but on the Roof of the Earth, somewhere in Tibet, where a yak-cow gives birth to a calf.

However, as often happens in animation, there are many cooks involved and everybody seems to have ideas of his or her own.

Awards: Gold Panda Award, Best Domestic Animated Feature Film, 2011.

Gold Panda Award, Best Screenplay, 2011.

2008

Kungfu Master/Wong Fei Hong vs. Kungfu Panda

Producer: Tsui Hark

Comment: Direct-to-video anime feature that, according to its title, was an unofficial sequel to DreamWorks' successful *Kung Fu Panda*, which featured folk hero Wong Fei-hung.

Legend of the Sea

Chinese-Singapore coproduction
Zhejiang Zhongnan/CHINAnimax Pte. Ltd./
Phase 4 Films
Producer: Jianrong Wu
Director: Benjamin Toh
Voice Actors: Rob Schneider, J. J. Lin, Jin Sha, Lin Yu Zhong
Synopsis: The Eastern Sea has been peaceful under the reign of the Dragon King. That is, until the evil octopus Ocho is freed from banishment and unleashes its vengeance. Prince Draco is about to stop all evil.
Comment: Produced by the Singapore-based distribution arm of a Chinese company. DVD buyers didn't react in favor: "The WORST MOVIE I have ever seen! Horrible animation that didn't even match the soundtrack" and qualified it "just plain stupid."

2008–2009

The Magic Aster/Man Lan Hua

Shanghai Animation Film Studio/Xiamen Shangchen Science and Technology Company/Shanghai Chengtai Investment Management Company
Voice Actors: Leon Lai Ming (Ma Long), Lin Chi-Ling, Yao Ming, Wu Kenji, Hsu Valen, Chen Hao, Zhou Libo, Gao Yuan
Synopsis: The Magic Aster is a flower that helps the brave and courageous. Xiao Lan, a hardworking woman, is married to the God of Flowers, Ma Lang, but then greedy Old Cat intervenes. He wants Da Lan, the jealous sister, to kill Xiao Lan to get the Magic Malan Flower, which luckily protects the innocent.
Comment: Animated folk tale.

Pleasant Goat and Big Big Wolf—The Super Snail Adventure/Xi Yang Yang Yu Hui Tai Lang Zhi Niu Qi Chong Tian

Creative Power Entertaining
80 Minutes
Director: Sung Pong Choo
Voice Actors: Liqing Zu (Pleasant Goat), Yuting Deng (Pretty Goat/Warm Goat), Ying Liang (Lazy Goat/Small Grey Wolf), Quansheng Gao (Slow Goat)
Comment: First feature film based on the most popular Chinese animation series.

2009

The King of Milu Deer

Zhonke Weiwo Digital Technology in association with CCTV
Director: Guo Weijiao
Voice Actor: Li Yang
Music: Wang Bei
Synopsis: Once-beautiful Yunmeng Kingdom is in severe drought. Ten years without rain have transformed the once blossoming country. In order to save the country, Prince Can leads an army to the mountain where the king of Milu Deer lives because the king's horn has magical power and can restore the lost beauty. The prince, however, falls in love with the king's daughter, who has transformed from a deer into a lovely girl.
Comment: CG-animated blockbuster based on a legend from an ancient literary classic, *Legends of Mountains and Seas.* The animated feature took in four million yuan in just one week after its release.
Award: Best Animation, Golden Rooster and Hundred Flower Film Awards, nomination only.

McDull, Kung Fu Kindergarten/Mai Dou Xiang Dang Dang

Bliss Pictures Ltd., Hong Kong
Director: Brian Tse
Voice Actors: Kwok Kwan Yin (McDull), Anthony Wong (Brother Panda), Sandra Ng (Mrs. Mak), Jan Lamb, Jim Chim
Narrator: Wan Kwong
Musical Score: Steve Ho
Synopsis: Due to economic hardships, Mrs. Mc decides to leave her home town in Tai Kok Tsui and settle in Wuhan, where she enrolls her son, McDull, in the Spring Flowers Gate, a Taoist martial arts academy in the Wudang Mountains. In the beginning McDull, coming from Hong Kong, is ridiculed.
Comment: Fourth entry in a series of feature films devoted to the popular pig character.

New Underground Tunnel Battle

90 Minutes
Screenplay: Ruan Jizhi
Synopsis: People in Wang Village are living a peaceful life. The children are fond of hide-and-seek. One of the best players is Little Bao, who can stay hidden till the last moment. However, the Japanese aggressors' "Massive Mapping-up" in Middle Hebei Base

Area in 1942 disturbs the villagers' tranquil life. One day when Little Bao, together with sister and classmates, is having class in school, he suddenly hears an explosion in the distance. Soon the school is informed by a militia uncle that all villagers have been caught by Japanese aggressors. The teacher immediately tells the children to hide in a cellar and himself tries to escape and seek help from a nearby village, but unfortunately he is observed and killed. Little Bao and his classmates hide in the cellar and search for a way out. Soon they find a hole that leads to a tunnel. Little Bao's grandpa is caught, and when he is tortured during interrogation, he learns that the Japanese are trying to find a Communist Party member who obtains all necessary strategic information. Little Bao and his friends quickly get familiar with the structure of the tunnel and swear to save their families and kick the Japanese out of the village. Then they begin to prepare proper weapons to fight the hated aggressors.

Strange Family

Its Cartoon/Its Happy Film and Television Institution
90 Minutes

Comment: Giannalberto Bendazzi writes, "For its new conception, original creation and high level professional team, *Strange Family* might be considered the new milestone of the Chinese theatrical animated production."[13]

2009–2010

Folks

Jilin Animation Institute
Producer: Zheng Liguo
4D Special Film

Synopsis: A girl from the northeast of China rescues and befriends a tiger. The tiger protects her from a huge bear.

Comment: A 4D Circling Screen film that applies a 180-degree circling screen, a 3D technique, moving chairs, sound, light, scent, water, fog, bubble and snow effects to let audiences feel as if they are in the real place and experience the grandeur and magic of Changbai Mountain. The film was screened as part of the Jilin Pavilion project of the 2010 Shanghai World Expo and is also part of tours through Jilin Animation Institute in Changchun.

Pleasant Goat and Big Big Wolf: The Tiger Prowess/Xi Yang Yang Yu Hui Tai Lang Zhi Hu Hu Sheng Wei

Creative Power Entertaining
84 Minutes
Director: Sung Pong Choo
Voice Actors: Zu Liqing (Pleasant Goat), Deng Yuting (Pretty Goat), Liang Ying (Lazy Goat), Gao Quansheng (Slow Goat), Liu Hongyun (Fit Goat), Li Tuan (Soft Goat), Zhang Lin (Grey Wolf), Fan Bingbing (Red Wolf)

Synopsis: Two dubious entrepreneurs, Crafty Gecko and General Tiger, plan to turn Goat Village into a theme park and Wolfie's castle into a public toilet.

2009–2011

Little Big Panda/Kleiner starker Panda

Benchmark Entertainment Picture Productions, Berlin/Angels Avenue/Juventy Films/ORB Filmproduktion/Yi Sang Media in association with China Animation Comic Game Group Co., Ltd., Beijing
84 Minutes
Stereoscopic (2D Animation)
Producers: Michael Schoemann, Xiao Xiong Chen, Hua Shen, Armin Timmermann
Co-producers: Daniel Zimmermann, Hilary Pujol
Line Producer: Dirk Hampel
Directors: Michael Schoemann, Greg Manwaring
Animation Department: Marcelo Fernandes de Moura (animation director), Victor Ens, Vittorio Pirajno, Christian Retzlaff
Screenplay: Jörg Tensing
Story Consultant: Rolf Giesen
Art Direction: Juan Japl, Miquel Pujol
Art Department (Storyboard Artists): Christian de Vita, Toby Schwarz, Richard Bazley, Jody Gannon, Satjit Matharu, Paul McKeown
Character Design: Christian Retzlaff, Harald Siepermann
Sound Editors: Christian Conrad, Detlef A. Schitto
Postproduction Supervisor/Editor: Erik Stappenbeck
Original Music: Detlef A. Schitto, Bernd Wefelmeyer

Synopsis: High in the majestic mountains, the survival of the panda bears is under dire threat as humans (Chinese, not to be seen in the final movie) encroach on their environment and at the same time the supply of the pandas' cherished sole nutrient, bamboo shoots, is steadily dwindling away. Unfortunately, the pandas become extremely apathetic when confronted with change and need a hero to guide them out of misery.

The one they need is Manchu (Chinese version: Pandy), a little panda known as the Chosen One, but stupidly he is rejected by his clan due to his hair-brained ideas. He finally gains confidence and leads his community, struggling for survival, to a better environment, a New Promised Land of Bamboo.

Comment: Long and complicated production history. In China the film was announced to be the most expensive domestic animated feature film up to date (with a budget of more than U.S. $50 million). It was actually produced in Europe (Germany, Spain, Belgium) for less than U.S. $10 million. Xiao Xiong Chen, a wealthy Chinese investor with no knowledge of animation but a network of good connections, bought into the project for a million and released the Chinese dubbing, which included well-known voice talent via China Film Group, with a big promotional campaign.

2010

The Dinosaur Baby

Nuclear Power Animation Studios
85 Minutes

Synopsis: There is a legend that on the distant planet Pangea human beings live harmoniously with dinosaurs, but soon peace and tranquility are broken by an evil force as the patron saint of this continent—God Dragon—is gradually losing his power. For saving Pangea, God Dragon divides his power into four parts and seals each in a dragon crystal. It is said that whoever obtains these four crystals will get great powers. A teenager named Longxiang living on Earth accidentally touches his Grandpa's Gold Dragon bracelet and travels through time and space, arriving on Pangea. First Longxiang saves little dinosaur Bao, realizing how the evil force occupies the forest and expels people. In order to maintain peace and stop the intentions of the evil, Longxiang bravely takes on the responsibility of protecting Pangea. On the way he meets naughty Guo, beautiful Fengling and the mysterious teenager Yu. Based on their potential power—confidence, braveness and unity—four fearless dragon warriors get together, infusing new vitality and energy into the magic forest and saving struggling Pangea.

The Dreams of Jinsha/Meng Hui Jin Sha Cheng

Shi Long Animation
Distributed by China United Film Company
Director: Daming Chen
Screenplay: Xiaohong Su

Synopsis: Xiao Long is a modern-day middle-school student who is transported three thousand years back in time to the ancient kingdom of Jinsha.

Comment: Chinese version of *A Connecticut Yankee at King Arthur's Court.* Nominated for an Academy Award.

A Jewish Girl in Shanghai

Shanghai Animation Film Studio/Shanghai Kenmite Tanghua Culture/Shanghai Film Group Corporation
80 Minutes
Producers: Wang Tianyun, Ren Zhonglun, Cai Hongzhuan, Shi Bixi, Wu Pei
Directors: Wang Genfa, Zhang Zhenhui
Screenplay: Wu Lin
Musical Score: Shi Jiayang

Synopsis: The turbulences in Europe make Rina, a Jewish girl, and her little brother Mishalli flee Europe and seek refuge in Shanghai in 1939. There Rina makes friends with Zhou A-gen, a Chinese boy, and his family.

Soon Rina's father Joseph joins them in Shanghai. At the same time Zhou Liang, A-gen's uncle, is arrested and imprisoned by the Japanese. A-gen and Rina try to save him, but in vain.

There is danger also for Rina as Mesinger, a German colonel, comes to Shanghai to persecute Jewish refugees.

In 2005, after more than 60 years, Zhou A-gen welcomes Rena back to Shanghai.

Comment: Written by Wu Lin, a former history teacher, who first became interested in Shanghai's Jewish community in 2005 when newspapers and magazines published stories of Jewish refugees to mark the sixtieth anniversary of the end of World War II.

Awards: Nominated for the Jewish Experience Award by Jerusalem Film Festival, Israel.

Golden Cartoon Award, Best Chinese Film Prize CICDF, China.

2010–2011

Chuangtang Rabbit/Brave Rabbit

90 Minutes
Screenplay: Zeng Xianlin

Synopsis: In warm and peaceful Chuangtang Town, a "wishing gathering" that is expected by all people in the town will begin. Chuangtang Rabbit and his friends are also engaged in preparing for it. At this moment, Chuangtang Rabbit happens to know that there is an evil force attempting to spoil the gathering. What makes him even more surprised is that this sudden crisis is closely related to the mysterious disappearance many years ago of his father, Dr. Rabbit.

The Excellent Rabbit Year of Pleasant Goat and Big Big Wolf/Pleasant Goat and Big Big Wolf—Moon Castle: The Space Adventure/Xi Yang Yang Hui Tai Lang Zhi Tu Nian Ding Gua Gua

Creative Power Entertaining
88 Minutes
Director: Sung Pong Choo
Voice Actors: Liqing Zu (Pleasant Goat), Yuting Deng (Pretty Goat), Ying Liang (Lazy Goat), Weitong Xie (Fat Goat), Quansheng Gao (Slow Goat), Na Zhao (Red Wolf)
Screenplay: Shi Jianna, Mai Zhicheng, Zhang Shengliang

Synopsis: One day a huge "candy spacecraft" lands on the green grassland and a little Brother Rabbit, who calls himself a magician, comes out of it. He identifies Pleasant Goat as the Moon Savior as soon as he sees him and tells about the mysterious family background of the Pleasant Goat, which has been kept secret for a long time. It turns out that long ago Pleasant Goat's parents transformed the originally deserted moon into a colorful candy world. However, the ambitious King Balsam Pear is now trying to change the sweet planet into a bitter one. In order to protect his parents' painstaking efforts, Pleasant Goat, heading his Goats Combating Team, boards the spacecraft to travel to the moon, with Big Big Wolf (who tried to catch the goats) being trapped as stowaway. Thanks to Pleasant Goat's intelligence and wit, King Balsam Pear's conspiracy of disguising the Queen of the Moon is debunked so that everyone narrowly escapes the danger. However, they are separated into different groups as King Balsam Pear's forces are after them. At the same time energy on the moon is gradually reduced as the lunar eclipse approaches. Unfortunately, King Balsam Pear learns about the bitterest thing in the world—the tears of Big Big Wolf. In order to turn Big Big Wolf into an ally and make him cry, King Balsam Pear uses every method, making the moon increasingly bitter. At this moment, Pleasant Goat finds the key that opens the Sweet Tree.

Comment: Another animated feature film inspired by the popular Chinese TV series.

Kui Ba

Beijing Vasoon Animation Co., Ltd.
83 Minutes
Director: Wang Chuan

Synopsis: Every 333 years, warriors in heaven and on earth fight fiercely, regarding it as their difficult but glorious mission. Every 333 years a grotesque creature named Kui Ba is reborn, armed with a nuclear weapon, to annihilate the world. But the Kui Ba Killers of Heaven and Earth Glory Union already have located the evil demon. To destroy him becomes the warriors' final goal. Nine States Union releases an enlistment order to call for young people joining the army to kill Kui Ba. Manji, a monkey boy who resembles the Monkey King, and his friends rise to the challenge of saving the world by fighting against the destructor, and thus the tug of war begins.

Comment: Its plot is a mess (eight writers spent six years refining the story), as is its animation, and, with a budget of RMB 35 million (U.S. $5.4 million), it was a dismal failure at the box office.

According to CCTV.com,

> The much anticipated Chinese animation "Kui Ba," or "Great Bug," has swept cinemas across the country during the summer season. The animated feature film, produced by Beijing-based Vasoon Animation, is China's latest attempt to showcase its homegrown cartoon talents.
>
> A mere look at this cartoon production might remind you of the signature styling of Japanese anime. But it is indeed a one-hundred percent Chinese original production.
>
> Although the fact that all the roles on the big screen with exaggerated big round eyes and long hair that resemble classic Japanese cartoon figures, has triggered mixed reviews from critics, director Wang Chuan says it's a genuine Chinese story enveloped in a Japanese visual cover.[14]

ChinaCulture.org was also positive in its review: "Among Chinese moviegoers, the film's Japanese styling has caused some controversy, but Vassoon's sincere and mature effort has touched many viewers and critics' hearts. For the first time, a Chinese animated feature is targeting general audiences, not just young kids."[15]

Legend of the Moles: The Frozen Horror/Taomee

Released by China Film Co., Ltd.
Director/Screenplay: Liu Kexin
  Comment: Another spinoff of an online game. Grossed approximately RMB 18 million ($2.8 million) in its August 2011 theatrical release.

The Legend of Silk Boy

Shanghai Red Motion Animation
90 Minutes
  Synopsis: In 1851, Mr. Xu Rong Cun, a Chinese businessman, brought his "Yun Kee silk" to the Great Exhibition in London. The pure, natural Chinese silk won him worldwide accolade and recognition and was awarded one gold and one silver medal.
  One hundred years later, at the Shanghai Expo 2010, one of Mr. Xu's offsprings, a self-centered boy called Silk Boy, finds himself obsessed with robotics instead of his family's silk business. Unfortunately, Silk Boy loses one of his important games together with his chance to enter the highest robotics school. But then, however, a magic, ancient silk world begins to unfold before his eyes after he has learned the secret of silk from his grandfather. With the help of a kaleidoscope of characters, Silk Boy embarks upon an adventure of beast-taming, treasure-hunting in ancient tombs and searching for holy relics.

Mao Tu: Phoenix Rising

Hunan Great Dream Cartoon Communication/China Film and Television Production Co., Ltd./Hangzhou Great Dream Cartoon/Beijing Jiaxin Time Culture Co., Ltd.
88 Minutes
  Synopsis: One thousand years ago, Dark Dragon rose in revolt but was taken down by Holy Phoenix with its "Septette" and sealed in the Lake of Heavenly Sound. From then on, every two hundred years, the Valley of Heavenly Sound would hold a Grand Phoenix Ceremony to reinforce the Seal of Dragon.

During the Fifth Phoenix Ceremony, however, a sudden change in the astronomical phenomena leads to the failure of Phoenix Nirvana. Instead of being reborn of fire it becomes a holy egg. Dark Dragon attempts to take the chance to rid himself of fetters and rise in revolt once again.
  The only way to stop Dark Dragon is to obtain seven musical instruments from the Valley of Heavenly Sound, play the "Septette" to crack the Phoenix egg, and tame Dark Dragon by heavenly sound.

Mr. Black/Black Cat Detective/Hei Mao Jing Zhang

Shanghai Animation Film Studio
86 Minutes
  Synopsis: The return of Inspector Black Cat: A gang of terrorists attacks a barn at midnight. Mr. Black tries to round them up and has a fierce battle. In order to escape arrest, the cunning One-Eared Mouse, leader of the gang, instigates an elephant and locusts to spoil the harmony of the community and divert Mr. Black's attention. He goes abroad to look for his uncle, the Cat-Eating Mouse, and ask him for help. Back at the police station the White Cat chief of police is being killed. After Mr. Back's return he immediately looks up the files. Mr. Black and his unit wear gas masks to catch the enemy. But One-Eared Mouse slips through again and hires fearful Monkey-Eating Eagle. The giant eagle kidnaps a lot of little animals but Mr. Black and his fellow policemen are on the way to save them from the eagle's claws.

Seer/Taomee

  Synopsis: Robots are hired to fight space pirates.
  Comment: Released in July 2011, *Seer,* based on a popular online game developed by Taomee, grossed approximately RMB 44.1 million ($6.9 million). "The success of *Seer* is neither due to its story nor any kind of refined production," movie critic Guan Yadi said. "The reasons are Taomee's market strategy. Through its success, instead of seeing the direction of the film industry, we see the victory of an internet revolution."[16]

The Tibetan Dog/Tibet Inu Monogatari: Kin'iro No Dao Jie/Zang Ao Duo Ji

K. K. Madhouse (Kabushiki-gaisha Maddo-hausu), Tokyo/China Film Group Corporation, Beijing/Ciwen Pictures

90 Minutes
Executive Producer: Masao Maruyama
Director/Storyboard: Masayuki Kojima
Anime Design: Urasawa Naoki
Adapted from the book *The Tibetan Mastiff,* by
    Yang Zhijun

Synopsis:

"You're bold and powerful, strong and vigor-
ous;
    you move like greased lightning,
    galloping on the vast grassland.
    You're the companion we never had;
    you're the friend we always need.
    You're Doogee.
    You are unforgettable."

"It was the year when I was ten,"
Tianjin [Tenzing] tells.
"I left Xi'an, my hometown, for Tibet.
My mother passed away two months ago;
I turned to the guide GaWang to help me
    find my father who's been living on the
prairie
    for years.
I hadn't seen my father since I was an
infant
    so that I couldn't even remember what he
looked like."[17]

Tianjin meets his father, LaGeBa, like an
alien. LaGeBa decided to stay in Tibet, where
he is the essential physician of the poor community he lives in; while his wife, who didn't
adapt to the local customs and the living conditions, has left, taking her son with her.

To help his father, Tianjin has to learn how
to herd sheep.

Life is difficult at first: "Terrible food, an-
noying sheep and offish father: I can't take it
any more"—till the day the young boy is attacked by a bear and saved by a stray gold-
colored Tibetan Mastiff. Some time later
Tianjin witnesses a fight between some Tibetan guard dogs and the golden-haired
stranger, who is going to become the boy's
companion.

Both Tianjin and Doogee, the big dog, help
each other as they try to adjust to the environment, with the dog eventually defeating
a huge snow monster and sacrificing himself.

"This is how the adventure ended; yet
Doogee is not dead."

There are tiny, cute puppies: "They look
just like Doogee."

"Those little ones are the extensions of
Doogee's life. Doogee is still alive. He inspired me with courage and braveness. He
taught me to be a man of strong will. I carried

on my dad's intention to be a doctor. I live in
Tibet for more than 50 years to help those
who live on the prairie. Humans treat dogs
as their companions while dogs take humans
as their friends. It was Doogee who showed
me how incredibly precious the friendship
is."

Comment: A Japanese-Chinese co-
production made in China, it premiered at
the Fifty-first Annecy Film Festival in June
2011, and was released in China on July 15,
2011, and in Japan on January 7, 2012.
Adapted from Chinese writer Yang Zhijun's
best-seller, *The Tibetan Mastiff.* Infused with
Japanese anime style and Tibetan sceneries,
the film is the first Sino-Japanese animation
feature. The director, Kojima Masayuki, did
the famed comic-book anime *Piano no Mori.*

Xibaipo/Xibai Slope

Hebei Xibaipo Film and Television Production
    Center/Shanghai Film Group, Shanghai An-
    imation Film Studio/China Movie Channel
    Program Center, Publicity Department of
    CPC Hebei Provincial Committee
73 Minutes
Director: Yin Xiyong
Screenplay: Wang Jiashi, Lu Chengfa, Yin Xiyong

Synopsis: Xibai Slope is the last village
command post for Chairman Mao and the
Party Central Committee conducting the
Peoples' Liberation Army on the march into
Beiping (now Beijing) and to liberate the entire nation. Here the Party Central Committee holds the National Country Meeting, organizes and directs three large battles (Liao
Shen Battle, Huai Hai Battle, and Ping Jin
Battle), and also holds the Second Plenary
Session of the Seventh Central Committee of
the Communist Party of China, putting forward the celebrated statement of "Two Ne-
cessities."

That's when the story begins: Walnut, the
head of a group of children, accompanied by
his little sister Jujube and friend Melon, secretly joins the front line without telling the
adults. On the way they accidentally see
enemy spies searching for Xibai Slope and
discover that the enemy forces plan to bomb
Xibai Slope Central Command Post, collud-
ing with reactionary elements in the area.
Walnut commands Jujube and other group
members to immediately return to the village
and inform the elders while he himself leads
the rest of the gang across rivers and through

caves, climbing over Baipo and Shenlong mountains while fighting the enemy. Finally, at the risk of his life, Walnut helps his friends escape while the conspiracy has been discovered, greeting the birth of New China.

Comment: "This film incorporates rich animation factors and a story full of children's fun to display the revolutionary tales of the Communist Party of China at Xi Bai Po," wrote the Sichuan TV Festival Jury.[18]

2011–2012

Legend of a Rabbit/Tu Xia Chuan Qi
Tianjin North Film Group/Beijing Film Academy
85 Minutes
Stereoscopic (3D Animation)
Producers: Dong Fachang, Xue Jiajing, Jiang Ping, Zhou Chao
Director: Sun Lijun

Legend of a Rabbit, **Chinese** *Kung Fu Panda* **copy.**

Screenplay: Zou Jing Zhi, Zou Han
Musical Score: Peter Kam

Synopsis: Tu, the rabbit, is a humble cook from the country—until the day he is given a very important assignment by a kung fu master who has been betrayed by his best pupil. He is to return a significant Kung Fu Academy document to the master's daughter. But in order to do so, Tu has to sneak his way into the academy, learn the art of kung fu, always be on the watch for the ruthless master-pupil Slash, and in the end save all of China!

Comment: Celebrating the Year of the Rabbit, the hero was made a porky rabbit and his adversary a villainous panda. A shameless rip-off of *Kung Fu Panda.* With the initial investment of 120 million yuan, the disappointing 16.2 million yuan score at the domestic box office marks the movie a giant flop.

Magic Wonderland
Zhejiang ZN Animation Company, Bluever International Media Company of Zhejiang Radio and TV Group, Five Star Oriental Television Investment Company of Anhui Radio and TV Group

Synopsis: A little girl looks for her mother.

Comment: The movie version of a TV series.

Pleasant Goat and Big Big Wolf: Mission Incredible: Adventures on the Dragon's Trail/Xi Yáng Yáng Yu Hui Tai Láng Zhi Kaixin Chuang Lóngnián/Xi Yang Yang Yu Hui Tai Lang Zhi Kaixin Chuang Long Nian
Creative Power Entertaining and Imagi Animation Studios
Distributed by Shanghai Media Group (U.S. release: Summit Entertainment Lionsgate)
Director: Sung Pong Choo
Voice Actors: Zu Liqing (Xi Yang Yang/Weslie), Gao Quansheng (Mán Yáng Yáng/Slowy), Deng Yuting (Mei Yang Yang/Tibbie), Liang Ying (Lan Yang Yang/Paddi), Liu Hongyun (Fei Yáng Yáng), Deng Yuting (Nuan Yáng Yáng/Jonie), Zhang Lin (Hui Tái Láng/Wolffy), Zhao Na (Hong Tai Lang/Wolnie), Liang Ying

(Xiao Hui Hui/Willie), Liu Hongyun (Bianselong "Chameleon"), Bichang Zhou, Ah-Niu, O Ti

Synopsis: Fourth entry in the popular feature film series: This one opens with an artificial, mechanical, giant dragon that invades the world of the goats and defeats Wolffy on his vain attempt to catch goats. All of a sudden, some cute dragons appear and ask for help as on their planet evil dragons have taken over.

Comment: Released to celebrate the Year of the Dragon. The dragon characters introduced include Bianselong, "Chameleon"; Hong Longlong, "Red Dragon" (Molle); Zuandi Long, "Drill Earth Dragon" (Orito); Mengmeng Long, "Deceive Dragon" (Quinto); Qiqiaoling Long, "No Human Head Feature (eye, ear, nostril, mouth) Dragon (Raho); Xiaho Heilong, "Little Black Dragon" (Drago); Dielong, "Butterfly Dragon" (Archaeo); and finally Xiao Shenlong, "Little Divine/Mysterious Dragon," who teaches goats and wolves kung fu (introduced according to *The Standard* on August 27, 2012: "to maximize monetization potentials").

The *Standard* continued: "Pleasant Goat and Big Big Wolf 4 'Mission Incredible: Adventures of the Dragon's Trail' achieved another record breaking performance in China with box office receipts exceeding HK$203 million (RMB$165 million). The first three movies series for Pleasant Goat and Big Big Wolf have recorded box office receipts of HK398 million, HK$147 million and HK$180 million respectively."[19]

Seer II

37 Entertainment/Mr. Cartoon Pictures/EE-Media/Hunan Golden Eagle Cartoon Co., Ltd./Taomee
Directors: Wang Zhangjun, Fu Jie
Voice Artists: Philip Lau, Angel Chang

Synopsis: Three unlikely heroes fight space pirates in a bid to maintain interplanetary peace.

Comment: Sequel to *Seer*, which was released in 2011. Taomee, the company that released the online game the movie was based upon, is one of the first companies in Greater China to develop animated franchises for children through online virtual worlds. It is backed by Saban Capital Group, whose other Asian media investments include Celestial Tiger Entertainment and Indonesia's Media Nusantara Citra.

2011–2013

Frog Kingdom (Working Title: *Frog Sport*)

Jilin VIXO Animation, Comics and Games Technology Co., Ltd., Changchun
Distributed by H. Y. Brothers (Huayi Brothers Pictures Ltd.)
90 Minutes
Producer: Zheng Liguo

Synopsis: In order to find the right fiancé for his daughter, the Frog King orders a sport contest to be held at the foot of Changbai Mountain. The actual aim is to protect Frog Country's prosperity and stability.

Kunta

Zhejiang Versatile Media Co., Ltd.

Synopsis: On a quickly desertifying planet, a boy named Boca seeks a path to survival.

Comment: Big-budget feature, reportedly U.S. $16 million.

2012

McDull, the Pork of Music/Maidou: Dang Dang Ban Wo Xin

Shanghai Toonmax Media Co., Sunwah Media, Well Talent Hong Kong
79 Minutes
Producers: Yu Jie, Samuel Choy, He Zhikai
Director/Original Story: Brian Tse
Voice Actors: Sandra Ng Kwan Yue, Anthony Wong Chau-Sang, The Pancakes, Ronald Cheng
Screenplay: Brian Tse, Alice Mak
Illustrator: Yeung Hok-Tak
Music: Ng Cheuk-Yin

Synopsis: This time McDull and classmates crash shopping malls and private banquets with their cutesy choir performances in order to raise funds for their debt-ridden school.
Comment: Musical farce.

Yugo and Lala/Adventure in a Strange World

Director: Wang Yun Fei
Music: Sébastien Pan

Synopsis: Yugo, a little naughty girl who considers herself a supergirl, has a fantastic dream about following a talking little bun animal, Lala, and other animals into the mouth of a giant Cloud Whale that transports them to an imaginary Animal Island somewhere in the clouds, where humans are not allowed to enter. A friendly bear tells her that she will change into an animal herself if she does not return to Earth within a period of three days. Finally Yugo, Lala and the bear confront evil General Tiger, who wants to punish all mankind for destroying nature.

Comment: Looks like a cross between Winsor McCay's classic *Little Nemo in Slumberland* and Disney's *Lilo and Stitch*. Its budget of RMB 2.6 million in 3D animation was not sufficient, but it certainly is a breakthrough in Chinese animation storytelling. The story is interesting throughout and the film never loses pace. To make a girl and not a boy the hero of the story proves that the perception of genders is changing in China too. While this book is being written, a sequel that is better funded is already in preparation.

2012–2013

The Prince and the Demon-Kings

Same Player (France)/Kayenta Production (France)/Gebeka Films (France)/France 3 Cinéma/Bidibul Productions (Luxembourg)/Scope Pictures (Belgium) in association with Fundamental, China

105 Minutes

Producers: Vincent Roget, Michel Pierre Pinard, Lilian Eche, Geneviéve Lemal, Marc Bonny, Daniel Goudineau, Mark Gao

Synopsis: China in the eleventh century: The Demon-Kings are terrorizing the countryside. To defeat them would require the courage of one hundred tigers, and outrageous luck. A small group is daring to master the impossible task: Young Prince Duan has only his fairy-tale illusions. Zhang the Perfect has nothing but his monk's stick. The little beggar-girl Pei Pei has only the gift of the gab and her voracious appetite. But Prince Duan, the old monk and Pei Pei don't know that the Demon-Kings are invincible. So they aren't held back by fear, and they vanquish them.

Comment: Expensive Sino-French co-production using motion capture and 3D animation to tell the classic story of the Water Margin.

Tian Keng

Comment: In production, but for lack of funds it is uncertain at this time if it will be finished. Very ambitious stop-motion project initiated by graduates of the Animation School of Beijing Film Academy. Scheduled for release in 2013 (which didn't happen), but sadly underfinanced. It deals with a doomed, polluted world run by giant robots.

2013–2014

Gui Chui Deng

Director: Wuershan

Producer: Chen Kuo-Fu

Comment: 3D animation. First in a planned series, based on popular Internet novels.

➣ Education in Animation ➤

All over the country are spread animation schools. At the end of 2010 there were 286. The premier schools are the Animation School of Beijing Film Academy, CUC Anima, also located in Beijing, and in Changchun the private Jilin Animation Institute, founded as Jilin Animation College in 2000.

Animation School of Beijing Film Academy

The Beijing Film Academy (BFA) is the leading institution of its kind in China. The largest film academy in Asia, it was founded in 1950. Some of the academic programs are film and TV literature; film directing; film performance (they say that you see the most beautiful girls in China on the campus); cinematography; film sound; film and TV art design; film and TV special effect design; advertisement; film management; photography and, of course, animation. The animation curricula includes history of Chinese and foreign film; an introduction to film technology; film analysis; foundation of screenwriting; foundation of film directing; foundation of sounding; film production and market; foundation of film theory; film genre; drawing; DH; audio-visual course; animation motion rules; animation technique; computer animation foundation; screenwriting for animation; nonlinear editing; animation film appreciation; MAYA design; marketing; animation design; animation modeling; animation production; master study in animation. The head of the department, Mr. Sun Lijun, is a prolific animation film director himself.

Since its establishment, the Animation School has been valued by the officials from the central and local governments who have given instructions to speed up the development of the animation program, thus pointing out the direction of and injecting momentum into its growth. Following the instruction that "measures should be taken to give strong support for the development of original products in Chinese animation and game industries, improve the cultivation of talents for production of animation and games, and speed up the growth of Chinese animation industry and game industry," the Animation School of BFA works enthusiastically in the spirit of the central government and uses advantages of BFA in talent cultivation to give impetus to and expedite talent cultivation throughout the animation industry and game industry, in an effort to build the Animation School of BFA into a talent cultivation base for China's original animation and games.

Teaching animation.

History

The predecessor of the Animation School is the animation program in the Fine Arts Department of BFA. Started in 1952, the program, during the period of more than fifty years, has maintained its leading position in the domestic teaching and research field with its outstanding achievements. It has helped to develop many famous Chinese animators, animation directors and production talents of different generations, among them A Da (*Three Monks*), Dai Tielang (*Cop Black White* series), Yan Dingxian (*Nezha*), Lin Wenxiao (*Snow Kid*), and Hu Jinqing (Chinese water color painting and paper cut animated short film, *Yu Bang Xiang Zheng*).

By cultivating the directors of animation films and TV programs and high-level talents for animation production, the Animation School combines digital technologies with traditional animation production skills in the educational program, to implement the integration of "production, study, and research" in the Animation School and to develop the students into artists with high creativity who master new technologies and produce good accomplishments.

Teaching Environment and Advantages

At present, the Animation School is equipped with nearly 150 computers with P4 or higher processors. During their studies, the students have access to the most sophisticated software, such as motion capture, Filmbox, Maya, and Softimage XSI as well as Avid MC8000, DPS Velocity, Betacam SP, DV-Storm and more. Besides that, the Animation School also has the Motion Analysis optical motion capture system, which adopts the FALCOON HR240 Camera provided by Motion Analysis with the highest resolution of 640:480 and highest capture rate of 240 fps.

In recent years, the Animation School has set up two animation production labs, one 5D (stereoscopic dynamics) animation film lab, one virtual reality game lab, one motion capture lab, and one animation industry research institute to provide a solid materials foundation for teaching, production and scientific research.

For the animation program, the following directions are included: four available for master's degree applicants (animation production and theory, animation production and multimedia application and research, animation history studies, and animation screenwriting, while professional animation production management is planned to be provided), four available for bachelor's degree applicants (animation arts, computer animation, cartoon production, and game design) and five available for those receiving higher vocational education (animation arts, computer animation, cartoon, motion design, and game design). In addition, there are classes for further studies and for upgrading from an associate degree to a higher degree.

The Animation School has also established a new type of education and research institution. With the Animation Arts Institute of BFA, the International Animation Industry Research Institute Beijing, and the Game Design Institute of BFA forming the core, Production Studio System 15 was implemented to promote the research in production theory and link it with production practice and teaching practice. On the other hand, active exploration into animation history, theory and technique is encouraged to give impetus to production.

The Animation School combines digital technology with traditional animation skills to cultivate talents for animation production while giving consideration to the students' studies in other subjects related to film, animation, games, and multimedia as well as their research in relevant theory and history. The curriculum arrangement sets store by the study of fundamental knowledge while stressing updated technology:

- Animation Program: Animation survey, animation of animation masters;
- Film Program: Film language, film technology survey, Chinese film history, film history, performing, film shooting and sound production; and
- Computer Multi Media Course: Fundamentals for computer animation, 3D animation, computer multimedia technology and synthesizing.

Activities

After years of teaching practice and summarization, the Animation School of BFA has gradually developed a series of curricula and a teaching system that combines effectiveness with distinctive features, with more than hundred teachers and experts to compile the "21st Century National Planned Teaching Materials for Animation and Game Program of Higher Education," which is the most comprehensive and most authoritative set of teaching materials in China on animation.

Foreign Exchanges and Cooperation

For cooperation with overseas schools, the Animation School makes full use of the advantages of Beijing Film Academy in terms of scope and scale. For instance, it plans to implement a system for routine exchanges between its own teachers and teachers in overseas schools, cooperate with overseas schools in educational programs, and promote international academic exchanges, so as to take in the teaching and production experiences from those famous universities and colleges at home and abroad.

Animation School of Communication University of China

CUC Anima, the Animation School of Communication University of China, seems to have good ties with the government. The Communication University of China is the leading media university in the country. It evolved from a training center for technicians set up by the Central Broadcasting Bureau in 1954. In April 1959, the school was upgraded to Beijing Broadcasting Institute and in 2004 renamed Communication University. The departments are the School of Television and Journalism, the School of Foreign Studies, the School of Advertising, the School of Presentation Art, the School of Information Engineering, the School of Science, the School of Computers, the School of Media Management, the School of Literature, the School of Politics and Law, the School of Chinese Teaching for Overseas Students, the School of Distance and Continuing Education, the Phoenix School of CUC (founded by both CUC and Phoenix Satellite TV), and, prominently, the School of Animation.

CUC Anima has an Animation Department, Digital Art Department, Game Designing Department, and Art Foundation, with the Asian Animation Research Center, Digital Art and Technology Research and Development Center and several other research institutions attached, as well as laboratories for mobile multimedia and NGN, etc. Currently the school has sixty-two professional teachers, among them eight professors and thirteen associate professors, with Ms. Gao Weihua being dean. The school compiles the *Chinese Animation Yearbook* and organizes an annual film festival, AniWow!

Jilin Animation Institute

Jilin College of the Arts–Animation School was founded with the approval of the education department of Jilin Province in the northeast of China in June 2000, and later renamed Jilin Animation Institute.

Most Chinese animators had been trained as painters or designers, according to the formula set by Te Wei and comrades. Nowadays the focus is on software. But the understanding of film language is still limited.

Beyond all the superficial software glory, in education—as in the rest of Chinese animation industry—there are severe problems in dealing with structure and story in animation. Several speakers at the International Animation, Comic and Game (ACG) Forum in September 2009 at Jilin Animation Institute talked in length about the lack of content and story in Chinese animation. One of the speakers was Barry Plews. Mr. Plews, a postgraduate from Flinders University in Australia, started to work in China in 1995 and is now based in Shanghai working on a range of collaborative projects, including a 90-minute 2D animated feature film co-produced with the Shanghai Animation Film Studio:

> Story development is one of the most pressing creative problems for Chinese animation studios today. The development of new animation stories is not keeping pace with the capacity of Chinese animation studios to physically make new animation. To my mind, many animation studios in China are still stumbling around in the dark when it comes to knowing how to go about developing new ideas and new stories for animation.
>
> The first task, as I see it, is to begin thinking about ways of creating a new generation of Chinese animation scriptwriters; scriptwriters knowledgeable about their craft and full of ideas for new stories? The task is easier said than done, of course, but we must begin somewhere. If we don't, the body of the animation dragon will only become larger and larger as production capacity increases exponentially, whilst the head of the dragon shrinks ever more until, for all intents and purposes, we will just be left with a blind giant dancing.

There were similar problems Barry Plews mentioned in his speech that I had to solve during my lectures and workshops at CUC Anima, the State Animation School of the Communication University of China (CUC) in Beijing (with more than twenty thousand students, by far China's most important media university).

Chinese animation contents are quite specific. Audiences in the West tend to find them sometimes too outlandish. One who understood was German dramatist Bert Brecht (1898–1956). Firstly, he recognized in Chinese dramaturgy a symbolic method and alienation effects: "It is well-known that Chinese theatre uses a lot of symbols.... Characters are disguised by particular masks, i.e., by simply painting. Certain gestures of the two hands signify the forcible opening of a door, etc."[20]

Brecht also "discovered the unique principle of formulaic representation of characters in Chinese drama, which is a kind of restrictive performance—the actor is not allowed to pour out his emotion naturalistically. Formulaic representation is a means to portray characters—the emotions of joy, anger, sorrow and fear have their own formulae."[21]

There is one axiom, however: If production companies from two different cultures unite to produce symbiotic media content, the result might be understood globally. This means that there also is an important economical factor to this type of creative work.

There are several ways to approach cross-cultural development, some of them easy, others that require extensive research. Here are some possible scenarios:

1. Characters from East meet characters from West (the *Lost in Translation* model).

2. A Chinese story is being rewritten and interpreted by Western storytelling—or a Western story is told in Chinese art style.

3. Story content (folk and fairy tales, mythology) has travelled centuries ago along the Silk Road from East to West and therefore is spread throughout the world. In a way, this literally is the classic *Journey to the West.*

4. Contemporary problems that affect the socio-cultural life all over the world, especially ecological and environmental problems.

The topic of ecology is what one of the most recent projects of CUC Anima to be produced by professors Lu Shengzhang (former dean) and Wang Lei in cooperation with Zurich University of the Arts in Switzerland (Dr. Martin Zimper, supervisor) is based on: the *Shanghai Super Kids.*

It all began with a simple question: Chinese audiences adore Spider-Man, Batman, Astro Boy and anime, but why don't they have their own brand of comic superheroes?

The *Shanghai Super Kids,* however, the result of our research, are no copies from Marvel or Manga. They are contemporary, mundane Chinese. They are no Supermen and Supergirls commanding superhuman features or super powers but have adopted an incredible, extraordinary awareness to explore nature and its miracles, particularly the underwater world in the Pacific Ocean, which is under general attack.

Selected Students' Work and Short Films

2002

About Life
Animation School of Beijing Film Academy
13 Minutes
Director-Animator: Yu Shui
Genre: Satire

Synopsis: Proving the popularity of German filmmaker Tom Tykwer's *Run, Lola, Run* in China, this short describes a chain reaction that reaches from China to the U.S.

2003

Pan Tian Shou
The China Academy of Fine Arts, Visual Art School, Animation Research Centre
5:22 Minutes
2D/3D Animation
Producer: Xu Jiang
Director/Executive Producer: Joe Chang (aka Chang Hong)
2D Animation: Wang Fuping, Joe Chang, Lu Jiangyun, Hong Wangli, Ruan Juntin, Jiang Binhong, Zhang Yu, Li Jiajia, Zhuang Yuoping
3D Animation: Tang Hongping, Tong Zhou
Consultant: Lu Xin
Genre: Experimental Animation/Biography

Synopsis: Experimental animation devoted to the life of Pan Tianshou (1897–1971), painter and art educator.

Comment: Joe Chang had been associated with the National Film Board of Canada for some time. In this short film he combines hand-drawing, ink painting, and 2D and 3D computer techniques to reproduce traditional Chinese painting style.

2004

Entropy
301 Studio
7:03 Minutes
Director: Zhang Hao
Writer: Zhang Han
Audio Editor: Duan Shunge
Genre: Fantasy

Synopsis: He wakes up and brushes his teeth, goes to the computer, leaves home. He smokes a cigarette as suddenly enormous tentacles, like those of Ray Harryhausen's giant octopus from *It Came from Beneath the Sea,* break through the ground and pursue him. He flees over the roofs but a tentacle is hot on his heels. Suddenly, as if waking up, he finds himself in bed next to a naked woman. They begin to have sex when the woman becomes green-eyed. The man takes his gun and shoots her. Then he is back at the computer screen, occupied with a shooter game when his alter ego returns. Sweating, he wakes up from the nightmare.

Comment: The boy flying like Superman is 2D; the tentacles are 3D animation.

The Lost Commitments

The Animation School of Communication University of China, Beijing
8:49 Minutes
3D Animation
Genre: Chinese Culture

Synopsis: You clap four times. I clap four times. Every single word in the letter contains "missing you."

A boy with his eagle kite. A storm threatens to blow it away. The kite is hit and burnt by lightning. The remnants of it float in the river. The desperate boy gets ill over it. Mother takes him home and cares for him.

You clap five times. I clap five times. Drum is beaten in the background of war flame maintaining combat readiness and rising up upon hearing the crow of a rooster. You clap eight times. I clap eight times. Soldiers fight and fall on the battle field. You clap nine times. I clap nine times. When could we expect the end of war? You clap ten times. I clap ten times. The kite is flying like white bird.

Comment: Like a Chinese poem in animation. Computer technology delivers the feeling of cut-paper animation.

2005

Dream in the Sky

Animation School of Communication University of China, Beijing
4:03 Minutes
2D Animation
Genre: Environment/Ecology

Synopsis: "It says that a long time ago we could see the blue sky on the earth. Even the earth was blue. There were pure water and green trees. But what does the blue sky look like actually?"

A teenage boy has a daydream. Father scolds him: "Blue sky. Enjoy your daydream! Damn!"

But the boy produces a rocket to ride sky high and see the blue that is above the grey dome of pollution. For a brief moment he sees the blue, then explodes into pieces of light that rain onto the grey earth. A glowing feather is the last thing his parents hold in hands.

Dedicated to "all the people who want to seek for the dream."[22]

Egg

4:14 Minutes
3D Animation
Director: Wang Xiaoyuan
Genre: Environment/Ecology

Synopsis: The adventures of a little chick that has just hatched and suddenly meets a mechanical hen and other hybrid chicken that live at a dump near a polluted factory. Finally, a man prepares scrambled eggs but instead of egg yolk has only screws in the pan.

Award: Copper Award, AniWow! Festival, 2006.

2006

Circus

Animation School of Beijing Film Academy
10:30 Minutes
3D Animation
Producers: Sun Lijun, Cao Xiaohui, Qi Xiaoling
Production Manager: Zhang Huijun
Director/Screenplay/Character Designer: Yin Yiao
Storyboard/Animation/Postproduction: Yin Yiao, Lu Ruidan
Art Directors: Sun Cong, Su Xia
Background Designers: Lu Ruidan, Yin Yiao
Character Modeling: Lu Ruidan, Yin Yiao
Scene Modeling: Lu Ruidan, Yang Li, Yin Yiao
Texture: Yin Yiao, Liu Yang
Lighting: Lu Ruidan, Yin Yiao, Yang Li
Music: Ding Yingfeng
Music Mix: Jiang Chong
Dubbing: Zhao Nanlezi
Genre: Parable

Synopsis: A little red-haired, red-eyed girl walks through desolated streets destroyed by war and finally enters the ruins of a carnival that includes a circus inhabited by two robots, a small fat one and a tall slim one. At first the girl is frightened, but then she relaxes to the friendly robots, who are going to make her happy and feel the sense of wonder producing artificial birds. But then the mechanized birds fall down and everything ends in what might be a nuclear catastrophe.

Comment: Dark and pessimistic. For modeling the students used Maya7, software render, and for texture, Photoshop.

Infinity on Your Hand

CUC Anima, the Animation School of Communication University of China, Beijing
3:50 Minutes
Director/Animation: Ding Meiyin
Production Coordinator: Lu Shengzhang
Pictures: Ding Ping
Sound Effects: Li Bo
Genre: Experimental Animation

Comment: Colorful hand and finger prints form characters that move to Viennese operetta tunes: chicken, swans, tadpoles, frogs, deer, kangaroo, sheep, panda.

Award: ASIFA China Award, AniWow! Festival, 2006.

Legend of Shangri-La

14:57 Minutes
2D Animation
Genre: Fantasy

Synopsis: In the mind of the Dong Jing people, Peach Blossom Valley or Shangri-La represents paradise on Earth and the desire to return to a life in harmony.

In the opening a man is being tortured because he has a valuable secret. Once a fisherman—we learn in a flashback—he sailed into Wu-Ling River and ended in a forest made up entirely of blossoming peach trees, a place of sheer beauty: "Ah, is it possible that the winter was over and the spring has come?" Filled with sheer amazement, he entered a dark grotto and finally reached a dreamlike valley with a village populated by animals and people of all ages: "I heard sounds and smelled all kinds of sweet fragrances."

The villagers, although surprised, welcomed him in a friendly way and with kind hospitality: "All encounters are karma." His old host told him: "Although this humble place is far away from the rest of the world the weather is spring-like all year round. We get peaches in all seasons." "May I ask how did you find his place?" the fisherman asked.

"During the war time of Qin Dynasty, my ancestor escaped with his wife and neighbors and found this exclusive place. We have never gone out ever since. We have been staying away from the outside world for many years. You are the first outsider who ventured into our village." The old man didn't know that the time of Qin Dynasty was over several hundred years ago. The fisherman told him that there were Han and Wei Dynasties in the meantime and now Jin Dynasty. The old man grabs his beard: "The Dynasties surely change fast outside the mountains."

Wu-Ling stayed in the village for several days: "I have never met people with such hospitality. They entertained me with their best wine and food in abundance. There was neither government nor tax looming over them. People treated each other with mutual respect and love. Even the water from the well tasted sweet like rice wine. I really wanted to stay." Next morning he decided to sneak out, return home and arrange things, then return to this paradise for good. But he is being met by the elder at the exit of the grotto: "Have a safe journey, my venerable guest. As you are leaving may I have a request? Would you please be discreet about what you have seen here? This place is really insignificant for outsiders to know."

"To make sure I could return I made road marks along my way back. After I arranged everything at home and tried to return to the peach blossom valley all the road marks were gone. I was so stupid. Why did I come back? I can never return to that place again," he said, telling an outsider his incredible story. This person promised him that together they would find the fabulous place. But all their attempts were in vain. Shangri-La remained lost. After the friend's death the fisherman began to wonder if he had ever been to that worry-free place or all was a dream. "Day after day, I kept fishing, paying endless taxes and no one believed my story anymore. But I still believe, one day I will find Peach Blossom Valley again."

Comment: Adapted from a poem, *The Peach Blossom Spring,* written by the most famous poet of Dong Jin Dynasty, Tao Yuan Ming. Traditional Chinese painting techniques are applied to CG backgrounds and Shan-Xi shadow-puppet-show style to CG animation.

Award: Handsome Monkey Animation Award, 2006.

First Place Golden Award, DigiCon6+2 Contest, sponsored by Japan Tokyo Broadcasting System, Inc., 2006.

The Memories About the Street

CUC Anima, the Animation School of Communication University of China, Beijing
Ours Animation Studio
7:54 Minutes
3D Animation
Director: Zhong Ding
Genre: Children's Story
   Synopsis: Through a shop window a little child admires and enjoys the antics of a living toy manikin. The kid returns, and a special relationship develops. When the kid grows older, however, he doesn't pay attention to the puppet anymore. But then a new kid comes and the show would go on, but the manikin is rusty and no more able to perform. The father of the child, however, recognizes the toy, as he is the little boy from the past.
   Comment: Sentimental children's story.

Mending the Sky

Lu Xun Academy of Fine Arts
7:40 Minutes
Director: Huang Yu
Genre: Experimental/Mythology
   Synopsis: The naked goddess Nuwa creates man.
   Comment: Animated woodcut mythology.

The Song of Ours

CUC Anima, the Animation School of Communication University of China, Beijing
6:58 Minutes
2D Animation
Director: Zccko (Li Bo)
Genre: Youth Culture
   Synopsis: A Chinese art student producing comics waits for a chance and turns in some samples of his work. And the miracle happens: His work is accepted and published. But then there is a fist fight between the student and a teacher who dislikes the rock music the students love to hear. His protest leads to the student's relegation. In the end it's all a dream.
   Comment: Anime-influenced style with rock songs.
   Award: Silver Award, AniWow! Festival, 2006.

2007

The Ants

Director-Animator: Guo Yuangyuan
Genre: Comedy
   Synopsis: In an ordinary house a fresh piece of cake causes a rush of ants.

Battle Cry

Animation School of Beijing Film Academy
Producer: Li Shijun
8:53 Minutes
Genre: History/Politics
   Synopsis: Fascist soldiers are attacked by what seems to be a U.S. combat team and create lots of bloodshed, with arms lying around. The Fascist troops fight back with bazookas. As the Fascists regard themselves almost victorious, an enemy bomb destroys them.
   Comment: Claymation anti-war short with all the soldiers wearing World War II steel helmets.

The Emerald Jar/Cool New Look

2D Animation
Director/Writer/Animation: Xi Chen
Genre: Fantasy
   Synopsis: A man comes with a basket of money to a killer and asks to have his wife murdered. In a dream sequence man and wife meet and hug each other in the sky, then the wife floats again. The man wakes up, tears in his eyes.
   Comment: Chen Xi started drawing comics at an early age. He graduated from Beijing Film Academy with a master's degree in 2010. The same year he was awarded at the Hiroshima International Film Festival.

Pure Color

CUC Anima, the Animation School of Communication University of China, Beijing
4:39 Minutes
2D Animation
Producers: Liao Xiangzhong, Gao Weihua
Director/Writer/Animation: Zhu Dan
Presented by Su Zhiwu
Faculty Advisers: Xue Janping, Li Jie, Zhang Yue, Luan Lian
Genre: Children's Story
   Synopsis: A story about a country boy entering a Buddhist temple and for the first time seeing the colorful shapes of the paintings. He takes an apple meant for sacrificial offering and outside gives it to an infant. He

finally joins his mother. Together they watch the nightly sky.

Shadow

CUC Anima, the Animation School of Communication University of China, Beijing
3:26 Minutes
Genre: Experimental Animation
　　Comment: Shadow play characters.

So

22:45 Minutes
2D Animation
Genre: Experimental Animation
　　Synopsis: An infant chooses the color orange for himself. The boy in orange meets a girl in pink. Growing up. Later the girl, now a woman in pink, returns. Getting older the man gets around and starts to drink and gamble, turning to a prostitute until he finds a lady in pink. As a result he is knifed. Next time the infant's color choice is green.

Sweet and Sour

The People's Republic of Animation/Shanghai Animation Film Studio/Reckless Moments/ iDraw Fast/The South Australian Film Corporation/The Australian Film Commission
17 Minutes
Writer-Director: Eddie White
Genre: Satire
　　Synopsis: The story deals with the prejudice that Chinese eat dogs (occasionally they do, but in rare quantities): Errol, a hungry stray dog, falls in love with the smells and tastes of Chinatown but begins to believe that the Chinese want to put him on the menu.
　　Comment: Australian production with animation outsourced to China.

Vase

Department of Digital Art and Design School of Software and Microelectronics, Beijing University
Director/Writer/Character and Scene Design/Animation/Editor: Zhang Xiaohua
Adviser: Ma Kexuan
Genre: Satire
2D Animation
　　Synopsis: On TV a vase is being offered. The wife watches intensely while her husband reads a newspaper. She dials a phone number and orders an object that all of a sudden appears on the table. Next comes furniture. Then the man orders designer chairs. And so on. Every article that is announced on TV is being ordered by the couple. Finally the flat is filled with stuff of all kinds. On TV they offer new partners. Man and wife consider it a splendid idea to change their partner and immediately fight for the phone.

2007–2008

Nancy's Morning

Animation School of Beijing Film Academy
10 Minutes
3D Animation
Genre: Youth Culture
　　Synopsis: A city girl gets up in the morning. Her friend who took a taxi in the end becomes victim of a car accident.
　　Comment: Demonstrates improvement of students' work in art and technology. Car accidents seem to be quite a topic in students' work.

2008

Amy's Happy Life

2:45 Minutes
2D Animation
Genre: Comedy
　　Synopsis: Amy tries to slim down, but when she finds out that the scale is not working correctly, while constantly showing 150 kg, everything is forgotten and she feeds herself.

Attaching Great Importance to Face-Saving

2:32 Minutes
3D Animation
Director: Schuck
Software: 3Ds Max 8.0, Cat 2.0, Combustion 4.0, Premiere Pro 2.0, Photoshop csZ
Genre: Parable
　　Synopsis: A character wearing a green mask and green clothes finds a red-colored mask. A purple character turns up who seems to like the other face better than his own. He asks for the mask, but the finder rejects him. They start to fight, but the object lands in the crown of a tree. Disappointed, the two part and continue to go their own ways. At least, they pretend to do so. Then they return and jump for it.

Choose

CUC Anima, the Animation School of Communication University of China, Beijing
4:37 Minutes
Directors: Jiang Miao, Liu Yuangyuan
Animation and Inbetweens: Jiang Miao, Liu Yuangyuan, Zhu Houlin, Wang Ruochen
Character Design: Gao Yuan
Cinematography: Xiang Yang, Jiang Miao
Special Effects: Xiang Yang, Wang Tenghuang, Liu Yuanyuan
Editor: Jiang Miao
Digital Compositing: Xiang Yang
Sound Design: Li Shuang
Faculty Advisers: Wang Lei, Hong Yu, Ai Shengying, Gao Weihua
Genre: Environment/Ecology
Comment: Simple animation to show how cars pollute our planet. Pastel animation over live backgrounds. Greedy Freon bottles. All kind of dangers for the environment of our planet are shown until the planet becomes red.

The opening titles say: *We can choose another way...*

Live action footage of father and child in front of batteries of wind turbines.

You could choose it, and you should be responsible for it. But before you choose, be responsible.

Darkness

3:19 Minutes
3D Animation (3D Max)
Director: Liu Jin We
Genre: Sci-Fi
Synopsis: Hollywood-style alien attack on some distant planet. A fight between alien and robot.

Deer Antlers and Hooves/Yingzi

7:08 Minutes
3D Animation
Genre: Parable
Synopsis: A deer, while thinking how to cross some water, is attacked by a lion and escapes into a green forest. It gets struck. The lion comes up. All that remains of the deer is the skeleton.
Comment: Box-like character design.

The Distance of the Hearts

D5 Studio
3:51 Minutes
2D Animation
Director/Screenplay/Animation: Alice Huang

Presented by Gareth C. C. Chang
Music and Sound Design: Xue Dong Hui, An Le
Genre: Comedy
Synopsis: A young man falls in love with the image of a woman on another guy's t-shirt. The girl manages the change and goes over to him as he offers her his heart. The other guy gets jealous and beats the young man up, but eventually he is with her on his t-shirt, where they can have love with each other. But her grip is so total that he would like to escape from this situation.

Dream

8:01 Minutes
3D Animation
Genre: Youth Culture
Synopsis: Late at night, a tired teenager sitting in front of his computer fights sleep. Suddenly he wakes up, deciding to woo his dream girl, but being shy he feels helpless and useless. But then he thinks: "I have not dropped down." He decides to fight, then keep on dreaming and falling asleep again.
Comment: Some good acting in animation.

Experiment Animation So

22:46 Minutes
2D Animation
Genre: Experimental Animation
Comment: Stylistically interesting little film about a boy who grows up with his dog.

The Falling Star

Animation School of Beijing Film Academy
5:06 Minutes
Genre: Youth Culture
Synopsis: The daily life of teenagers. Out of a situation that a girl is bitten by a snake, love evolves between the girl and her helper, a boy, after she has recovered in the hospital.

Father

3:58 Minutes
2D Animation
Genre: Family
Synopsis: Father is chain-smoking and recalls the times when his son was young but there was all kind of disagreement between them. Now he is looking desperately for the son and in doing so is struck by a car. Finally, in death, his ghost finds the boy sitting on a park bench while the ambulance is picking up the father. The boy now is alone.

Fatman and Moto

2:40 Minutes
3D Animation
Director/Screenplay: ZP686
Genre: Comedy

Synopsis: A fat man in bathing trousers chains his motorcycle but finds it gone on his return. Only the wheels are left. Next is a bicycle. He takes this as a consolation prize.

Comment: ZP686 is originally from Baotou, Inner Mongolia. He graduated from Beijing Fashion Institute's New Media and Animation School in 2008. Although trained as an illustrator and animator, he is currently employed in Beijing by an American VFX company as a concept art designer.

The Finger Prints

5:56 Minutes
2D Animation
Director: Chen Hansing
Story: Koo Hsinming
Screenplay: Chen Hansing, Yen Lily
Design: Chen Hansing
Postproduction Editors: Chen Hansing, Koo Hsinming
Consultant: Ling Tsing
Genre: Fantasy

Synopsis: Can destruction of evidence remove the evil?

A fight to the death between two street boys. There is blood on the hands of the knife thrower. With his knife he tries to cut the finger prints from his hand. An old lady appears on the dark street. From behind a trash can he watches her taking some drugs from a bottle. The characters on the capsule: "Longevity." He sees her transform into a young woman. He gets the bottle. This time the characters read: "Composition: fingerprints and palm prints, etc." He passes into the street under a lantern. The characters on the lantern: "Pawn the career line." Imaginary lanterns lead him: "Pawn the finger print." "Pawn the sentiment line." One lantern in hand, he ends up at a pawnshop/clinic. He sees a hybrid—half robot, half human—lift his own fingerprints, then scan him. The lantern obviously belongs here. The characters on the balance: "kindness—justice—benevolence—crime." The old shopkeeper passes energy that changes the young criminal's fingerprints. Suddenly he feels free again. He sees the balance: crime vs. life span. (Note: Ancient Chinese people believed that the length of the three most obvious palm lines could control a person's career, love and life span.) But now that he is without prints or lines, his hands deteriorate. Balance: "Innocence." And he fades away. The shopkeeper collects the absorbed energy and locks it in a capsule that reads: "Longevity."

Fish Kite

5:13 Minutes
3D Animation (2D Look)
Genre: Fantasy

Synopsis: A girl has a kite shaped like the goldfish in the bowl and starts to fly it. Suddenly, inside the house, she hears a cat and finds out what happened. The bowl has been destroyed and the goldfish lies on the floor. She takes it in her hands and buries it outside near a tree in the sunset. At night she cannot sleep. There, at the tree, she experiences some magic, with a giant ghost-like kite-fish coming to her and making her fly on its back.

Comment: Miyazaki-style. Also may have been inspired by the German *Laura's Star.*

Freak Huazha Fantasy

Academy of Fine Arts and Design
4:43 Minutes
Genre: Experimental Animation

Comment: Just a mix of beautiful images set in peacock garden.

God's Bliss

20:07 Minutes
Genre: Experimental Animation

Synopsis: A boy and his family. The boy befriends a sheep and brings it home, much to the dismay of his parents. More animals follow: a cat, a giraffe. And right in the house a tree starts to grow out of the floor. The old parents have to cut out the roof to let it grow. A cow is bound to the ceiling, while the old man starts doing paintings under the cow. Later the cow falls down and has to be fixed again. The boy sleeps and dreams surrounded by sheep. Sheep carousing in the breakfast room. Chicken flown by balloons. The house is lifted on the growing tree up to the sky.

Comment: Surreal claymation short in the tradition of Aardman Studios and Švankmajer.

Grandpa and I

Animation School of Beijing Film Academy
7 Minutes

2D Animation
Director: Ying Ma
Genre: Family/Childhood Memory
   Synopsis: Scenes from life of a grandfather and little granddaughter.
   Comment: Dedicated: "To my grandfather."

Green

Animation School of Beijing Film Academy
8:52 Minutes
2D Animation
Producer: Li Shijun
Genre: Sci-Fi/Environment
   Synopsis: A three-eyed alien king is going to have his one-eyed and robot-like troops absorb all green energy from this planet, but a vegetable-like creature fights back and makes them work for green environment and not steal it.
   Comment: Crude claymation short with colorful, animated 2D graphics.

A Half of Newspaper

Shanxi University of Technology
1:26 Minutes
2D Animation
Genre: Comedy
   Synopsis: Three boys, side by side, sit on toilets, but there is no toilet paper, only half a newspaper. Two boys start fighting for it, while the third one is going to read the paper.

Head

4:10 Minutes
Genre: Parable
   Synopsis: Those he meets on his way to work, even animals, have a light bulb instead of a head. He decides to get rid of his head and puts a light bulb in. Now he is in between, neither man nor animal nor artificial. He decides to use his head again.

Home

A Noway Animation
3:35 Minutes
Genre: Experimental Animation
Photoshop Ulead GIF Animator
   Synopsis: Things, animals, people and sets keep changing in black and white, with two or three protagonists in color.

Kid Coming

Media College of Nanjing Arts Institute
8:29 Minutes
3D Animation

Producers: Zhang Chen Zhi, Zhuang Yao
Director/Screenplay/Animation Supervisor: Yue Feng
Technology Supervisor: Yu Jie
Sound Design: Zhuang Yao, Zhuang Xiao Ni
Genre: Family
   Synopsis: "If you are going to have a boy, let him be healthy, smart and wealthy.
   If you are going to have a girl, let her be pretty, lucky and witty.
   If you are going to have a boy, let him be healthy, smart and wealthy."
   A man asks his wife: "Honey, what do you think? We'll have a son next year?"
   She objects: "Girls are more considerate."
   "But I prefer a son."
   "I want to have a lovely daughter."
   They drive into the countryside and have sex in their campervan.
   She: "A daughter is perfect."
   He: "But I prefer son."
   Suddenly outside the van there is a little boy.
   "Whose baby is it?"
   The boy gets inside the vehicle and honks, making a terrible noise.
   This boy is a real nuisance.
   While they still are struggling and trying to catch the boy, the van starts rolling towards a cliff, heading downwards.
   The woman screams. Finally she gets hold of a tree and the vehicle comes to a stop. Three other kids, girls, take care of the little rascal.
   The couple watches them, relieved.
   "It seems a girl might be better," the man agrees with his wife.
   But the wife says: "Both good. Both good."
   Comment: One has to realize that traditional Chinese society had a lot of reservations against girls.

The Love Song of Tong Nationality

7:08 Minutes
Genre: Chinese Culture
   Comment: Traditional song with experimental animation of singers.

Memory of a Lover

Wang Qianru's Works
4:16 Minutes
2D Animation
Director/Story/Storyboard/Character and Background Design: Wang Qianru
Key Animation: Liu Nana
Genre: Fantasy

Synopsis: "I often feel like a stranger being set unwillingly in this world." Dream moments of a girl taken by a whirlwind and flying, accompanied by mice and bats and other animals. "My heart is full of unknown terror. I become confused more and more."

Comment: Surreal visuals.

Morning, Noon and Evening

4:42 Minutes
Genre: Experimental Animation
   Synopsis: Elephant on a whip; a squirrel; a snake lighting a candle.
   Comment: Colorful cut-out animation.

My Family

Design School of Jiang Nin University
7:28 Minutes
3D Animation
Director/Screenplay/Design/Rendering: Zhao Gui Sheng
Animation: Wu Xiang Hua (Dog), Wang Bing (Man), Zhao Gui Sheng (Wife)
Rendering Assistant: Xu Quan Bing
Genre: Family Comedy
   Synopsis: Family life complete with husband watching sports on TV, and the wife and dog, ends in a conflict between the couple about the dog.
   Comment: Inept 3D animation with a 2D look.

The Next

Ours Animation Studio
7:14 Minutes
3D Animation
Director: Zhao Ronghao
Screenplay/Modeling/Texturing/Lighting/Animation/Music and Sound Effects/Postproduction/Editing: Zhao Ronghao, Zhong Ding
Faculty Adviser: Ren Jiazhen
Genre: Fantasy
   Synopsis: A little girl kicks a tin on the street. In a corner street there is an automaton with tins, one with her own image. She puts a coin in the slit, then another one, but nothing happens. More coins follow. The girl is upset that she doesn't get the tin, and wants to break the machine open. Finally a coin is returned and the automaton starts to move and turn around. A big ball appears, scanning her, then offering her a dream world full of toys inside, but when she is in she is trapped and the box closes.

Old House

CUC Anima, the Animation School of Communication University of China, Beijing
3:49 Minutes
2D Animation
Director/Screenplay/Art   Director/Animation/Music/Editor: Li Danni
Presented by Su Zhiwu
Producers: Liao Xiangzhong, Gao Weihua
Faculty Advisers: Lu Shengzhang, Yu Haiyan, Zhang Yuejin
Genre: Everyday Life
   Synopsis: Daily scenes that repeat in an old house.

Paradise Under Water

Animation School of Beijing Film Academy
7:37 Minutes
2D Animation
Producer: Zhang Huijun
Production Supervisors: Sun Lijun, Yiauling
Executive Producers: Ai Tong, Li Min
Director/Screenplay/Storyboard/Art Design: Li Min
Assistant Director: Ai Ming
Art Direction: Sun Cong
Animation: Li Min, Zhang Liao
Music: Liu Wei
Editor: Li Min
Genre: Fantasy
   Synopsis: Little girl and animals ride in a train under water, with the vehicles forming a giant wheel and the girl riding in a bubble beside it.

The Private Pressure

Animation School of Beijing Film Academy
15:31 Minutes
2D Animation
Director/Screenplay/Art Direction/Animation: Zhang Zheng
Producer: Zhang Huijun
Adviser: Sun Lijun
Filmmakers: Sun Lijun, Qi Xiaoling, Li Jianping, Sun Cong, Cao Xiaohui
Photographer: Zhang Yueyin
Sound: Wu Chunlin
Technical Support: Zhang Yueyin, Fu Bo
Administration and Logistics: Li Liang
Genre: Parable
   Synopsis: "City people are under pressure from all aspects. The pressure will appear in dream, finally, be resolved."
   A man sleeps and snores, has nightmares, is being pursued on the stairway by a rhinoceros, wants to kill a duck and is almost devoured by it. The moon transfers into coin image.

Comment: Daily pressures become evening's nightmares.

The Promise

Animation School of Beijing Film Academy
22:50 Minutes
2D Animation
Producer: Li Shijun
Director: Peng Qingzheng
Genre: Children's Story

Synopsis: Sentimental story of a boy and a little girl who were raised in the countryside. Their imagination circles around an orange and the final growth of a tree when they have grown up themselves. Then the boy goes abroad and the girl waits for his return. The enemy attacks the country, and she has nightmares of demons, thunder and lightning. Only the tree is left. Eventually, when both are old, the man returns to his love and they hold hands under the moon as they did when they were kids.
Award: ASIFA China Award, Aniwow, 2009.

Red Scarf

Art Academy of South China Agricultural University
5FID Animation Studio
4:41 Minutes
2D Animation
Genre: Fantasy

Synopsis: The story of a boy who wears a red scarf like all the other Chinese pupils. In his imagination he and his friends ride a Miyazaki-like giant cat (right out of *My Neighbor Totoro*) that wears a red scarf too and jumps with them around houses.
Comment: Teaser for a film that apparently was not finished.

The Return

CUC Anima, the Animation School of Communication University of China, Beijing
6:50 Minutes
3D Animation
Producer: Gao Weihua
Director-Writers: Shang Zhuo, Hu Haowei
Genre: Parable

Synopsis: Suicide attempt: Desperately alone on an island, a man finds a magic trunk. Soon after, he will embark on a journey to the moon.
Comment: Nightmarish quality.

Rian Xing Jin Gang

Animation School of Beijing Film Academy
14:03 Minutes
2D Animation
Producer: Zhang Huijun
Production Supervisors: Sun Lijun, Qi Xiao Ling, Li Jian Ping, Sun Cong
Director: Ruan
Screenplay: Xiao
Logistical: Li Liang
Animation: Guo
Music: Wu
Sound Recording: Chun
Sound Effects: Lin
Genre: Sci-Fi

Synopsis: Some giant superhero characters on board a spaceship get into a fight; then their spacecraft crash-lands on Earth where they get loose, with no way to stop them.

September

4:39 Minutes
Comment: Classic Chinese style done in claymation.

Shinobi

Animation School of Beijing Film Academy
5:30 Minutes
2D Animation
Producer: Zhang Huijun
Production Supervisors: Sun Lijun, Liu Dong
Director/Screenplay/Art Designer/Animation/ Music/Sound Recording: Liu Dong
Genre: Fantasy

Synopsis: A fox and a wildcat have a game of dice, with the fox winning all the coins.
Comment: Study in animal character animation.

So.So

1:28 Minutes
Genre: Environment
Synopsis: Martial Arts Girl stops another female who wants to throw away tin under the bridges and makes her aware of waste paper baskets.
Comment: Experiment in motion capture.

Sunshine

3D Animation
8:14 Minutes
Executive Producer: Zheng Li Guo
Director/Screenplay: Standing
Art Director/Compositing: Ranyi
Animation Director/Instructor: Matthew
Character Design: Xiao Lie, Li Bo, Standing

Scene Design: Standing
Administration of Networks: Lin Yan Qiang
Editor: Standing
Genre: Sci-Fi Parable

Synopsis: An old man, naked to the waist, is beside a dying flower. Around them is a dark environment. There is no sun in this underworld, only despair. He shoulders a shovel, and starts to feed and repair a huge, dirty machine.

Suddenly a bully, his boss, turns up, chomping a cigar, checking the work, throwing him a coin for his work.

A situation similar to *Metropolis.*

The worker lets the boss have the coin so that he can put it in a slit.

Suddenly a gate opens and sunshine bursts in, and the flower recovers in the light.

But after a few seconds and brief moments of light, the gate closes. Darkness again.

The worker continues in a world that is without light.

While the end credits roll we see the worker hunting the boss with his shovel. A revolutionary situation.

A Thief's Story: Hurling Himself Willingly into the Net

3:15 Minutes
2D Animation
Genre: Drama

Synopsis: A thief knocks, then breaks open a door. But the flat owner is in. They are eyeball to eyeball. The apartment owner attacks the thief. A martial arts–worthy fight begins between the two of them. The thief lies on the floor.

The Winter Solstice/The Midwinter

Congrongfilm
11:17 Minutes
Executive Producer: Liang Zhang
Producer: Jian Jiang
Directors: Xi Chen, Xu An
Voice Actors: Fan Chen, Yuan Yuan, Xuesheng Liu
Character Design/Animation: Xi Chen
Background Design: Xu An
Sound: Xi Chen, Xu Chang
Genre: History

Synopsis: In snowfall a man tries to light a cigarillo. He is sitting in all the snow in a little pavilion with a soldier (Japanese?) behind, aiming his gun at him. The man smokes while he is shot.

The man, bleeding and severely wounded,

rings at a nearby door. A pregnant woman opens and hugs him. Tea water. A record player. The two dance to some Chinese tunes. They fight, then they kiss each other. The man gives the woman a drug. They sleep together and have oral sex. Then the man is outside again, dying. Everything is in the imagination of a person dying, who longs to see his newborn child.

2008–2009

Water Brain

Ani7me Animation Studio/Guangzhou Academy of Fine Arts (GAFA)-Academy of Art Design
15 Minutes
3D Animation
Director/Art Supervisor: Johann Pu (Zhou Jan Rui)
Art: Zhang Chun Li, Su Jing Xin
Music: Sun Hua
Music Score: Wall-E
Sound Design: King Kong
Genre: Parable

Synopsis: Covers the unbelievable performance pressure faced by pupils in China. "When overstressed, their brains boil and give off steam that serves as food for the schoolbag monsters (parents/teachers) 'enslaving' them in energy factories (classrooms/bedrooms)." The fears appear behind them shaped like monsters while they do their homework. Each kid has to carry a steam monster. A burning paper flyer symbolizes the kids' dream of more freedom.

Comment: A bizarre student work distantly influenced by Miyazaki. Although it is not much, compared to him, it does have some strength. Remarkable for its Chinese take on steampunk.

Award: Best Graduation Award, GAFA. Presented at SIGGRAPH, 2009.

2009

Anna

7:30 Minutes
2D Animation
Genre: Kid's Fantasy

Synopsis: Daily life of a little girl. Her puppet becomes huge and suddenly is alive and has flowers for her. The benign creature becomes very friendly and even prepares breakfast for her, then rides with her on a broom and travels in a balloon. Then she realizes that she is in the hospital. She was involved in a car accident and the toy was the last thing she saw before the accident happened.

The Birthday Gift/Birthday Present

8 Minutes
Director: Li Pin
Genre: Family
Synopsis: Set in the small town of Liuzhou in the 1970s: Three ordinary people prepare a birthday present for a little boy.

Candy Storm

Hirain Technologies
12:12 Minutes
3D Animation
Genre: Fantasy
Synopsis: We hear Mother Bear and Kid Bear talk about a land of milk and honey and see illustrations of chocolate floods and cake and lollipops. Of course, the kid wants to find this wonderful land. Another animal overhears the wish and climbs a giant beanstalk up to the sky, like that of the fairy tale, and reaches the fabled country, where he causes a candy storm to fall down to the little guy.

Chase

CUC Anima, the Animation School of Communication University of China, Beijing
Director: Mu Jianhong
Award: ASIFA China Award, Aniwow, 2009.

Chasing Butterfly

China Academy of Art, School of Media and Animation
6:17 Minutes
2D Animation
Director/Scene Design: Zhang Jie
Screenplay: Fueng Ziejang
Music: Zhang Jing
Genre: Fantasy
Synopsis: A little girl draws on walls. A colorful butterfly appears in her grey environment. With her fingers she touches it; then she begins to chase it and all of a sudden realizes that she is able to fly over the skyscrapers of the city, following the butterfly. She falls into the ocean. She flies up and sees sea gulls. Climbing on the shore, she enters a most beautiful garden. There is a storm coming up and skyscrapers grow up to imprison her again. The leaf of the last sunflower she holds is blown away in the wind.

Comment: Dream of a life in free, clean environment. Fear of big cities.

Chicken Wants to Fly

Jilin Animation College
Presented by Zheng Liguo
10:30 Minutes
2D Animation
Director-Animator: Zeng Yigang
Consultant: Chang Guangxi
Genre: Chinese Culture/Fable
Synopsis: A little chicken tries to find out about its own identity and eagerly wants to fly.
Comment: Watercolor animation inspired by Te Wei and his *Where Is Momma?*

Combatant

Animation School of Beijing Film Academy
11:43 Minutes
2D/3D Animation
Producer: Sun Lijun
Director/Writer/Storyboard: Lidina
Voice Artists: Lidina, Frank
Assistant Screenplay: Cayman
Presented by Zhang Huijun
Instructors: Li Jianping, Xian Liu
Music/Sound Effects: Frank
Genre: Adolescence
Synopsis: Daily life of a teenage girl who has problems with her parents. She has a nightmare of herself in a martial-arts computer game with all-powerful, gigantic representations of her parents, who fight themselves by firing rockets. The girl intervenes as an angel of peace. Then, one day, her father is hit by a motorcycle and brought to the hospital to undergo an operation. Mother is happy when he gets well again and so is the daughter who brings, tears in her eyes, a flower.

The Cooperation Project

Animation School of Beijing Film Academy
6:30 Minutes
2D Animation
Director/Screenplay/Layout/Graphic Design: Rang Bo
Genre: Students' Life
Synopsis: The cooperative project of the Animation School of Beijing Film Academy is explained by the dean of animation, Sun Lijun: "In the cooperative project 4 or 5 persons make up a team. They work together on the same project but doing different things. At the end you will produce an animation short film. This is the Animation School."

Scenes of animation students' daily routine: "I announce that the junior year animation Cooperation Project of 2005 level of Animation Art of the Animation School of Beijing Film Academy starts now!"

All students: "Hooray!"

"Good. You have two weeks. I hope every team will bring a satisfactory script to the class!"

Time to hand in the script. An empty page. The students seem to have problems developing and writing a coherent storyline. The guy they have chosen to do the job was not able to hand it properly. "Director! Is the script ready?" the other students want to know. Instead of working they clown around and beat him up with plastic clubs: "Damn you, don't scream like hell! Go, explain this yourself!"

In his imagination he sees an angry, upset teacher: "Where's your script? It's been half a month! Where is it?!"

He confesses: "Professor, I have not finished the script!" And promises: "Next time!"

Dreaming Prisoner

3:44 Minutes
Genre: Parable

Synopsis: In his prison cell, every day the prisoner receives another child's drawing.

Comment: Stop motion.

Dui Ling Yi Ge Zi Ji Shuo

Communication University of China at Nanjing
   Animation Department
6 Minutes
2D Animation
Executive Producer: Liu Jinan
Director: Kong Guangxia
Writers: Kong Guangxia, Su Yalin
Executive Supervisor: Ding Haiyan
Presented by Zhang Huilin
Production Manager: Liu Liangtoo
Mentors: Xu Dingkai, Zhang Huilin, Bo Lin
Color Designer/Matte Painting: Su Yalin
3D Compositing and Editing: Wang Yuanyuan
Narrator: Qin Shanying
Genre: Kids' Story

Synopsis: After a train accident a boy has to stay home and lie in bed:

All the other kids in Longtang go to school while I am still sleeping in bed lazily. They wish they could be me, but I'd rather go to school. Mom and Dad say I'm not the same as other kids. I know that. I can't go to school, and I have to take a lot of pills every day. I have hundreds of toys. Every day when I wake up, I see them. No one has more toys than me in Longtang. They used to come and play with me a long time ago, but they haven't come since then. Mom and Dad already have gone to work when I wake up. There's only Grandpa and me at home, having breakfast with our nanny. This is the nanny my parents hired for Grandpa and me but I don't like her because she makes noises when she eats. I find it boring to play alone. So I started to look for some fun. I found many funny things in my parents' room (holds woman's clothes and high heels in front of a mirror). Dad told me Grandpa's aging and he's not energetic enough to handle affairs. I began to expect my parents to leave early in the morning every day so that I could play some game that I want but I can't tell people what it is. (Has sexual fantasies.) Grandpa still pees in his pants every day and nanny will settle for him. I know she doesn't like to do this stuff at all. What's more, I know she doesn't like Grandpa; neither do I like her. (We see him masturbating while dreaming of having sex with a woman.) It's a totally different feeling, and I like this kind of feeling. (We see him falling, like into water, onto a floor of sucking boobs.) One day, the nanny happened to find out about my secret. I promised to steal Mom's cosmetics for her in order to keep her mouth shut. If I'm caught by Mom, I should say I wanted to use the cosmetics myself. She's really a bitch. I don't want to stay in this house anymore. I ran once I opened the door. For the first time, I ran so desperately I felt as if I could run a long, long time. I saw the place outside Longtang. No wonder they all like to play outside here. I like it here too.

Comment: Dedication: "I would like to dedicate this film to those hard working and diligent parents and those big post–80s kids who do not want to grow up." In a way, a plea for sexual freedom as well.

Escape from the Temple/Shuang Xia Shan

The National Academy of Chinese Theatre Arts
5:48 Minutes
2D Animation
Director/Producer: Zhou Xing
Voice Actors: Jiao Jingge (Monk), Lu Jie (Nun), Ma Hongbo (Midi), Wang Xiqiao (Singer)
Faculty Adviser: Yu Shoafei
Art Adviser: Zhou Zhilong
Music Adviser/Bamboo Flute: Xu Dajun
Pipa: Huang Shan

Erhu Fiddle: Jiang Ying
Three-String Fiddle: Lou Jlali
Reed Pipe Wind Instrument: Liu Fusheng
Genre: Peking Opera

Synopsis: The story of a young monk who escapes from his temple and dreams of marriage and of a Buddhist nun who does likewise because they both have had the same experiences.

This is what they sing: "When I was young, I was sent to the Buddhist temple."

Girl: "I was suffering a lot."

Boy: "I was beaten and scolded by my master."

Girl: "Then I escaped."

Boy: "One or two years later I will have longer hair."

Girl: "Three or four years later I will be a common person."

Boy: "Five or six years later I will be married."

Girl: "Seven or eight years later I will have a baby."

Suddenly the former monk meets the nun: "Armitabha Buddha."

They part, but then the boy starts talking to a squirrel:

"When I saw this Buddhist nun, I was attracted by her beauty. When I glimpsed her, she turned her head and looked at me. I feel she is very nervous, it must have a reason."

The girl also feels emotions: "When I saw this Buddhist monk I thought he was very gentle. He turned his head, looked at me several times. It seems that he knows what is in my mind. Is it possible that...?"

The monk calls her. She hides behind a tree.

"Buddhist nun. Buddhist nun. Buddhist nun. Where is she? When I find her, I will tell her that her master is coming. If she escaped from her temple, she will panic. Ha ha..."

She turns up behind his back: "Hey, your master is coming."

The monk reacts terrified: "Amitabha Buddha."

He looks around: "Where is my master? Oh Buddhist nun, do you know that I escaped from my temple?"

"Buddhist monk, do you know that I also escaped from my temple?"

They touch each other in love. He carries her away.

Song:

The monk likes the nun, and the nun likes the monk.

No matter how hard it is,
we will escape together.
The monk loves the nun, and the nun loves the monk.

Comment: A traditional Peking Opera tale drawn and animated in classic Chinese watercolor style.

Award: ASIFA China Award, Aniwow, Beijing, 2009.

Every One, Every Day

Animation School of Beijing Film Academy
3:43 Minutes
2D Animation
Producers: Zhang Huijun, Sun Lijun, Cong Lin
Director: Xu Xiaoxun
Writers: Sun Lijun, Xu Xiaoxun
Music Theme: "The Very Thought of You," arranged by Jia Ruichuan
Genre: Environment/Ecology

Synopsis: A man waits for a seed to grow, in sunny and stormy days, watering it until it becomes a tree liked by everybody.

Comment: Simple caricatures.

Evil Thought

Animation School of Beijing Film Academy
8:34 Minutes
2D Animation
Director: Zhou Xiao Ran
Genre: Drama

Synopsis: In a war a soldier gets wounded. While hospitalized he falls in love with the nurse. They have a baby. But their love is in danger when the man doubts that he is the father of the child. For the murder of his child he is sentenced to the guillotine.

Fantasy Naheya/Na He Ya

Animation School of Beijing Film Academy
Octopus Team
11:28 Minutes
2D Animation
Producer: Zhang Huijun
Directors: Su Haotian, Liu Kuang, Wan Fang, Zheng Xuezhi
Voice Director: Liu Siwei
Voice Actors: Li Min, Wan Fang, Wang Yifei, Zhang Linhan, Chi Cheng, Chen Xinrui, Jiang Ruoxin
Writers: Li Jian, Su Haotian, Li Qingshan
Storyboard: Su Haotian, Zheng Xuezhi
Production Managers: Sun Lijun, Qi Xiaoling, Li Jianping, Sun Cong
Unit Manager: Li Liang
Production: Zhang Miao
Scene Design: Liu Kuang, Zhang Miao

Key Animation Principals: Zheng Xuezhi, Wan Fang, Su Haotian
Sound Design: Wang Yuqin
Music: Liu Cong
Software: CAS Animo 5.0, Adobe Photoshop CS4, Adobe After Effect 7.0, Autodesk Maya 2009, Autodesk 3DsMAX, Steinberg Nuendo 3, Adobe Premiere Pro 2.0
Genre: Kid's Fantasy

Synopsis: Kids on the playground play with murmurs. One murmur gets lost in the sewers. The other kids are angry with the boy who lost it, who has a wet nose. They beat him and he loses a tooth. He is going to tell Miss Sun, and is already afraid of the dentist. Then they follow a mysterious man. The other kids leave. But the boy stays and watches. For him this man is a monster, and he has all kind of nightmares about what's going on in his kitchen. Tiny creatures come from the man's mouth. The boy flees, with the creatures and tea pots, knives and spoons on his heels.

The God on the Moon
Animation School of Beijing Film Academy
6:31 Minutes
2D Animation
Genre: Fantasy

Synopsis: A rabbit looks to the night sky and sees a gigantic rabbit enclosed in the full moon. For the rabbits on Earth he is like a god sitting on the moon. The rabbits do everything to worship the enormous shadow in the sky. They sacrifice a huge carrot and the rabbit god, with watering mouth, makes it fly to him on the moon and eats it like a cherry. Then he makes a little rabbit fly to him from earth to become the next rabbit in the moon.

Haven of Peace
7:30 Minutes
Producer: Han Hui
Director: Jia Haoxiang
Animation: Song Liu, Jiang Ping
Genre: Environment

Synopsis: A reflection on how traditional (originally rural) Chinese life is giving way to the automobile "culture" of the cities.

Hold Out
Media College of Nanjing Arts Institute
4:47 Minutes
3D Animation
Director: Lu Xi

Storyboard: Li Li, Lu Xi
Animation: Wang Mingxing, Lu Xi, Li Li, Zhuang Jing, Du Chao
Adviser: Xue Feng
Editing: Lu Xi, Wang Mingxing
Genre: Comedy

Synopsis: A guy throws a dart at home. Suddenly there is something like an earthquake. No, no earthquake, but passenger planes taking off and landing and shaking the house. With a catapult he starts to attack but to no avail. So he builds a ramp and lifts off with his car but fails the landing plane.

Kidbot
4:15 Minutes
3D Animation
Genre: Comedy

Synopsis: A tiny, walking, ball-like kid robot composited into live action backgrounds waits for days, weeks and months at a bus station, rusting, and dirtied by birds' droppings. He gets angry and is shot at, and is hit by a standing post. Then the "bus" arrives: a snail carrier.

Mole on the Face
CUC Anima, the Animation School of Communication University of China, Beijing
6:48 Minutes
2D Animation (Live Action Prologue and Epilogue)
Supervising Producer: Liao Xiangzhong
Producers: Lu Shengzhang, Shi Minyong, Jia Xiuqing, Ye Jing
Executive Producer: Gao Weihua
Directors/Writers: Jiang Miao, Liu Yunyuan
Presented by Su Zhiwu
Faculty Advisers: Wang Yaping, Luan Lian
Art Director: Jiang Miao
Animation and Inbetweening: Jiang Miao, Liu Yuanyuan
Sound Design: Luan Lian
Recording and Audio Production: Li Shuang
Editor: Jiang Miao
Genre: Parable

Synopsis: A boy who has a mole on his face feels different. A girl laughs as she spots it. Others seem to laugh and ridicule him. He feels like an outcast and starts to run from the masses. In his imagination the mole seems to get larger and larger, like an infection. An operation will bring change. But there is a fly nesting on the spot, and others laugh again. He tries to chase it away but it returns.

Finally it is revealed that an ancient Chinese book said that a mole next to the mouth means you will have lots of delicious food or you are very popular. Moles in different parts of the body mean different things.

Comment: A plea for difference.

Nalaku

AI.Studio
8:28 Minutes
2D Animation
Genre: Youth Sci-Fi

Synopsis: Kids on futuristic city streets in a polluted environment see flowers coming down.

Comment: Partially inspired by *Akira.*

On the Way

Beijing School Digital (Cartoon) Art Workshop
4:07 Minutes
2D Animation
Genre: Kid's Memory

Synopsis: A boy (filmed in live action) sits in the chair and recalls daily events in 2D animation: Bicycling through the forest, breaking a wheel, and carrying the bike through the forest.

The Return of the Sun

Sichuan Fine Arts Institute, BaoZi Art Studio Production
4:21 Minutes
2D Animation
Filmmakers: Li Na, Cia Jia, Wang Xiao Chen, Liu Mo, Cheng Peng
Genre: Mythology

Comment: Mythological tale in cut-out animation style.

Self Portrait

Flowcolor Animation Studio
4:31 Minutes
Stop Motion
Genre: Experimental Animation

Synopsis: An artist sits down in front of the canvas and starts a simple bear drawing in nice colors. All the paintings around are naive and childlike, toys and similar things that put together make a self portrait of the man.

Super Baozi vs. Sushi Man

Director-Animator: Sun Haipeng
Genre: Comedy

Synopsis: Baozi has had enough of his short-lived existence in gastronomy. He longs to be a second Bruce Lee and confronts Sushi Man.

Comment: Delightful spoof on martial arts films and Chinese cuisine.

The Tree Seed

Beijing Institute of Graphic Communication
4:31 Minutes
2D Animation
Producers: Qiao Dong Liang, Tian Zhong Li, Yang Hang, Shi Ming Feng
Director/Writer/Storyboard/Character Design/ Animation/Background Art/Editor: Hong Qiu Li
Tutors: Liu Feng, Li Xiao Yuan
Music: Crysand Lovhappy
Genre: (Green) Fantasy

Synopsis: Spirits of the forest carry nuts. One nut gets lost. When they have left, another spirit appears and takes the nut. Out of the nut grows a green plant but it is tiny, not as huge as the plants around.

2010

Beauty

4:20 Minutes
Director: Mao Qichao
Genre: Chinese Culture/History

Synopsis: Beauty is the story of a girl who tries to assassinate the emperor of the Qin Dynasty.

Comment: Animated in the meticulous style of ancient Chinese painting.

The Bird and the Prisoner/Prisoner and Bird

Jingdazhen Ceramic Institute, JCI Animation, Digital Media Art Design Section, XCM Animation Studio
17:41 Minutes
3D Animation
Executive Producers: Kang Xiuji, Wang Wanxing
Co-Producers: Ning Gang, Yan Fei
Director: Zhong Xuejun
Directors of Art: Zhong Xuejun, Zhang Sanchong, Li Feng
Character Design: Yu Chengfeng
Scene Design: Liu Jing, Gao Chunqian, Shen Yu
Animation: Gao Chunqian, Yu Chengfeng, Liu Jing, Yu Shen
Dynamics: Han Linjun
Compositing: Liu Jin, Yu Chengfeng, Zhao Longfei
Sound: Gao Chunqian, Shen Yu
Editor: Shen Yu
Genre: Parable

Synopsis: While the birds are free, the prisoner is not.

Once upon a time, there was a castle deeply sleeping in the middle ages. An old man who tried to wake it up was put under arrest for a long time. He was sentenced to be hanged by the rulers and had only three days of life left. As he is led to the gallows, a bird leaves a flower. When the old man wants to pick it up, one soldier stomps it with his foot. The bird is in the old man's cell. The soldiers try to chase it away. The old man plays a harmonica (like Charles Bronson) when the white bird returns. One soldier shoots it. Next day the gallows are prepared for hanging the old man. A soldier shoots the bird. The old man confronts him and the bird attacks the soldiers. The other soldier lets the old man escape. The bird is in a cage; the old man returns and opens the cage to free it. This moves him to fly away.

The Black Wasp

College of Communication and Art Tongji University
4:21 Minutes
2D Animation
Director/Production/Screenplay/Animation: He Dong Cheng
Genre: Child's Story

Synopsis: Based on the author's childhood experiences. Ordinary sheep farmers in northern China pick up their own sheep manure. One day a mountain wasp attacks a farmer. All attempts to get rid of it fail and rouse a whole swarm of black wasps.

The Blue House

Graduates' Studio
6 Minutes
Genre: Fantasy

Synopsis: When a person spots freaky shadows distorted by all kind of desires, he flees out of the blue house that was built by lust and greed.

Comment: The work reflects the desires and natural instincts deep in people's hearts through abstract figures such as a shadow and a house to create a feeling reminiscent of Edgar Allan Poe's stories.

Bruce Lee

Chongqing Technology and Business University Design Institute of the Arts
2 Minutes

Director: Shen Zhengzhong
Genre: Comedy/Parody
Comment: A stop-motion Bruce Lee.

Chang Ban Po

Animation School of Beijing Film Academy
7:16 Minutes
Director: Ou Yan Zhonghong
Genre: Chinese Mythology

Synopsis: A warrior named Zhao Yun saves his young master.
Comment: Based on the historical novel *The Three Kingdoms.*

Chapman and Roger

China Academy of Art
Director: Dou Hongbin
Genre: Friendship

Synopsis: Scarecrow Chapman befriends a string puppet he calls Roger.

Childish Snail's Diary/Fool Snail Diary

Jilin Institute of the Arts
2 Minutes (3:13 Minutes)
2D Animation
Director: Lin Yu
Supervisor: Zhao Gui Jing
Team: Wang Jia Yin, Lv Zheng, Zou Lei, Li Dan Dan
Genre: Comedy

Synopsis: The misfortunes of a humanoid snail sitting on a chair with a nail inside. Tries to pick it out in vain. It needs an infant bee to come to drill it out.

Cicada Knows

8:47 Minutes
2D Animation
Producer: Zhao Xing
Director/Storyboard/After Effects: Seezr (Shi Zhe)
Animation: Ares, Zhao Xing, Wang Wen Jie, Hao Shuang, Co Co Lee, Li Tian Xiao, Tian Meng, Zheng Ji Shu, Zhang Yu, Guo Xue Ying, Cheng Yao
Voice Actors: Gang Zi Hui (Zhang Xiao Han), Lee Yun (Teacher), Seezr (Fu Xiao Yu)
Writers/Character Design: Seezr, Li Tian Xiao
Sound Recording/Sound Mixer: To To
Music Mixer: Face Off
Genre: Adolescence

Synopsis: Adolescent boys in love. A boy draws a girl. Together, on paper and in imagination, they sit on a cloud and kiss each other. The boy starts masturbating. He begins to watch the girl in class intensely. His teacher sees his drawing, and he is sent outside, then confronted by the teacher after class. The girl finds his drawings of her in a wastepaper basket and seems to like receiving attention. She shows the drawings around. The boy intervenes and tears the drawings. Eventually he takes revenge, hitting the girl in rainy weather with his bike.

Comment: In a vaguely anime style.

The Colors
Hubei Academy of Fine Arts
4:28 Minutes
Director/Writer/Producer/Art Design/Animation/Postproduction: Pang Shengyong
Supervisor: Yuan Xiaofan
Music: Whatever Rola Wants
Genre: Parable

Synopsis: Lines of digital people, blue, orange and green, march in endless uniformity. One boy leaves his home. He looks different, more human than all the others, and nevertheless appears to be an alien. They change grey people into orange. Color determines the conscience. The boy joins grey people and is showered in blue.

Comment: A reflection on the social environment.

A Day of Elevator
Beihang University School of New Media Art and Design
12:56 Minutes
Director: Wei Shilei
Genre: Experimental Animation

Synopsis: An ordinary day. The elevator carries group after group up and down. We watch what happens in the box-like elevator.

Comment: Artistic, short film.

Dec. 21st
Animation School of Beijing Film Academy
5:15 Minutes
Director: Zhou Yan
Genre: Parable

Synopsis: The life of a peasant when the end of the world is near.

Comment: The story tells us that we should be tolerant in our daily life and not regard ourselves as the center of the world. If this world comes to an end and doomsday is near, everybody will die. So why don't we live in happiness and harmony?

Decisive Battle
College of Science and Technology Ningbo University
Node Studio
4:08 Minutes
2D/3D Animation
Director/Writer/Storyboard/Editor: Yan Ming Zhou
Art Direction: Cheng Long Zhao
Concept and Character Design and Art Style: Liang Xiang
2D Animation: Liang Xian, Yan Ming Zhou
3D Animation/Sound Effects: Zhen Yang
Genre: Chinese Culture/History

Synopsis: Battle scenes.

Comment: Ink is used to depict the original historical spirit of battle scenes.

Dog's Jail
CUC Anima, the Animation School of Communication University of China, Beijing
7 Minutes
2D Animation
Director/Editor: Li Huimeng
Writers/Storyboard/Art Direction/Animation: Li Huimeng, Wang Chao
Presented by Su Zhiwu
Supervising Producer: Liao Xiangzhong
Producers: Liu Shengzhang, Shi Minyong, Jia Xialong, Ye Jing
Executive Producers: Gao Weihua, Liu Dayu
Faculty Adviser: Hong Yu
Sound: Wang Chao
Original Music: Wu Tong
Genre: Comedy Parable

Synopsis: The guards in this jail are anthropomorphic dogs. One delinquent, feeling not guilty, tries to escape through the toilet, by digging a hole in his cell, and when he succeeds he is pursued by a dog officer like in a Tex Avery cartoon. With a light sabre he attacks him but is being beaten, as the officer has his own light sabre like Darth Vader. In the end it turns out to be just a dream; he is a guy working with many others in an office. By the way, his boss looks a little bit like the dog officer and in his hands he holds a tiny pup, meaning that the guy feels jailed in his job.

Dormitory 111
9 Minutes
Directors: Wen Xue, Jiang Xiaojia

Synopsis: The lives of six college girls who share the same dormitory and in there become a sort of family.

The Dust

Jilin College of the Arts/Ani-Com School
6:50 Minutes
3D Animation
Producers: Zhao Qinghua, Shi Guojuan, Liu Saoyong
Director/Writer: Hu Hao
Presented by Feng Boyang
Music: "The Sorcerer's Apprentice" by Paul Abraham Dukas
Genre: Experimental Animation

Synopsis: The incredible journey of a speck of dust in the sky, through the sea, among all kind of fish.

Comment: One of the most memorable pieces of student work coming from China.

Eat Your Breakfast

CUC Anima, the Animation School of Communication University of China, Beijing
5 Minutes
2D Animation
Director: Su Yi
Assisted by Li Jing
Genre: Family/Personal Story

Synopsis: Eating is the main cultural activity in China, but in spite of mother's admonitions, a girl doesn't want to eat her breakfast.

Comment: A student's personal account of a childhood problem.

Every Dog Has Its Day/Every Dog Has Its Dreams

CUC Anima, the Animation School, Communication University of China, Beijing
Presented by Su Zhiwu
4:30 Minutes
Executive Producer: Gao Weihua
Supervising Producer: Liao Xiangzhong
Producers: Lu Shengzhang, Shi Minyong, Jia Xiuqing, Ye Jing
Director/Writer/Storyboard/Art Direction: Zhang Xiang
Faculty Advisers: Wang Lei, Sue Yanping, Suo Xiaoling
Character Designer: Duan Giuzi
Recording: Lei Weiting
Sound Design: Liu Luwei
Genre: Comedy

Synopsis: A dog—a carlin—is thrown out by his master out of the camper. Hungry, it dreams of food and particularly pizza. In its imagination the moon is being darkened by an enormous pizza and it dreams of getting up there, via fireworks and a self-made flying saucer–shaped trash vehicle. Police turns up as it flies around, aiming at him.

Comment: Farce.

Fate in Control

Beijing Forestry University
2D Animation
3:05 Minutes
Director: Ma Henan
Writers: Huang Long, Ma Henan
Genre: Parable

Synopsis: About a man who can't control his own fate. Each step he takes in life turns out to be a disaster, from birth to death.

Comment: Colorful, in style vaguely reminiscent of *Yellow Submarine.*

Fearless

6:41 Minutes
Genre: Adventure Drama

Synopsis: A swordfighter confronts a troop of soldiers commanded by Redbeard.

Comment: Intended as a teaser for a series or feature film.

Floating World

Northeast Normal University
3:45 Minutes
2D Animation
Director: Wang Li
Genre: Kid's Fantasy

Synopsis: In her dreams a little girl becomes the heroine of fairy tales she has read such as Cinderella and Snow White.

Comment: Illustrating the pure innocence of children's hearts.

Flower

7:53 Minutes
Director: Lu Weiming

Comment: A short made in Guangzhou with an environmental background.

Half of the Bowl

Sichuan Fine Arts Film-Video-Animation School
4:06 Minutes

Synopsis: Tu Gen, a villager, realizes the importance of a bowl that he has abandoned.

Home

Chongqing Technology and Business University Design Institute of the Arts
1 Minute
Director: Shen Zhengzhong
Genre: Environment/Ecology

Comment: The environment of the Antarctic is used to remind people to protect nature.

Journey

Beijing Forestry University
5:34 Minutes
2D Animation
Director: Dai Wenchao
Genre: Fantasy

Synopsis: A boy running around in nature sniffs at a flower, sneezes and is, like Alice into Wonderland, catapulted in transformed identity into a microscopic universe. He is chased for a while by a bazille, or germ, monster, then becoming so huge that the opponent gives up and runs away terrified. The transformed boy chases him, whale sized, devouring everybody and everything, swimming the imaginary ocean, up to a giant beanstalk. The boy realizes that all this is in a single butterflower.

Life is a journey.

By comparing the microscopic world with the real world, we can reflect on how small we are. Actually, in the universe we are like dust in the microscopic world, but after you manage to master your destiny you are full of strength to prove your values and change the world.

Comment: Compositing chalk-style animation and live action footage.

Last Piece

Tangshan Branch, Hebei University of Technology
3:39 Minutes
Director: Li Xiaoyun
Genre: Environment/Ecology

Synopsis: Protecting the Earth and the last piece of pure soil that exists.

Launch/Set Out

College of Art and Design of BJUT (Beijing University of Technology)
13:38 Minutes
Director: Huang Tianyu

Synopsis: A retired engine driver, in the late 1980s, lives in a town near the German-French border.

Comment: For two years a group of six students worked on this stop-motion film.

Letter from Grandma

Art School of Northwest University
11 Minutes
Directors/Filmmakers: Zhang Hui, Zhu Yunbo, Cheng Weijia, Kou Ye, Wei Jianan, Wu Jing, Cai Zongwei, Deng Yuanyuan, Xu Fangbi, Lin Weijing, Jiang Fei
Genre: Family

Synopsis: In wintertime, Grandmother's house seems very lonely. Grandmother takes time to write a letter of blessing.

Lollipop Knows

Animation School of Beijing Film Academy
10:20 Minutes
Director: Zhao Nan
Genre: Fantasy

Synopsis: By accident, A Sheng enters a strange world. In this dangerous environment the only thing he has in hand is a mysterious lollipop. How will he return to the real world?

Memory

International Ani-Com College of Hangzhou Normal University
1:40 Minutes
Stop Motion
Director/Producer: Li Jiaoyao
Screenplay: Shao Lin
Art Design: Wu Zhijing
Genre: History

Synopsis: Set during the late Republic of China, when life was chaos. People set their hope on the color red.

Comment: Stop-motion film using Plasticine models.

The Metamorphosis/Transform

CUC Anima, the Animation School of Communication University of China, Beijing, in cooperation with Sheridan
0:50 Minutes
Directors: Yin Zhenlun, Mo Zhu, Yuan Zichao, Xu Chen, Quan Zhou, Liu Yilin
Faculty Advisers: Hong Fan, Yu Haiyan, Dave Quesnelle "DQ," Zhang Yue
Genre: Comedy

Synopsis: A monster animator, as it turns out at the end (see Chuck Jones' *Duck Amuck*, in which the animator doing harm to Daffy Duck is revealed to be Bugs Bunny at the end) directs transforming animals who are chasing each other: "I love animation."

Comment: The basis of every animation is the metamorphosis.

Moon Eclipse

Beijing Institute of Graphic Communication
3:39 Minutes
2D Animation
Director: Chen Dafang
Genre: Kid's Fantasy

Synopsis: About a boy who has no confidence and always makes mistakes. One day he sees a rogue bullying a puppy dog, and he sums up all his courage to stop the brutal act. He is knocked out, but the dog is grateful to no end, understandably. At lunar eclipse time he finds the dog eating the moon and realizes that even a weak guy can shock the world.

Naval Heroes

Tianjin University
Director: Hao Lian Jianhui
Genre: History
12:19 Minutes

Synopsis: Scenes from the Sino-Japanese War of 1894. The Chinese navy resists Japanese aggressors.

Nian

CUC Anima, the Animation School of Communication University of China, Beijing
9 Minutes
3D Animation
Supervising Producer: Liao Xiangzhou
Producers: Lu Shengzhang, Shi Minyong, Jia Xiuqing, Ye Jing
Executive Producers: Gao Weihua, Liu Dayu
Directors: Liu Tianshu, Shan Keliang, Yang Yang, Wang Zaiyue
Voice Actors: Shi Yilei (the Little Boy), Wan Tao (the Watchman), Ge Jian, Ding Tianxin, Yan Liwei, Li Xueping (Villagers)
Writer/Character Design/Storyboard: Liu Tianshu
Presented by Su Zhiwu
Faculty Adviser: Liu Dayu
Design Advisers: Yu Haiyan, Li Wei
Matte Paintings: Cao Yan, Liu Tianshu
Animation Supervisor: Liu Tianshu
Character Animation: Liu Tianshu, Yang Yang, Wang Zaiyue
Digital Compositing Supervisors: Yang Yang, Liu Tianshzu
Original Music: Yuan Sihan, Billy Larriviere
Sound Design: Zhang Yue, Billy Larriviere, Yuan Sihan
Recording: Jin Cong, Sun Sisi
Editor: Shan Keliang
Genre: Fantasy

Synopsis: In ancient Chinese folklore, there is a monster. Every New Year's eve, it will appear and wound and injure people. Therefore, people drive it away by discharging fireworks and making noise. This monster is called Nian.

Warning voice: "New Year's eve is approaching. Alert! Kids, go home!" "Got it! Got it!" "Mom, open the door!" "Come in quickly. It's so late, Nian might eat you!"

One little boy doesn't seem to be afraid. He thinks that the adults just want to scare them. He has some fireworks, but on the roof Nian watches him already. One final firecracker is left, but Nian steals it.

All of a sudden, the boy spots the monster, which doesn't look that monstrous at all, more like a pet dog with glowing eyes. But to his horror he realizes that the little one is only an infant, while the real monster is on its way. The terrified boy runs away with the monster on his heels. Luckily Little Nian is on his side, and the monster turns out to be friendly.

Together they celebrate the New Year.

Suddenly an old watchman sees them: "Nian! Nian is around the corner! Nian eats children! Everyone light the fireworks!"

The boy is disappointed when the creatures are chased away but at the same time is happy to have seen the creatures.

"Nian is gone! New Year is coming! Next year will be safe! Let's light the fireworks and celebrate!"

The camera pans back and we see, in the mountains above the village, that Nian has not one but three kids. He's a real family guy.

Comment: The filmmakers hope to interest viewers into Chinese folk tales. Eerie atmosphere and some good POV shots.

Oh

The Central Academy of Drama
4:45 Minutes
Director: Li Dongqing
Genre: Parable

Synopsis: There is a man of few words born with a bad eye. His life is as tasteless as pure water. Facing a hard and ruthless life, he resists but cannot change it. The only choice is to live a simple life.

The Old Man and the Piglet

Animation School of Beijing Film Academy
9 Minutes
2D Animation
Producers: Sun Lijun, Li Jianping, Sun Cong
Director/Writer: Sun Yiran
Assistant Director: Wang Xing Chen
Storyboard: Sun Yiran, Wang Xing Chen
Presented by Zhang Huijin
Production Coordinator: Li Liang
Executive Producer: Chen Xi
Layout/Background: Su Yiran, Zhang Yi
Art Directors: Liu Xian, Feng Wen
Key Animation: Wang Xingchen, Cheng Lingzi, Sun Yiran, Chen Xi

After Effect: Chen Xi
Music: Chen Gong
Editors: Chen Xi, Sun Yiran, Zhao Xiadian
Genre: Parable

Synopsis: Waiting for his lover a lifetime, an old man's only hobby is to do wood-carving. One day a cute little piglet with a four-leaf-clover logo on its hip comes along. It changes the old man's life and brings joy to him. However, when the old man dies, magic things happen during a snowy night.

Comment: The poetic little film was created by six female students from Beijing Film Academy.

Award: Cyber Sousa–Xiamen International Film Festival, 2011.

Oops!!!

Beihang University
3:52 Minutes
3D Animation
Director: Huang Xiangnan
Genre: Comedy

Synopsis: A pilot's dream. He lands and pees on a cactus. A second pilot arrives, having his Polaroid in front of the propeller plane. Only one Polaroid turns out well. Happily he hops away on his riding animal, but he has damaged the propeller, and when the other one lifts off he crashes, burning the Polaroid.

Comment: Short 3D film.

The Pack Star War/War of Planet Pack

Institute of Guizhou University
2D Animation
5:34 Minutes
Director: Chen Kai
Genre: Sci-Fi

Synopsis: After one hundred years the Planet Pack that populates earth is attacked by a spacecraft manned by two humans. They wish for a hero who will defeat the Pack, and a three-eyed superguy turns up and is hailed with John Williams' *Star Wars* theme.

Comment: Opens with the "Also sprach Zarathustra" theme as used in Stanley Kubrick's *2001,* then changes to very simple animation.

Papa Is a Crocodile/Fear of Fear/Pa Pa Bu Pa

Animation School of Beijing Film Academy
2D Animation
11:32 Minutes

Producer: Sun Lijun
Director: Tan Xiaojia
Genre: Parable

Synopsis: Little Crocodile's family has moved to Cat World, but Little Crocodile remains an outcast who finds no friends. Like all other children she longs for red bean ice cream, but she is too shy to approach the vendor. Suddenly a friend with a crocodile face turns up and helps her get some ice cream. Under the mask of the sudden friend turns up a cat boy. From then on, Little Crocodile will have a friend.

Comment: Lovely children's film, almost Japanese-2D style. There are fifty-six ethnic groups living in China. Crocodile girl speaks with a heavy accent that characterizes her as one of them. The little antiracist film promotes friendship.

Pencil Showdown

Shanghai University
3:13 Minutes
3D Animation
Directors: Huang Yi, Zhao Jiacheng, Yang Huina
Genre: Comedy

Synopsis: Two pencils, a large blue one and a small red one, fight at midnight for an eraser by drawing different weapons that fight for them on the paper. Becoming totally exhausted, they find out that the eraser has his own love interest.

Perky

Beijing Institute of Graphic Communication
5:15 Minutes
2D Animation
Director: Li Xueting
Genre: Fantasy

Synopsis: Perky is a hero born among the sun elves, which look faintly like a Chinese version of the *Teletubbies.*

The Polar Team/A Team to the Antarctic/Ji Di Tuan

Animation School of Beijing Film Academy
8:30 Minutes
2D Animation
Producers: Sun Lijun, Qi Xiaoling, Li Jianping, Sun Cong
Directors: Zhang Jialin, Xu Ning
Screenplay: Zhang Jialin, Kang Yang, Xu Ning
Presented by Zhang Huijun
Line Producer: Zhao Yang
Production Secretary: Li Liang
Tutors: Sun Cong, Ren Tianchun

Art Directors: Zhang Jialin, Zhang Weiwei, Xu Ning

Animation: Zhang Jialin, Xu Ning, Ye Xiaomeng, Zhang Henyuan, Kang Yang

Music: Zhang Jialin, Xu Ning

Genre: Comedy

Synopsis: The polar team consists of an Eskimo girl named Little Love and her polar bear friend. Riding on an ice floe they reach the big city and, joined by a teenage boy, create all kinds of unbelievable havoc. They have a car race that ends by crashing into a ship; they go to Japan, hanging on top of Tokyo Tower and making it fly like a helicopter; they go to China, where they have a fight with hunters whom they overcome with the help of a Chinese boy; and they have more such stunts.

Puppet

Beijing Institute of Graphic Communication
3:20 Minutes
Director: Li Xin
Genre: Anti-War

Synopsis: A wounded soldier while in military hospital under the influence of anesthetics dreams of himself back in childhood playing a war game. Now he knows how horrible war is, not at all like the games they played as kids.

Comment: War game memories in black and white.

Pursuit of Life

4 Minutes
Director: You Jia

Synopsis: A little girl evolved from a microbe tries to cross the ocean. She is bothered by the octopus pig, witnesses love between frog and globefish, and is chased by the shark rabbit. Finally she finds the tree of life with the support of some fish. She enters the tree and discovers many plants that look like human organs. In the end she arrives at a giant organism made of branches. Connecting the navel line with the life ball in the tree, the little girl eventually understands life and becomes a baby in the body of a mother.

Rabbit and Tiger

Animation School of Beijing Film Academy
14 Minutes
Director: Wang Tianshi
Genre: Parable

Synopsis: A little animal has the important task of waking up the other animals in the Lunar New Year, but by nature it is too polite and careful. So it wakes up the Tiger instead of the Rabbit.

Rain

Art Institute of Guizhou University/Beijing Institute of Graphic Communication
2:45 Minutes
Director: Li Ye
Genre: Love Story

Synopsis: A city girl looking in vain for true love.

A Rainy Night

Jilin Animation Institute
4:28 Minutes
3D Animation
Directors: Zhang Rui, Zhu Jing
Genre: Modern Tragedy

Synopsis: On a rainy night a pregnant woman tumbles down, but no passerby comes to help her—until a beggar woman gives her a helping hand.

The Red

CUC Anima, the Animation School of Communication University of China, Beijing
4:41 Minutes
2D Animation
Directors: Li Xia, Cheng Teng
Presented by Su Zhiwu
Supervising Producer: Liao Xiaozheng
Genre: Youth Culture/Student's Life

Synopsis: A shy, bespectacled primary student, apparently addicted to the comic world of the manga, dreams of being a powerful superhero but is caught in the act by his strict female teacher, who doesn't appreciate his imaginative world. Between both, in the boy's imagination, a martial art fights ensues. The teacher seems to be well adapted. In the end she studies the manga book confiscated from the boy.

Comment: If you are able to read between the lines—and Chinese online viewers certainly are—you will find criticism against the unimaginative Chinese system of education, which is based on repetition. Aesthetically, the young filmmakers know manga quite well and appreciate anime, like most Chinese animation students.

Red Scarf and Exercise Books

Animation School of Beijing Film Academy
11:27 Minutes
2D Animation

Director/Writer/Animator: Zhu Hui
Sound: Zhang Xuan
Music: Li Xing Yu
Song: "Our Fields," Composed by Zhang Wen Gang
Genre: Kids

Synopsis: About a little kid with a failing memory. A story about going to school, play and games. While playing, the girl ends in a small, green bamboo forest. In the end there are some tears on the girl's part, but the other kids console her.

Comment: Colorful, imaginative style.

Rosemary

High School Affiliated to the China Central Academy of Fine Arts
7 Minutes
Director: Guan Xiaomei
Genre: History

Synopsis: Set in old Shanghai. The story of an artist torn between misunderstanding and focusing on his work.

Secret of Mechanical City

Jilin Animation Institute, Animation and Cartoon School, 3D Animation First Studio, Changchun
12:56 Minutes
3D Animation
Producer: Zheng Liguo
Executive Producers: Jackie Liu, Ada
Director/Storyboard/Production Design/Music and Sound Effects/Compositing/Editor: Jackie Liu
Animation Supervisor: Ada
Animation: Gu Kai Hua, Sally, Shark Xu, Sun Jing Jia, Cao Dong, Huang Huaqing, Chi Xiaofan, Ton Song, Cat, Wei Jian, Luo Chuan Huan, Nara, Xie Peng Ju
Writers: Niko Zhang, Jackie Liu
Effects Supervisor: Rita
Genre: Sci-Fi Fantasy

Synopsis: Life in Mechanical City is peaceful until, out of a mysterious Magic Cube, Devil King (who faintly looks like a minotaur) enters and makes people live in danger. Superboy has to find means to stop the evildoer and takes off in his rocket plane to find the king's palace, which is guarded by robots. The boy needs all his martial arts skills to fight back and confront Devil King himself. Eventually, Robot Girl, Superboy's friend, uses the Magic Cube to ban Devil King.

Comment: Mix of *Robots*, *Wall-E* and *Star Wars*. Very much like a computer game.

Soil (4D version titled The Seed)

Jilin Animation Institute, Changchun
Animation and Cartoon School / 3D Animation Third Studio
8:30 Minutes
3D Animation
Producer: Zheng Liguo
Executive Producers: Jacob, Jackie Liu, Ranyi
Directors: Jacob, Jackie Liu
Screenplay/Character Designer: Ranyi
Storyboard: Jacob, Jackie Liu
Production Designer: Jacob
Modeling Supervisor: Alvin Zhang
Texture and Lighting Supervisor: Jackie Liu, Wang Lulu
Animation Supervisor: Jacob
Effects Supervisor: Rita
Animation: Li Yang, Wang Guanxiang, Zhang Yingjie, Yu Zhixin, Liu Shiqun, Adrain, Zhou Zhe, Wang Yitao, Sun Jiayi, Zou Fen, Doven, Adam, Jin Fuel, Windy, Sally
Music and Sound Effects/Editor: Jacob
Genre: Sci-Fi/Environment

Synopsis: Opening lines: "Life is great. Yet at the same time, it's a struggle to an extent. Any form of life has its own rule of survival like air to human and water for fish. As for the seed, it requires SOIL."

We see a seed, then cut to a spaceship that seems to hold memories of man. The space traveler receives a signal and lands on a deserted planet, which is polluted. The space traveler passes the relics of civilization such as the broken head of the Statue of Liberty. Somewhere he learns via old film footage about the destruction of the planet due to atomic warfare. Eventually he finds a box that contains a single precious seed. While he holds it the seed begins to creep, wind and twine around his body and leaves him motionless, as though crucified by strangling vines.

Comment: Showpiece to demonstrate the skills of staff members and students of Jilin Animation Institute in Changchun. In theme parks it was screened as 4D entertainment with rotating seats and special effects added under the alternate title *The Seed*. It's an environmental sci-fi piece about nature striking back against humans, who brought destruction.

Soldier

Animation School of Beijing Film Academy
11:43 Minutes
Director: Li Huangge
Genre: Family

Synopsis: A family is just a small world. In this case it is tested in a car accident.

Comment: Family means the most in Asia. Family conflicts are common, and the purpose of this film is to make people realize and amend the problem.

Step Away

Tianjin University
China Stop Motion Animation Forum
5:20 Minutes
Stop Motion
Producer: Zhou Tian
Executive Producer: Li Xing
Director/Set Dresser/Prop Maker/Stop Motion Animator: Liu Shasha
Writer/Puppet Design/Lighting and Camera/ Editor: Zhang Hongming
Puppet Makers: Liu Shasha, Zhang Hongming, Wu Xianzhou
Visual Effects: Gui Yanxue
Music: Li Yuchen
Genre: Life and Death

Synopsis: An old man, sitting at sunset in his house, watches photos and films and misses his dear one. He decides to dance to the tunes of the song "One Step Away," imagining she is dancing with him.

A Team to the Antarctic

Animation School of Beijing Film Academy
8:30 Minutes
Directors: Zhang Jialin, Xu Ning
Also known as *The Polar Team/Ji Di Tuan*

Synopsis: An Eskimo girl named Little Love and her friend Polar Bear want to go to the Antarctic. On the way they meet two guys and befriend them. They defeat poachers and together reach the Antarctic.

Teeth and Teeth

Animation School of Beijing Film Academy
2:17 Minutes
Directors: Chen Yusi, Wangyan
Genre: Health Care

Synopsis: Through hard work, a decayed tooth becomes a healthy tooth again.

Together

Sichuan Fine Arts Institute Film-Video-Animation School
4:55 Minutes
Directors: Wang Qin, Zhang Wenxian, Shen Haifeng, Xiong Xuancong
Synopsis: The hero while trying to rescue

rabbits falls into a trap himself, right into a horror forest.

Comment: Watercolor-style art short.

Traveling Together Too Long to Say Farewell

5 Minutes
Director: Zhang Wen
Screenplay: Yang Yiyong
Genre: Youth Culture

Synopsis: Liang Shanbo and Zhu Yingtai are reluctant to leave. During their long farewells, Yingtai keeps borrowing things to express her affection to Shanbo, but being too honest and too sincere, Shanbo fails to understand Yingtai's purpose.

Tree

Dalian Polytechnic University
3:50 Minutes
2D Animation
Director: Zheng Xunxing
Genre: Family

Synopsis: An old woman remembers the tree she planted when her son was still small. He grows up. At different times of the year she cares for the tree in the garden. Now that she is old a storm comes up and shakes the tree. She tries to stabilize it. When she is about to die, her son returns and holds her hand. The tree has new leaves.

Undated Diary/A Diary Without Date

Kunming University of Science and Technology
24ers Studio
6:04 Minutes
Director/Writer/Scene Design: Meng Xiaoyu
Storyboard/Character Design/Animation: Zhao Jingjing
Instructor: Li Bong Jiang
Original Music: Guan Xin
Genre: Experimental Animation

Synopsis: Experimental film.

Comment: The story's inspiration came from a dream. It describes the conflict of the protagonist between reality and a dream world.

Variations of Life/Melody of Life

4:30 Minutes
2D Animation
Directors/Storyboard/Background Art/Color Style: Li Fan, Gao Dongmeng
Nonlinear Edit/Sound Effects: Gao Dongmeng
Genre: Parable

Synopsis: A frustrated young man accidentally kicks some piece of roadside trash, starting a series of encounters.

Comment: The story may seem ridiculous but actually has deep social roots. The intense pressure of public opinion makes it impossible to live freely.

The War of Chinese Chess

Jilin Animation Institute, Changchun
6:34 Minutes
3D Animation
Producer: Zheng Liguo
Directors/Executive Producers: Jackie Liu, Jacob
Animation: Wang Yitao, Sun Jiayi, Zou Fen, Li Yang, Wang Guanxiang, Yingjie, Windy, Doven, Adam, Liu Shiqun, Adrain, Yu Zhixin, Jin Fuel, Zhou Ze
Martial Arts Director: Jackie Liu
Screenplay/Character Designer/Storyboard: Wang Pengfei
Production Designer: Jackie Liu
Modeling Supervisor: Alvin Zhang
Texture and Lighting Supervisors: Wang Lulu, Jackie Liu
Animation Supervisor: Jacob
Effects Supervisor: Rita
Theme Song: Zian Ziu Yue Bie Xi Chu Jiang
Arranger: Hei Shi
Music and Sound Effects: Jackie Liu
Genre: Comedy

Synopsis: Rolling titles:

Xiangqi is a two-player Chinese board game. It originates from the Warring States Period in China and is therefore commonly called *Chinese Chess.* The ancient board game has evolved in the course of history and reached a stable form in North Song Dynasty. The game represents a battle between two armies, with the objective to capture the enemy's "general" piece. All in all, there are 32 pieces, each with a Chinese character, sometimes engraved into the surface. Half are in red color, half in black. They are made of wood, animal teeth or bones. Each player in turn moves one piece from the point it occupies to another point on a board that is 9 lines wide by 10 lines long. Dividing the two opposing sides is the river. The river is often marked with the phrase Chu He, meaning "Chu River," and Han Jie, meaning "Han border." In 203 BC, Liu Bang, the Han leader, attacked Xiang Yu, who led Western Chu. Xiang Yu was defeated and he was forced to split the state into two parts. Chu River and Han border were emerged. Chinese chess, as part of the nation's culture, is being enjoyed by Chinese people and will be passed on as a cultural heritage.

The film opens with a young woman asking her husband to play a game of Chinese chess. Both get angry at each other and feel themselves traveling back in history to ancient war times, with explosives, chariots and sword fights. Finally, the male points with the sword towards the chin of the female, already feeling victorious. The wife looks desperate and for a moment the husband loses control. The woman uses the moment to regain the upper hand and throws him down a cliff. The man lands hard on the floor. The price is to clean the toilet.

War on Vegetables

College of Science and Technology Ningbo University
2:54 Minutes
2D Animation
Directors: Zhang Di, Wang Shu
Genre: Comedy

Synopsis: The humorous efforts of struggling vegetables inside a fridge.

The Wedding Dress/Wedding Garment

Beijing Institute of Graphic Communication, Department of Fine Arts, Animation Work
6:51 Minutes
2D Animation
Directors/Writers/Storyboard: Chen Jieting, Yang Yue
Character Design/Animation/Editor: Chen Jieting
3D Background/Effects: Yang Yue
Genre: Parable

Synopsis: A story about a wedding. A girl in the rain is thinking about her wedding: "I'm the one who is getting married. And I wanna get dressed as I like. You promised me to have our ceremony at the church, right? Don't be naive! Getting married is not just about you and me. I don't trust you any more. You wanna get whatever you want? Don't be childish! You're not a kid anymore. You can't think like this. You can't settle up this little tiny thing." Holds ring. "I'm so annoyed by your hesitance!" She enters the clothmaker's shop for her wedding dress. "Ah ... I like this one." She points to a photo on the wall. "This is how girls wanna marry—wearing a wedding dress." She touches the silk of a garment. "I wanna try this on." She stands in front of a mirror and feels like a princess." To the dressmaker: "My fiancé and I are arguing about the dress at the ceremony." Through a door she enters the dressmaker's room. An old television set is running. She sees the sewing machine. The girl feels hypnotized by the dress lying in front of it: sparkled, getting wings. The dressmaker: "This one was to be my wife's dress when we got married. But it hasn't been finished yet." "It doesn't matter. I want this one." The dressmaker is going to finish it to meet her order, and will harm another life.

Comment: Anime.

Wild Clear Water Bay/Kuang Ye Qing Shui Wan

2:40 Minutes
3D Animation
Director: Xue Shanwu
Genre: Comedy

Synopsis: At the lake a caveman tries to fish but has some problems with a rather slimy fish.

The Wind of Cypress Hill

Jilin Animation Institute, Changchun
9:25 Minutes
Producer: Zheng Liguo
Directors and Photographers: Christophe Peladan, Ludovic Berardo
Story: Susanne Baekby Olesen, Christophe Peladan
Lead Animator: Ludovic Berardo
Additional Animators: Micky, Menggang
Animation Assistants: Yang Lei, Guo Pu
Musical Score: Li Bai
Genre: Comedy

Synopsis: Each morning a monk leaves the monastery accompanied by his dog to care for the cemetery. Over the years, the dog passes away. Eventually, at witching hour, the monk, older now, returns and meets the ghosts of his dog and all the others who rest in peace in this graveyard.

Comment: Elaborate stop-motion piece done by professional guest artists with the help of Chinese students. Christophe Peladan, the director, had been working all over Europe, in Germany, France (Folimage) and Switzerland. Ludovic Berardo is known as an accomplished stop-frame animator who later was involved in the making of Aardman's *The Pirates!* and *ParaNorman*. In the summer of 2012 he returned to Jilin Animation Institute for more stop motion.

Wish Piano

Predecessor of Luxun Academy of Fine Arts
4:46 Minutes
Stop Motion
Director: Liu Yihong
Genre: Kid's Fantasy

Synopsis: A girl has not only injured her legs in an accident but has also lost all confidence and memory. Sitting in a wheelchair, she abandons her piano and is left with a diary only and a rabbit that silently cares about her. One day she hears a melody that revives her memory and brings her back to the piano. The tunes make her move and walk again.

The World Should Be Like This

Animation School of Beijing Film Academy
3:46 Minutes
Director: Chen Yanlai
Genre: Kid's Fantasy

Synopsis: With her parents asleep a little girl feels free to do some experiments of her own. She thinks bread should float in the water like a boat and transforms the bed into bread.

Comment: The purpose of this short is to make adults aware of the needs of children.

Ya'er

Academy of Arts and Design Tsinghua University
28:58 Minutes
Director: Du Pengpeng

Comment: The author wants to express a heartwarming story about the love of life.

Zhong Kui's Sister Got Married

13:34 Minutes
Cut-Out Animation
Director: Lu Yue
Genre: Mythology

Synopsis: After his tragic death Zhong Kui, a famous folk god, engaged himself in catching ghosts and became known as the ghost-catching god. This story is adapted from an episode titled "Zhong Kui Married Off His Little Sister," in which a bunch of demons try to kidnap the girl before her marriage.

Comment: Adapted from the folk legend of same title. Fantasy creatures and elements.

2011

A Bu Wants to Grow Up/A Bu's Story/ A Bu Yao Zhang Da

The Art College of Sichuan University/Inimage Studio

Director: Li Wenyi
Genre: Child Story/History
2D Animation
9:39 Minutes

Synopsis: Set during the period of early reform and opening up in China, it describes the desire of children, A Bu (with a tooth missing) and friends, all wearing the typical red scarves, to grow up. With their umbrellas, they fly up sky-high and fall, the national anthem playing, with the blood of the People's Liberation Army tinting the flag red. Visiting the zoo. Watching TV. Playing early video games. His father urging A Bu to learn and study hard as most Chinese parents do, slapping him in the face. Celebrating the New Year with fireworks.

Comment: Includes, in simple drawing style arranged in a photo book, toys and games that were popular in China in the 1980s and early 1990s.

Angel and Giant

6:40 Minutes
Genre: Fantasy

Synopsis: In a fruit forest a little angel is being helped by a giant.

Are You Hiding Yourself, Grandpa?

Animation School of Beijing Film Academy
10:19 Minutes
2D Animation
Producers: Sun Lijun, Li Liang, Li Jianping, Sun Cong
Director/Screenplay/Executive Producer/Storyboard/ Voice Direction/Editor: Sui Jinyun
Presented by Zhang Huijun
Art Consultant: Ling Jingdong
Character Design: Li Guanyu
Designer: He Jinyong
Music: Yin Bin
Sound Recording: Li Shunxing, Lu Ling
Genre: Family/Kid's Memory

Synopsis: "I was born in a small town in the north of China. This is my mother." Mother hangs the washing. "A woman indulged in an orgy of housework."

"This is my Grandpa—a man infatuated with opera. He is a super opera fan. But I don't like listening to his singing. I like to play *ZuoDatang* [a game] with him." Pulls him away. "Grandpa was sitting in the court hall with whiskers a thousand inches long. Feifei came to the hall and complained something wrong. Who and why will you accuse?" Granddaughter interrupts: "I accuse my grandpa, for he didn't buy sweets for me."

"Look at your teeth. No one would like to marry you."

"My Grandpa is always impartial and incorruptible like *BaoDaren*."

"I will not give you sweets. Retreat."

To console the girl grandpa suggests to play hide-and-seek. The little girl starts to count: "Because no matter where my grandpa hides I can always find him."

But this time she has problems in finding him, not even in the pot or inside the drawer. She plays. She wants to fly: "Grandpa, can you show me how to fly?"

Grandpa has a glass sitting at the table: "All right, wait a minute until I finish it." Impatiently she grabs the glass and finishes herself. But that was not water. She starts to cry.

Mother consoles her: "Feifei, what are you doing?" "I am playing hide and seek with my Grandpa." "Shall Mom play with you?" "No."

When the little girl sleeps, out of her small piano a flying spirit with a mouthful of piano keys appears. He leads the girl out to Grandpa, who is sitting in the crown of the tree. The girl complains that she still cannot fly to the sky.

Grandpa: "Have a try again, now."

And once she tries she starts to fly up to the tree, joining Grandpa, flying with him to the sky, around the moon.

How did Grandpa accomplish the miracle? Well, he has gleaming magic drugs: "Ah, they are sweet."

Next day: "Feifei, where did you get the sweets?" "I ... I picked them up." "Mom, are my sweets on the table?" "Please return the sweets to your brother Niuniu."

Feifei feels guilty and runs away. In her dream the gleaming sweets let beautiful flowers grow. Next day the girl wakes up and the tree has beautiful cherries.

Grandpa tells her that if they will play hide-and-seek she may find him in heaven.

Years later. The girl is older. And grandpa dead. But the memory remains.

This short video is dedicated to my dear Grandpa in heaven.

Comment: It was Stanley Kubrick's widow Christiane who told me that as a little girl she wanted to fly too: "Every little girl wants to." Miyazaki-style.

Back to the Monkey Island

4 Minutes
Director: Luo Hongyang
Genre: Comedy

Synopsis: There are two islands in the boundless sea not very far away from each other, with baboons on the desolate island and monkeys living on the flourishing one. One day, a monkey falls from the sky on the baboons' island and disturbs the quiet life. The baboons decide to send the monkey back to Monkey Island, but on the way across the sea various difficulties and obstacles appear.

The Balcony

Animation School of Beijing Film Academy

3:20 Minutes

Producers: Sun Lijun, Qi Xiaoling, Li Jianping, Sun Cong

Director/Screenplay/Photography/Post-production: Xu Ning

Adapted from a classic joke

Storyboard: Xu Ning, Zhao Hang

Presented by Zhang Huijun

Advisers/Tutors: Sun Lijun, Huang Yong

Art Designer: Chen Yijie

Matte Painting: Jiang Juncheng

Sound Design: Yan Long

Synopsis: At a castle's window we see a character hammering. Two of his fingers are bandaged already. He loses his hold and falls, but can hold tight to a balcony. But suddenly two other hands appear and push him into the deep. The man lands hard but is still alive. The hands belonged to a knight. To kill the craftsman he pushes a heavy box over the railing, but when it shatters downstairs there is a crack that rips off the balcony and the knight falls into the deep himself.

Comment: Stop motion. Bizarre story that takes place in a castle.

Ballet Dancer Under the Streetlight

10:44 Minutes

Genre: Kid's Story

Synopsis: A ten-year-old who loves ballet pursues her dream.

Beacon

CUC Anima, the Animation and Digital Arts School of Communication University of China, Beijing

11:38 Minutes

Supervising Producer: Liao Xiangzhong

Producers: Lu Shengzhang, Shi Minyong, Jia Xiuqing, Ye Jing, Zheng Weilin

Both photographs: *Beacon* (2011) (courtesy CUC Anima).

Executive Producers: Gao Weihua, Suo Xiaoling, Xue Yanping
Director/Screenplay/Art Direction/Storyboard/ Animation/Sound Design: Lixia
Presented by Su Zhiwu
Faculty Adviser: Ai Shengying
Music: Douwei
Genre: Experimental Animation

Synopsis: When the protagonist, a strange human with a face somewhat like a panda, was a child, he wanted to go all the way through heavy snowfall to a towering lighthouse. Standing atop, to him, was the biggest challenge of all, but finally, dreaming of love, he found out that life there was only a stop.

Comment: Story of adolescence in stylistically pleasant, soft sepia tones, that shows a change towards better quality in recent Chinese shorts.

The Brave

CUC Anima, the Animation and Digital Arts School of Communication University of China, Beijing
5:20 Minutes
2D Animation
Directors: Liao Xinzhou, Lu Hongchen, Zhang Chu
Genre: Kid's Story

Synopsis: A little boy who travels back and forth between reality and a game world.

Brother: A Book of the Covenant

Jilin Animation Institute/Jilin College of the Arts
Animation School
Animation Academy Pengfei Animation Studio
9:04 Minutes
3D/2D Animation
Producer: Zheng Liguo
Directors/Screenplay/Editors: Kobe, Shen Yu
Animation Director: Kobe
3D Animation: Shen Yu, Pang Zhuo, Neil, Laky, Liyan, Song Ge, Lilan, Jia Li Cheng, Linan, Long Zeyu, Wang Zan, Lili, Zhao Dong Yang, Song Guanglu, Wang Zixi, Xuhai Zhou, Liu Li Rong, Zhu Jian, Song Yang, Fujian Zhou, Zhang Yuan, Jing Liyan, Jin Qiao Zhen, Wang Qian Feng, Hou Jun, Hou Zhan Hong, Feng Youfa
2D Animation: Shen Yu, Lu Kun, Hu Bing, Liu Li Wen, Han Xiang Long
Modeling: Niminjin
Art Director: Ranyi
Effects: Zhang Rui
Genre: Fantasy

Synopsis: A boy's fantasy dream inspired by the mysterious *Book of Covenant:* In a decayed abbey the boy, first clad in monk's wear, then undressing as a skeleton, fights a two-legged ghoul demonstrating some martial arts skills.

Comment: The fantasy world is presented in 3D animation while the boy's daily world is shown in 2D.

Button

Director: Ma Tengei
Genre: Childhood Memory

Synopsis: While at class a student has a winter dream of building a snowman using

The Brave (2011) (courtesy CUC Anima).

buttons for eyes: "For me childhood is just like snow."

The Can

Animation School of Beijing Film Academy
5:55 Minutes
2D Animation
Production Managers: Sun Lijun, Li Jianping, Sun Cong
Executive Producer: Fan He
Directors/Screenplay: Fan He, Yun Li, Xiangbin Jin, Yisai Tu, Chu Wang, Kexin Wang
Animation Supervisors: Tu Yisai, Wang Kexin
Animation: Wang Kexin, Jin Xiangbin, He Fan
Storyboard: Wang Kexin, Wang Chu
Presented by Zhang Huijun
Stage Manager: Li Liang
Mentors: Xian Liu, Wen Feng, Zheng Zu
Art Design: Yun Li
Sound Design: Wang Shuangshuang
Editors: Wang Chu, Chen Angcheng
Genre: Experimental Animation

Synopsis: A quiet morning. A mysterious figure enters the canneries with a can and disappears in the crowd.

Comment: Van Gogh–like skies. There is a scene in which a pig couple dances at a soiree at Wonder Dream Club, which is inspired by a similar dance scene in Disney's *Beauty and the Beast.*

Circle of Life

CUC Anima, the Animation and Digital Arts School of Communication University of China, Beijing
10:44 Minutes
2D Animation
Producers: Lu Shengzhang, Shi Minyong, Jia Xiuping, Ye Jing, Zheng Weilin
Executive Producers: Gao Weihua, Suo Xiaoling, Xue Yunping
Director: Zhu Jing
Written/Storyboard/Animation by Zhu Jing
Presented by Su Zhiwu
Supervising Producer: Liao Xiangzhong
Faculty Adviser: Li Zhiyong
Genre: Student's Life

Synopsis: Three chapters are extracted from the university comic diary, relating to three topics: a bicycle, a roadside store and fireworks over Olympic Games 2008, seen from afar; Sisi's magic cube, given to an old man.

Comment: Simple-style line characters. Very grey, not much color used, except for the Olympic Games and the magic cube.

Cold Heart

5:11 Minutes
Black and White
2D Animation
Directors: Shiwei Ding, Liang He
Genre: Horror/Experimental Animation

Synopsis: A female driver goes into a forest at night and has an encounter with a psychopath.

Confusions in the Morning Reading Class

7 Minutes
Director: Xiang Jiaheng
Genre: Youth Culture/History

Synopsis: With the nostalgic colors of the 1970s and based on a closed inner world, the work recalls the old days from a morning reading class. It uses the memory of the old books and stationery to express the confusion in the heart. Actually, the memory of the past is always tinted with sentiments and depression. We grew up in happy old days but now, being adults, we seem to lose ourselves in the demands of reality. The song of Cui Jian may express our sentiments and feelings—*It's not that I don't understand but the world just changes so fast.*

The Covenant of God

9:12 Minutes
Genre: History
Synopsis: Brothers' story in war years.

Cricket

8:36 Minutes
Genre: Farce

Synopsis: The hero is a famous scholar. At the behest of the magistrate he orders the arrest of a cricket, which leads to a bizarre, grotesque farce.

The Cube Redemption

CUC Anima, the Animation and Digital Arts School of Communication University of China, Beijing
3:05 Minutes
2D Animation
Supervising Producer: Liao Xiangzhong
Producers: Lu Shengzhang, Shi Minyong, Jia Xiuqing, Zheng Weilin
Executive Producers: Gao Weihua, Suo Xiaoling, Xue Yanping
Director/Animation: Liu Yan
Presented by Su Zhiwu
Faculty Adviser: Yang Xiaojun

The Cube Redemption (2011) (courtesy CUC Anima).

Character Design: Liu Yan, Ascher Bi
Genre: Fantasy Comedy
   Synopsis: In an ice cave an explorer finds a precious cube and escapes with it, with a snowman yeti in hot pursuit. The cube is sheer magic and transports them to different places, even into a scene with the Monkey King. Finally he ends on board a spaceship, being photographed and placed on intergalactic eBay for $477.37.
   Comment: Some characters in this short were taken from the classic *Havoc in Heaven.*

Cutting Paper for Window Flower Decoration

4:19 Minutes
Genre: Chinese Culture
   Synopsis: Another Shanxi folk song describes describing an optimistic attitude towards life in general.
   Comment: Paper-cutting performance.

Dad

3:03 Minutes
Genre: Family
   Synopsis: A hymn to Dad.

Dance

5:45 Minutes
Genre: Kid's Story
   Synopsis: A girl with a disabled leg has always dreamed of becoming a dancer.

Darling

6 Minutes
Director: Jia Bing
Genre: Chinese Culture
   Synopsis: Expresses the philosophy of love through the changes of seasons. Set in the north of China.

Di

6:09 Minutes
Genre: Sci-Fi Environment
   Synopsis: A little robot on Earth carefully protects plant life and finally the last of the small fish in order to survive.
   Comment: Maybe inspired by Douglas Trumbull's sci-fi movie *Silent Running*, in which robots on board of a space ark fulfill a similar task, but more likely by Pixar's *Wall-E.*

Dream as a Kid

16:59 Minutes
   Synopsis: The story of a child's dream.

Dream Chronicles

3:32 Minutes
3D Animation
Genre: Childhood Memory
   Synopsis: A lovelorn boy who feels out of control collides in heavy rain with a bus and is launched into childhood memories. Reality and memory constantly switch.

Dream in the Deserted Garden (2011) (courtesy CUC Anima).

Dream in the Deserted Garden

CUC Anima, the Animation and Digital Arts School of Communication University of China, Beijing
4:36 Minutes
2D Animation
Supervising Producer: Liao Xiangzhong
Producers: Lu Shengzhang, Shi Minyong, Jia Xiuqing, Ye Jing, Zhang Weilin
Executive Producers: Gao Weihua, Suo Xiaoling, Xue Yanping
Director: Wang Lin Hui
Presented by Su Zhiwu
Faculty Adviser: David G. Ehrlich
Music: Lotus by Secret Garden
Genre: Peking Opera

Synopsis: A girl from ancient times falls in love with a boy who appears in her dreams. Their love is expressed in metamorphoses. They transform into birds. Then the dream is over and the girl weeps.

Comment: Adapted from a classical Chinese opera, *The Peony Pavilion.* Ink-like 2D animation.

Dududu

8:03 Minutes
Genre: Kid's Story

Synopsis: A little fat boy's favorite team wins the championship in the World Cup. He is going to tell the exciting news to his father, who works overseas.

Face

CUC Anima, the Animation and Digital Arts School of Communication University of China, Beijing
7:33 Minutes
2D Animation
Supervising Producer: Liao Xiangzhong
Producers: Lu Shengzhang, Shi Minyong, Jia Xiuqing, Ye Jing, Zheng Weilin
Executive Producers: Gao Weihua, Suo Xiaoling, Xue Yanping
Director/Screenplay/Digital Composition: Zhang Tongye
Presented by Su Zhiwu
Faculty Advisers: David G. Ehrlich, Li Zhiyong
Original Music: Fang Xin

Synopsis: Jia is diagnosed with OCD. She can't stand any folded things, including her own face, so she keeps it wrinkle-free by the use of Botox until she cannot move her muscles anymore. To smile she has to fix her mouth with tape.

Comment: Black and white animation.

Fat

7:27 Minutes
3D Animation
Genre: Comedy

Synopsis: A boy by the name of Fei is overweight because he loves to eat. To win a girl's heart he decides to lose weight, but the God of Cookery, who appears like Aladdin's Ghost in his imagination, challenges him constantly

Face (2011) (courtesy CUC Anima).

with images of tasty food. Fei works hard against being seduced. At the end everything is locked and the spirit of food defeated. Now he is almost slim but the girl of his dreams is fat.

The Fate of Mosquitoes

3:05 Minutes
Genre: Kid's Story
   Synopsis: Mosquitoes and a little girl.

Fickle Snake

3:38 Minutes
Genre: Comedy
   Synopsis: A snake changes shapes to satirize fickle people.

Flight

5:12 Minutes
Genre: Fantasy/Youth Culture
   Synopsis: Determined to follow his own dream, a boy decides to quit school and to fly over the well to find the green pastures that are in his mind.

Floater

5:12 Minutes
3D Animation
Producer: Zhou Chuan
Software: Autodesk Mayam Autodesk 3D max, Adobe After Effects; Adobe Photoshop, e-on Vue, eyeon Fusiom
Genre: Environment/Ecology
   Synopsis: In his imagination a pupil rides on a train of trash over the walls to a green island.

Flying Jar

4:23 Minutes
Genre: Environment
   Synopsis: Warning people to cherish our environment.

Fresh Green

7 Minutes
   Comment: Inspired by the filmmakers' years spent at university, with youthful vigor and joy.

Friend

3:05 Minutes
Genre: Parable
   Synopsis: In order to get the highly prized ivory, a hunter kills an elephant that had rescued him from a lion's attack and was his best friend in childhood.

Garden

9:30 Minutes
Genre: Fantasy
   Synopsis: In a quiet forest a lonely monster desires to communicate with humans.

Get a Lift

5:30 Minutes
Director: Gaoxiang Li
Genre: Comedy
   Synopsis: The road to his beloved is long and mountainous. On the way, a biker trying to pass a truck (which is laden with pigs) finally decides to become a stowaway and have himself pulled by the truck, which ends in a disaster.
   Comment: For background the short makes use of nice Chinese landscapes and also has a traditional score that makes it quite sympathetic.

Gift

9:13 Minutes
Genre: Kid's Story
   Synopsis: Instead of sending his mother a barrette for Mother's Day, a small boy from a poor family has another idea for a gift.

Graduate Work

6:38 Minutes
Genre: Student's Life
   Synopsis: A group of sophomore students is given a difficult task—to do their graduate work together.

Grandpa

Tianjin University, Institute of Animation Software
8:30 Minutes
Director/Screenplay/Character and Scene Design/Storyboard/Puppetmaker/Photographer: Wu Xianzhou
Compositing/Special Effects: Wang Heming
Music: Su Yang
Producer/Instructor: Zhou Tian
Genre: Personal Story
   Synopsis: A freshman admits to his college the reason for his visit home. His grandfather is ill and going to die, and the boy has to stay with Grandma.
   Comment: Stop motion.

Hair Growth Diary

4:16 Minutes
Genre: Comedy

Synopsis: A handsome man is eager to become a model but he has an obstacle: He is bald.

Happy Anniversary

CUC Anima, the Animation and Digital Arts School of Communication University of China, Beijing
8:51 Minutes
2D Animation

Supervising Producer: Liao Xiangzheng
Producers: Lu Shengzhang, Shi Minyong, Jia Xiuqing, Zheng Weilin
Executive Producers: Gao Weihua, Suo Xiaoling, Xie Yanying
Directors: Cheng Teng, Liang Fan
Presented by Su Zhiwu
Faculty Advisers: Gao Weihua, Li Wei
Storyboard/Animation/Digital Composition and Editing: Cheng Teng
Art Director: Liang Fan

Happy Anniversary **(2011) (courtesy CUC Anima).**

Original Music: Li Hui
Sound Effects: Zhang Yue, Wei Junhua, Cheng Teng, Liang Fan
Genre: Family

Synopsis: A woman at home carefully prepares a meal to celebrate her wedding anniversary with her husband, but he is late. She calls him, but there is no answer. The sensitive, worried woman gets into a series of imaginative scenarios about what might have happened to him. Maybe an accident. Buying flowers he could have gotten into a fist fight with some bad guys; escaping from them, he accidentally ran into a car. Or might he have met with a mistress and danced with the blonde? She dreams of when she was a little girl and met the boy for the first time. Getting flowers from him. Marrying him (in a Catholic church). Still he is not showing up. She waits and waits and gets old. But then there he is, smiling, holding flowers ... and she hugs him.

Hi! Baboon

The School of Media and Animation, China Academy of Art
4:12 Minutes
3D Animation
Director/Screenplay: Kevin Law
Associates: April, Chen Zheng, Yunkun Du, Chang Li, Changming Liu
Motion Graphic Design: Joker.D
Original Score: Shuo Yuwen
Sound: Wang Tao
Genre: Comedy

Synopsis: The story of a baboon who encounters a little monkey who asks for help in returning to his home island. There is a shark lurking on the way home. But the hoped-for paradise island is a colony of monkeys who have made baboons their slaves to build their monuments.

Homeward Bound I Go

9:45 Minutes
2D Animation
Genre: Childhood Memory

Synopsis: The main character is transported from the present time back to childhood to re-experience those happy days that have been forgotten since. On his way he meets strange, humanoid animals. Then, looking at his watch, the young man is back in reality, back at work, out of the land of wonder.

Comment: The score contains Miyakazi elements. There are some aesthetic parallels to Miyazaki as well.

How to Eat a Whole Family

11:50 Minutes
Genre: Comedy

Synopsis: A carnivorous bird is going to eat up a whole family.

How to Make Fun

CUC Anima, the Animation and Digital Arts School of Communication University of China, Beijing
2:32 Minutes
Director: Zhang Zhe
Presented by Su Zhiwu
Genre: Comedy

Synopsis: In a painting class, a (live action) teacher censures the students for doing unsatisfying work while knocking the blackboard on the head of a caricatured chalk boy. This unintended action provokes the chalk boy, and a fierce fight ensues between the animated cartoon and the teacher (who cannot stand any fun).

I Saw Mice Burying a Cat

Jilin Animation Institute
5 Minutes
Director: Dmitry Geller
Producer: Zheng Liguo
Art Director: Anna Karpova

Synopsis: A bittersweet story about the eternal struggle between cats and mice that ends in a nightly procession of mice literally burying a feline.

Comment: On a regular basis Jilin Animation Institute invites foreign filmmakers to join them and, together with students, make a short film in Changchun that is intended to tour various national and international festivals. Among those invited was Russian animator Dmitry Geller. Geller, born in 1970 in Sverdlovsk City, as a painter participated in exhibitions in his home town as well as St. Petersburg, Moscow, Copenhagen and Washington. In 1990–1995 he worked as assistant animator for animation studio A-Film, then studied directing and scriptwriting in Moscow.

Awards: Grand Prix, Hiroshima Animation Festival, 2012.

Grand Prix, Festival "Animator" Poland, 2012.

Best Short Film 2011, National Award of China Association of Animators, Golden Monkey.

Special Jury Prize, Festival "Suzdal," Russia, 2012.

How to Make Fun (2011) (courtesy CUC Anima).

Special Jury Prize, Festival "Window to Europe," Vyborg, 2012.

I Wanna Be

3:32 Minutes
Genre: Kid's Story
   Synopsis: A little girl wants to show the innocence of children to different animals.

In Poster/Poster Rhapsody

CUC Anima, the Animation and Digital Arts
   School of Communication University of
   China, Beijing
3:52 Minutes
Supervising Producer: Liao Xiangzhong
Producers: Lu Shengzhang, Shi Minyong, Jia
   Xiuqing, Zheng Weilin
Executive Producers: Gao Weihua, Suo Xiao-
   ling, Xue Yanping
*Director/Writer/Art Director/Animation/3D
   Effects:* Yuan Zhichao
Presented by Su Zhiwu
Faculty Advisers: David G. Ehrlich, Vincent Lee,
   Ray Wong
Genre: Comedy
   Synopsis: Teenage boy and teenage girl are

lost and have to find their way together in the colorful world of posters, such as from *Finding Nemo, Day and Night, Cars, Up!, Les Triplettes de Belleville* (German Poster: *Das große Rennen von Belleville*), *How to Train a Dragon, Cloudy with a Chance of Meatballs.*
   Comment: Lively touches are references made to animation and Pixar posters (although some titles are misspelled).

Insomnia People

4:47 Minutes
Genre: Comedy
   Synopsis: A man angrily destroys all the city's bells desperately trying to get the unnerving sound to stop.

It's All Because of Your Dad

CUC Anima, the Animation and Digital Arts
   School of Communication University of
   China, Beijing
4:17 Minutes
2D Animation
Director: Zhao Xizhe
Genre: Child Fantasy/Comedy

Synopsis: In the carriage of a train, all the animals sit together and talk about how they were born. When the chicken is asked, Mom tells her in a very funny way how Dad overcame all difficulties and how she was born. After the story is finished, the train arrives at the station and the chicken excitedly runs to Dad, who is waiting to pick them up.

Comment: Simple but effective 2D caricatures that are well suited to a child's imagination.

Kung Fu Cooking Girls

8:40 Minutes
Director: Xie Ning
Genre: Comedy

Synopsis: Two females (experienced in martial arts techniques), offering food, fight for the attention of a male.

Kung Fu Dunk

Global Digital
3 Minutes
Director: Shen Yu
Genre: Fable

Synopsis: There is a kind of faith called perseverance and a kind of pursuit called dreaming. Basketball player Panda Fei Pan always desires the feeling of dunking. He admires his friends, Kangaroo Ku Dou and Pig A Can, who usually show various dunking actions. Fei Pan tries hard. He even puts up a jumping platform. Finally he climbs up the basketry, but can he accomplish what he has dreamed about for so many nights?

The Last Key/Way to Heaven

MUMA Animation Studio
6:25 Minutes
3D Animation
Director/Storyboard/3D Layout/Sound Effects:
   Jeam Li (Li Junliang)
Artistic Director: Ronghua Huang
Art Director: Teng Chen
Advisers: Shuzong Huang, Ding Zhong, Xiangrong Liao
Music: Ziwen Cao
Genre: Comedy

Synopsis: Before they are allowed to enter heaven two brothers, sinners who have recently passed away, a fat one and a thin one, are tested at heaven's gate in what looks like a computer game of their deeds. But the last key to open the gate is denied by an old female guard because they have not done enough tasks and there is only one free seat in heaven. So they are transferred downstairs to collect more points by doing good deeds. Both try to remove a cow from the street and thus save it from traffic. They start a competition to accumulate their points. In the end the cow passes away too and receives the last key.

Lian Sheng Dian

8:20 Minutes
2D Animation
Genre: Peking Opera

Synopsis: A candidate for the civil service examination asks a landlord in Liang Sheng Dian to have a first-class room for one night. But the landlord refuses to give him a good room, instead showing him one with mice in it. "What a mess!" the candidate complains. "It's not for humans!" The landlord remains unimpressed: "It's all up to you. You can just leave, and I am not gonna force you!" "I think I have to agree. I have nowhere else to go."

Next day. A messenger arrives and asks to see a certain official. The landlord asks: "Who is it?" "Mr. Wang." "What is the official seal?" "It says *Ming fang*." "Where is he from?" "Pei County Xu Zhou." "We do not have a Mr. Wang here, except that cracker over there who came in when we were about to close. He cannot be the man you are asking for. Whatever, it's time to get him out." The official still sleeps. The landlord wakes him up rudely: "You! It's late in the morning. You should go and get some fresh air outside. By the way, what's your family name?" "My family name is Wang." "I see: Tang, right?" "No, it's Wang." "It's Yang, isn't it?" "No, no, it's Wang." He spells: "W-A-N-G. Wang." "You are lying. Look at you. No one will believe you have the family name Wang but WANG." (He uses a different pronunciation.) "My family name is Wang and it means honor, not the WANG you refer to, which has the meaning of 'water.'" "Oh boy! Your family name is WANG! You are *the* Mr. Wang they are looking for just now! How can you still be here? Follow me! Hurry up! Hurry!"

Realizing that he has made a mistake, he pushes Mr. Wang out, who wants to know where they are going. "Please go to the first-class room." "The first class? I thought you said I did not deserve it before!" "It is just for you, before and now!" "Step back! My mouth smells!" "What? No, it smells great. Just follow me, your honor." In a better room the landlord asks Mr. Wang to sit down: "Mr.

Wang. Congratulations! You are the new Zhuang Yuan. The messenger just came, Milord! You cannot just wear these clothes in case someone will make a mistake." "I do not have new clothes." "Don't worry, Milord," the landlord says obsequiously. "We have plenty of them." He brings better clothes: "Let me serve you. Your family name is WANG, isn't it?" "Yes, it is." "What is your official seal?" "*Ming fang*!" "And your hometown?" "Pei County, Xu Zhou." "Right! It's you. Definitely you! Good news! Good news! Mr. Wang has won the 8th prize." The landlord is ashamed and apologizes: "I did not mean to hurt you. Sorry!" "Hum. Ha-ha-ha. I am going to be an official." "Let me walk you out, my lord. Let me send you off." "Where are you going to send me?" "I am planning to send you off the stage!" The landlord appears again and addresses the audience: "You cannot just judge a person simply by his appearance and clothes."

Life as a Game

4:33 Minutes
Genre: Youth Culture
   Comment: Graduation is a process of confusion.

Lin

4:57 Minutes
Genre: Kid's Story
   Synopsis: Monster child Xiao Lin escapes

to find his dream but eventually is forced to give up on it.

Little Bear Hiding Behind the Tree/ Little Bear and Balloon

4:09 Minutes
3D Animation
Director: Chen Feiyi
Genre: Fable
   Synopsis: A little bear is hiding behind the tree and staring at a clown's balloons. But he is too shy and too timid to ask for one, as he is not human. All of a sudden a boy in a bear's overcoat approaches the clown and gets a balloon. The little bear thinks the boy is a real bear, so he gets up the courage and goes to the clown himself. The kind clown doesn't see any difference between humans and animals and hands the bear a balloon too. But the bear's claws cannot hold the balloon, and the balloon flies away. Next time the clown ties the balloon to the bear's claw. Happily the little bear takes the balloon home to the forest.

The Love Between People and a Dog

CUC Anima, the Animation and Digital Arts School of Communication University of China, Beijing
Genre: Animal
6:58 Minutes
   Synopsis: A story about a pet dog.

Little Bear Hiding Behind the Tree (2011).

Little Bear Hiding Behind the Tree (2011).

Background for *The Love Between People and a Dog* (2011) (courtesy CUC Anima).

The Love Story

CUC Anima, the Animation and Digital Arts School of Communication University of China, Beijing

6:14 Minutes

2D Animation

Supervising Producer: Liao Xiangzhong

Producers: Lu Shengzhang, Shi Minyong, Jia Xiuqing, Ye Jing, Zheng Weilin

Executive Producers: Gao Weihua, Suo Xiaoling, Xue Yanping

Director/Animation: Zhang Yan

Screenplay: Yan Liwei, Zhang Jie, Zhang Yan

Storyboard/Sound Design: Yan Liwei

Presented by Su Zhiwu

Faculty Advisers: Gao Weihua, Li Wei

Art Direction: Zhang Jie, Zhang Yan

Genre: Love Story

The Love Story (2011) (courtesy CUC Anima).

Synopsis: After being hit by a car a woman, not pleased with her love life, transforms into a character like Snow White and encounters a prince in four different fairy-tales. But the princes are not to her liking. In the hospital, when she wakes up from a coma, her life companion is waiting with flowers.

The Magic House
2:50 Minutes
Genre: Fantasy
Synopsis: Mr. Magic welcomes visitors and uses his magic skills to transform the life of his visitors.

Maya Era
4:33 Minutes
Genre: History
Synopsis: Set at the time of ancient Mayan tribes, who worshipped the sun.

Me?!
3 Minutes
Director: Han Jin
Genre: Fantasy
Synopsis: Shows growth, transformation, and the fear of losing "me" in a surreal way: Little "T" creates a world in the water. "I" flies to the sky by a balloon and plays in the clouds. "T" slips down the rainbow, and a Big "I" comes out of "me" and swallows clouds, rainbow and everything else.

Meet on the Bridge of Magpies
7 Minutes
Director: Cui Baoli
Screenplay: Chen Chunhua, Zhang Chun
Genre: Classic Love Story
Synopsis: Adapted from the traditional Chinese folktale *The Cowherd and the Girl Weaver,* two characters who guard their love.
Comment: The work integrates Chinese paper-cutting with shadow play in art-style design to express people's desire for free love and happiness as well as to promote the unique appeal of traditional Chinese culture.

Men Sanye
14:11 Minutes
Genre: Parable
Synopsis: Men Sanye is lazy and loves hunting, but eventually he changes and gives up hunting for ordinary, hard-labor farming.
Comment: Based on folklore.

Migrating West
4:31 Minutes
2D Animation
Genre: Chinese Culture
Synopsis: A traditional song, illustrated. The mourning of a wife whose husband is leaving:

My honey, you're migrating west.
And I, your sister, can't hold you.
Hand in hand

I see you off at the gate.
I would rather die than release your hands
Tears well up in the eyes
and stream down my face
You just married me in January
Then you migrate west in February
I am loath to part with you and say good bye to
    you
My honey, you turn and go away.
My tears... The tears pour down non-stop
I can only see you leaving step by step an early
    date
stomping, stomping, stomping
and disappearing in the distance.

Comment: Colorful Chinese design.

Military Training

2:23 Minutes
Director: Ma Tengfei
Genre: Comedy

Comment: Military drill in a short that proves how popular *South Park* is in China.

Miss Rabbit

2:35 Minutes

Synopsis: The psychology of spinster groups.

Mr. Cock

CUC Anima, the Animation and Digital Arts School of Communication University of China, Beijing
11:55 Minutes
2D Animation
Supervising Producer: Liao Xiangzhong
Producers: Lu Shengzhang, Shi Minyong, Jia Xinqing, Ye Jing, Zheng Weilin
Executive Producers: Gao Weihua, Suo Xiaoling, Xue Janping
Director/Writer/Animation/Compositing/Editor: Victor Xu
Presented by Su Zhiwu
Faculty Advisers: Li Zhiyong, David G. Ehrlich
Sound Design: Zhang Yue
Original Music: Crystal Ai
Genre: Parable

Synopsis: Only one little chicken is left after the other has been slain accidentally on the farm. The chick picks and finally becomes a rooster. He sees the farmer shooting birds and his dog returning them. He falls in love with a cow. Then a war breaks out and everything is destroyed. Only the rooster survives, among unknown soldiers. Then other soldiers come and shoot the enemy. Tanks roll upon the ground, and the rooster takes

shelter. The ground has become a graveyard until he exits to heaven himself.

The Mizzle of Pipa

7:51 Minutes
2D Animation
Genre: Kid's Story

Synopsis: Scenes from a Chinese girl's childhood.

Comment: Traditional Chinese ink painting is used to express the feeling of youth that is ignorant of love.

Moving Westward

3:48 Minutes
Genre: Chinese Culture

Synopsis: A Shanxi folk song from the northwest area of Fugu, titled "Moving Westward," depicts a woman left by her husband feeling desolate, listening to the song with tears in her eyes.

Natural War

2:35 Minutes
2D Animation
Directors: Zhu Yunbo, Wei Jianan
Genre: Anti-War

Synopsis: Boundary disagreements lead to a war between two different countries that is represented by two caricatured guys and their troops. They arm themselves in red and blue castles, respectively, and fire rocket arms until a volcano spits green smoke and engulfs them.

North Drift

5:25 Minutes
Genre: Comedy

Synopsis: The life of penguins in the Antarctic. A ship arrives, and its captain tells a little penguin about his home, where trees are. To prove it he gives the penguin a leaf. Out of ice he builds himself a boat to go there, and arrives at the country that is full of plants and green life. He meets a koala who wants to leave in the opposite direction in a boat as well.

Palmistry

20:47 Minutes
Genre: Kid's Story
Synopsis: A little girl and a fortune teller.

Peach Feast

4:20 Minutes
Genre: Animal

Synopsis: A monkey turns out to be an unexpected visitor at the Peach Feast.

Qualitative Change

6:51 Minutes
Genre: Kid's Fantasy

Synopsis: One morning, in the countryside, a boy chases a caterpillar, ready to stomp it with his feet and feels like Mr. Universe doing so. But all of a sudden, the small worm transforms into a mighty, powerful dragon and chases the frightened boy. Luckily, it all was a dream but the boy has learned his lesson when he sees a caterpillar that transforms into a beautiful butterfly.

Comment: A variation on the traditional Chinese proverb: "Don't miss doing any good no matter how insignificant it looks."

Race and Bull

1:45 Minutes
Genre: Comedy

Synopsis: In order to prove their strength, two bicycle riders in a small town start a competition.

Room 403

20:47 Minutes
2D Animation
Genre: Youth Culture/Student's Experience

Synopsis: Youth culture in a students' dormitory. A world of telecommunications changes youth: iPhones, interactive games, sound and music. In between they smoke, use the toilets, eat noodles in the cafeteria, go to the supermarket, and drink beer.

Semicircle

2:17 Minutes
Genre: Parable

Comment: In life it is usual that a thing develops from many possibilities.

Shangri-La

10 Minutes
3D Animation
Director: Weiqiang Ling
Genre: Fantasy

Synopsis: According to an old proverb, everyone will find his or her true calling in the fairy-tale land of Shangri-La.

Shoes

13 Minutes
Director: Mao Qichao
Genre: History

Synopsis: Set in a beautiful seaside town during World War II and adapted from a short novel, *Soldiers and Shoes*, the film tells a story about war, militants and love, including fifty characters such as a shoemaker and the son of his dead comrade, a soldier and his distant lover, a mother and her son in the battlefield, and a general and a soldier.

Shop

4:35 Minutes
Genre: Kid's Story

Synopsis: For a little boy, the shop holds lots of surprises.

Single for a Long Time

2 Minutes
Genre: Kid's Story

Synopsis: The activity of a little girl's inner mind.

Sky Blue

MAM Film Studio Entertainment
15:10 Minutes
3D Animation
Director/Screenplay: Ma Yingjie
Music: Ludovico Einaudi
Genre: Anti-War

Synopsis: Time changes. The world changes. People change. A story about a red girl and her father, a green soldier, who leaves her behind to go to war. The girl is waiting in vain for his return. Only the sky remains unchanged.

Smart Lee

Jilin Animation Institute
5:36 Minutes
2D Cut-Out Animation
Producer: Zheng Liguo
Director: Oleg Dergachov
Genre: Environment/Fantasy

Synopsis: In what turns out to be a nightmare, a little boy sees how a consumption-oriented society pollutes and destroys nature and the environment and reduces the biosphere of birds and animals. Even Noah's Ark seems to be part of that system.

Comment: Made by Oleg Dergachov with the support of animation students in Changchun. Oleg was born in 1961 in Rostov. In 1984 he graduated from the Ukrainian Academy of Print, Graphic Art and Book Design. In 2005 he moved with his family to Canada. Oleg views himself as cosmopolitan and refers to an old Chinese proverb: "The more you travel, the longer life your life will be." This little film was based on a picture book (*Smart Boy*) he had published in 2010.

Smoker

4:23 Minutes
Genre: Health Care
   Comment: Animation is used to warn of the health hazards of smoking.

Story of Information/Communication

3:20 Minutes
Directors: Zhou Qinghua, Feng Jianing, Xu Yuan
Genre: Experimental Animation
   Synopsis: Today, highly developed information technology has united us in a world that is small and smaller. From the hieroglyphs in ancient times to today's 3D technology, all this appears as the crystallization of human wisdom.
   Comment: Object animation, using natural raw materials such as mung (green) beans and jumby (red) beans that evolve and change frame by frame to illustrate the process of modern-day communications.

Swallow

4:15 Minutes
Genre: Parable
   Synopsis: The swallows live a carefree life but when the enemy comes, they don't know what to do or how to protect themselves.

Tangram Story

5:26 Minutes
Genre: Kid's Story
   Synopsis: An adventure story caused by a little girl who plays tangram.

Tapir of Dream

7:49 Minutes
Genre: Kid's Story
   Synopsis: A small girl dreams to fly away with a balloon.

I Teach My Grandma Reading Words

3:30 Minutes
Genre: Personal Story
   Synopsis: Grandma is illiterate. Her little niece is determined to teach her to write and read. The learning process is difficult, but in the end Grandma succeeds in writing the little girl's name.

Teapot

4:06 Minutes
Genre: Parable
   Synopsis: The story of a teapot, from its initial beautiful condition to its final complete breakdown.

Thrush

8:38 Minutes
Genre: Fantasy
   Comment: Adapted from *Fantasy Magazine*, April 2005.

Travel Life

Zhejiang Sci-Tech University, Art Design Academy
4:54 Minutes
2D Animation
Producers: Zhuang Xiao Wen, Huang Wen Shan
Script/Character Design/Animation Director: Kong
Genre: Parable
   Synopsis: Travelers are compared with their luggage:

> Every person possesses their own luggage for carrying cherished recollection.... We exhaust our whole lives through travelling. From city to city, from strangeness to strangeness.

   Comment: Through the leading roles' internal monologues, it expresses reflections on drifting lives and hasty journeys.

A Tree Disappeared

6:36 Minutes
Genre: Environment/Ecology
   Comment: About ecology and the harmonious relationship between man and nature.

Went to School

6:17 Minutes
Genre: Youth Culture
   Comment: Drastic action video.

Wu Feng Wu Ji

8:07 Minutes
Genre: Fable
   Synopsis: Fox and dog looking for the right way.
   Comment: Uses Tibetan culture as background.

Yao

6 Minutes
Genre: Kid's Story

Synopsis: In a remote mountain village lives a poor family. One day their small boy, Yao, becomes seriously ill, and the parents don't know what to do.

Zen

5:45 Minutes
2D Animation
Genre: Fantasy

Synopsis: A child monk's magical and wonderful dream world, exploring a natural world of flowers and lotus. Suddenly there is thunder and lightning. The monk fights his way through the storm to save a broken plant, but he cannot repair it. His tears water the ground and produce a garden of new green plants that move skywards and engulf him in a rain of red flowers. Gratefully he gives one to the Buddha.

2012

Alive Is Paradise

3:25 Minutes
Genre: Kid's Story

Synopsis: While doctors and surgeons fight for the life of an infant, other children discuss the precious gift of life.

Box Home

Animation School of Beijing Film Academy
3:49 Minutes
Producer: Zhang Huijun
Production Managers: Sun Lijun, Li Jianping, Sun Cong
Director/Animation/Sound Effects: Huang Sijia
Art Direction: Liu Ko
Music: Yoko Kanno
Genre: Parable

Synopsis: A couple lives with their pet in a flat that actually is a box. The volume of the box is just the volume of the couple. Although the box is too small to live in, they try their best to move and continue their routine, with him reading newspaper or her wiping dust or even having a shower, then going to sleep. One morning they are woken up by seven birds pecking outside on their nutshell, then flying away. All of a sudden, the box breaks up. The couple starts to rebuild but are unable to do so. But instead of using their freedom, they continue as if still living in the confined box.

The Castle of Sand

3:41 Minutes
Director: Fan Zhengi
Genre: Experimental Animation

Comment: Experimental music-video clip.

Chameleon

Animation School of Beijing Film Academy
3:53 Minutes
2D Animation
Director: Xu Xiaoxu
Producer: Zhang Huijun
Production Managers: Sun Lijun, Li Jianping, Sun Cong
Guidance Teachers: Sun Lijun, Zhang Li
Genre: Parable

Synopsis: A chameleon lives in a black-and-white world and therefore doesn't know about the characteristics of colors. One day, a chicken falls into the chameleon's black-and-white world and turns him yellow. Then the chameleon kisses a goldfish and turns reddish. For the first time the animal realizes the colorful world around. Finally it colors the black-and-white palm tree under which it was living on the tiny island, which actually is the back of a huge turtle.

The Creed/Impermanence

6:27 Minutes
3D Animation
Director/Animation: Miao Tien-Tu
Supervisor: Yu Wei-Cheng
Producer: Chen Chia-Ying
Sound: Chen Chia-Wei
Genre: Fantasy (made in Taiwan)

Synopsis: The main character wakes up in the ruins of his town. He tries to remember his own past and creed. When he finds out the ruin of town is being swallowed by the time flow, he tries to escape, until he sees the temple where he used to worship. As he is about to be swallowed by time flow himself, he attempts to save it from destruction.

Creep

CUC Anima, the Animation and Digital Arts School of Communication University of China, Beijing
7:05 Minutes
Supervising Producers: Huang Xinyuan, Zheng Weilin
Producers: Lu Shgengzhang, Jia Xinqing, Shi Minyong, Tan Xiao
Executive Producers: Suo Xiaoling, Gao Wei-hua, Chen Jie

Director/Art Direction: Liu Siyu
Animation: Liu Siyu, Liu Yujie
Screenplay: Liu Siyu, Liu Yujie, Zhao Puling, Han Xiao
Character Direction: Liu Yujie
Presented by Su Zhiwu, Liao Xiangzhong
Faculty Advisers: Ai Shengying, Li Wei, Gao Weihua
Digital Composition: Liu Siyu
Sound Design: Liu Siyu, Zhang Yue
Genre: Sci-Fi Fantasy

Synopsis: The deteriorated city is often attacked by a four-legged monsters. Over time, people have gotten used to the existence of these monsters and have developed a comprehensive defense strategy. The story's hero, however, is a boy who has no knowledge of the case. While warning sirens give signals he innocently feeds a cute little monster with three green eyes and makes it his pet, wondering about the green slime. The pup is found to be a threat and put into a cage, but it outgrows the bars. The military misinterprets his affection for the boy as aggression and eliminates the creature by force on a bridge, leaving a sad boy behind.

Dandelion

2:39 Minutes
2D Animation
Genre: Fantasy

Synopsis: All things are in a cycle; anything that starts will inevitably have an ending. A little girl sees a giant flower grow, then the spores like an umbrella drift away with her through day and night. Then she lands, back at the flower, finding a boy watering it. The two come together. The girl lets go of the umbrella, which is found by another girl.

Double Hunting/Gear Studio

7:58 Minutes
3D Animation
Genre: Satire/Environment

Synopsis: Set in a forest that is surrounded by human industrial civilization. A hunter who looks faintly like Hitler and has a deep-rooted urge to conquer ignores the sign forbidding hunting and thrusts himself in the forest. However, those targeted preys have been taken away preemptively by a humanized wolf. After noticing that, the hunter gets angry and utilizes a lamb as a bait to start chasing the wolf with a chainsaw. Where he goes, the environment starts to change and the forest vanishes, becoming buildings and skyscrapers. In the end there is a showdown between hunter and prey, a fierce fistfight with the pseudo–Hitler put into a cage inside the last green resort in an otherwise totally artificial environment.

Fairwell [sic]

3:30 Minutes
2D Animation

Synopsis: Announces a series concept about the future. A teenage girl watching a (Chinese) space rocket launch.

Comment: In the great turning points in human history, everything seems as it should be ... self-sacrifice, separation, blind courage, all shrouded in the aura that everything must be sacrificed for the sake of community. However, all those people who are involved, even if they understand what's going on, cannot stop their primitive, selfish emotions. They are confused about future and doubt their own choices.

Fox

CUC Anima, the Animation and Digital Arts School of Communication University of China, Beijing
7:39 Minutes
Stop Motion
Supervising Producers: Huang Xinjuan, Zheng Weilin
Producers: Lu Shengzhang, Jie Jinqing, Shi Minyong, Tan Xiao
Executive Producers: Suo Xiaoling, Gao Weihua, Chen Jie
Directors/Art Direction: Feng Wen, Ma Wei
Screenplay/Storyboard: Feng Wen
Presented by Su Zhiwu, Liao Xiangzhong
Faculty Adviser: Xue Yanqing
Stop Motion Animation Props/Photography: Wang Xintong
Original Music: Zhao Mingchi
Sound Design: Luan Lian
Editor: Ma Wei
Genre: Experimental Animation
Synopsis: A fox character performs in a Japanese Kabuki-like play, holding a fan.
"There are always ancient legends about the unknown which people are curious about and make subjective speculations. But ultimately, is there anyone who wants to know the truth? And lay down their grudges to accept it relievedly? Have you heard about the story of the fox? It is rumored that the fox will hold a wedding in sunny rain. If people see that then they will die."
Scenes of a stop-motion fox holding an

umbrella to protect himself from sunny rain on stage, with couples around.

"His curiosity blooms into an exotic flower with twisted sprays which leads him alone to sleep in the mysterious forests. Attend a secret banquet."

A child follows the fox into the forest and becomes witness to a strange ceremony executed by the fox community disguised with human masks. They discover the boy, who runs away.

"Soft thunder rolling in the wind, the shoes of the dead are still walking. Explore the truth of the unknown and desire in the deadness and struggle of being exposed. Sigh for the groundless longing."

Out of breath, the boy comes home and seeks protection from his mother. But mother is not mother. She mutates in front of her son into an evil spirit.

Concealed by the world, create the game, then curse it. And finally, back into freedom and silence. Persistent, leave, and delusion. From then on, do not believe any words."

Next morning:

"Left the cloudy night sky.

Shadow is the dumbness afterwards.

It's time to greet the sun, which is harsh and never to be looked directly in the eye.

Let it be.

A song of praise goes from the bottom of the heart.

Story ends."

Comment: In China, the fox symbolizes the afterlife and is connected with the spirits of the deceased.

As this story is completely Japanese—even the mountain in the background painting looks like Fujiyama—it looks as though Chinese and Japanese students working jointly at CUC Anima, although there is no hint of this in the credits.

The Fox

Animation School of Beijing Film Academy
3:10 Minutes
2D Animation
Genre: Fantasy

Synopsis: An animator who lives in the bottom of the city creates a little fox in animation, but the boss is not pleased by the result and throws the cels out of the window. The animator storms out of the room to save the paper, but to his surprise finds out that the images of the fox are gone. He looks around and, right, sees the tail of a living fox. The fox is alive. The artist follows him into the subway, onto the roof of the train. He is shocked and chases it until the fox grasps him and, as a product of the artist's imagination, flies him up to the top of the city, where they both experience a wonderful, unforgettable sunset.

Good Night!

Xian Academy of Fine Arts
Motion Picture Photography and Animation
7:49 Minutes
2D Animation
Genre: Macabre Parable

Synopsis: An old man is closed in a room on the night of his death. His two pets are a dog and a cat. These two animals have different attitudes about the death of their host, which lead them to make opposite choices in this extreme environment. Eventually, both of them die. The dog kills the cat (conscience) and prepares to die too.

The Green Land

Animation School of Beijing Film Academy
9:59 Minutes
2D Animation with 3D Elements
Producers: Sun Lijun, Li Jianping, Sun Cong, Huang Yong
Executive Producer: Wang Chenying
Director: Yang Mu
Key Animation: Bai Xi
Animation: Bai Xi, Longdemao, Gu Fangyu
Story: Tian Yu, Yang Mu
Storyboard: Yang Mu
Presented by Zhang Huijun
Production Manager: Li Liang
Tutors: Liu Xian, Xu Zheng
Art Directors: Bai Xi, Peng Xiao
Character Design: Bai Xi
Background Design: Peng Xiao
3D Models and Rendering: Cheng Che, Guo Mingyue, Yang Mu
Music: Bozy, Wang Wei
Postproduction, CG Effects and Editor: Yang Mu
Genre: Parable

Synopsis: The film opens with a little boy caring for flowers. All of a sudden he sees a stranger approaching on the bridge who sits in a mobile, carousel-like device. The stranger has a present for the village: a blue artificial kind of flower. When the boy comes and accepts it, the man and device disappear mysteriously. The boy takes the flower home with some other flowers in his little cart. The gift makes a tremendous impact on the villagers, just like a virus. Well, in fact there is a big secret linked to it. Everything that once was blue now turns green, while people line up in front of the stranger (who has returned) to ask for more. Finally everything is cold and blue. The boy, looking around, falls into a mine where he finds his flower being transported, cut down and sprayed to become one of the blue plants.

The King

7:18 Minutes
2D Animation
Producer: Guo Ji
Director/Screenplay: Wu Xiaoyue
Executive Director: Jiang Qinhao
Production Director: Jing Shaozong
Art Consultants: Wang Qiang, Li Jianping
Animation Design: Cheng Hao, Zhang Ze, Qi Zaiqiang, Shan Xiuyin, Zhao Xuejing, Li Bingchi
Music: Liu Jia
Genre: Parable

Synopsis: There is a mysterious castle located in the sky above a beautiful planet. Every night, the King of the Stars has fireworks that light up the whole planet. Toutou is most obsessed with the castle, and he never misses any fireworks show. He always imagines himself in the role of the king. But with his imagination stopped, Toutou would become desperate. Fortunately, his best friend, Meimei, a girl, always will find a way to cheer him up. One day a crown falls from the sky that turns Toutou into the king of his dreams (as the original king has had enough). Wearing the crown, he is extremely excited to climb to the castle and sit on the king's throne. However, a king's life is nothing compared to his imagination. As time goes by, Toutou begins to understand why the old king has abdicated and thrown away his crown. At the same time, he regrets that he has to give it up all and smashes the crown to return to Meimei.

Krum

Animation School of Beijing Film Academy
5:35 Minutes
2D Animation (Prologue), Stop Motion
Presented by Zhang Huijun
Producers: Sun Lijun, Li Jianping, Sun Cong
Genre: Fantasy

Synopsis: A boy who is faintly reminiscent of the *Little Prince* and a dinosaur-like creature share all kinds of joy and play. A story about friendship and wishes.

Lion Dance

CUC Anima, the School of Animation and Digital Arts, Communication University of China, Beijing
4 Minutes
3D Animation
Presented by Su Zhiwu, Liao Xiangzhong
Supervising Producers: Huang Xinyuan, Zheng Weilin
Producers: Lu Shengzhang, Shi Minyong, Jia Xiuqing, Tan Xiao
Executive Producers: Gao Weihua, Suo Xiaoling, Chen Jie
Directors/Screenplay/Storyboard: Duan Wenkai, Mai Weijia
Voice Actors: Gu Zi, Liu Lu, Peng Yao, Hu Xiaoyue, Gao Chong, Sun Megqing, Sun Wenxin, Zou Con, Xu Ziyao, Kang Yan
Faculty Advisers: Wang Lei, Zhang Yilong
Character Design: Ma Weijia
Character Animation: Duan Wenkai
Group Animation: Ma Weijia
Music: Yuan Sihan
Sound Design: Hu Tinglan
Foley Recording and Sound Editing by Hu Tinglan, Zhang Yue
Genre: Comedy

Synopsis: Boy and girl are circus actors and play a lion. The boy, who is taller, always performs the lion's head and the girl the lion's back, which makes the girl very unhappy. A fierce competition ensues. The girl tries to grab the lion's head during the performance, which causes a lot of trouble while dancing on the rope, as all things start to break while they are up there. Finally, they work together to solve the problem and win the applause of the audience.

A Little Pond by the Great Wall

Jilin Animation Institute
6:50 Minutes
Producer: Zheng Liguo
Director: Dmitry Geller
Screenplay: Vladimir Geller
Art Director: Anna Karpova
Genre: Fantasy

Comment: After *I Saw Mice Burying a Cat*, this is the second work by Russian filmmaker and painter Dmitry Geller. Produced in Changchun, China.

Love: The Lost Thing

Animation School of Beijing Film Academy
5:06 Minutes
2D Animation
Music: King of Convenience
Genre: Urban Life/Family

Synopsis: Images of polluted cities and environment:

"My name is Xiaoli Wang, 27 years old, Scorpio, and I am currently working as a tech support in a common design company. From Monday till Friday, depart at 7:10 am., from 'Mudanyuan' to 'Guomao' (Line Ten), then change to Line One till arriving at 'Yonganli' Station, and after a 10-minute-walk, here I am, the place where I have to stay and work for 8 hours a day: The Huarun Technology Limited Company. Oh, yes, and we're not the only company in this building, which is also the reason why I often see new or unknown faces in the elevator, but there were also warm moments, e.g., a phone call from my girlfriend: "Darling, do you want to have dinner with me this evening?" As one sits down on one of those chairs one will notice immediately that a very stressful and boring day is about to begin. Looking at the table that holds a bunch of disorganized files, looking at the notepad where there is an unfinished work record, instantly one feels like a wound-up robot with a specific and accurate workflow: Program, edit, decipher, decode, apply, upload, etc.... Yeah, that's exactly what I do. I don't really care about food, adhering to a principle: a low price, daily special, radically reduced. A simple combination like [images show canned food and drink]. Usually I take my work seriously, but I am not that patient with parents. Typical Scorpion Zodiac sign. Phone ring. It's the protagonist's mother: Well, ok, I know you like the kind of apple sold here. I'll remember that and bring you some home. Hangs up: I was determined to hang up the phone, will return to the keyboard. Can't stand the peaceful and silent attitude on the other side of a phone. When Coco puts her high heels on and leaves the office she may have noticed that we all again managed to pass a stressed day. And of course, again shutdown, elevator, subway, open door, falling into bed... Yes, this is my life."

A nightly phone call interrupts: "Hello? Is this Xiao Li? I'm afraid that your mother... Before your mother passed away, she still talked about that apple... Do you know what that means?"

Xiao Li opens the fridge and there is an apple in the back.

Title: "There are often moments when we ignore simple things, especially those that can be done by one person. Because we didn't take it seriously enough, happiness will often slip away from us. A seemingly minor thing, but different people view the meaning differently.

It is no small matter to make our lives have more well-being and happiness, less sorrow and regret!"

Comment: Graphically designed using a black-and-white multiple-image screen; for instance, on the left the narrator working frantically, on the right a humanized robot.

Make a Wish

Animation School of Beijing Film Academy
7:32 Minutes
Producer: Zhang Huijun
Director/Scenarist: Luo Qiuyi
Storyboard: Li Yun
Production Managers: Sun Lijun, Li Jianping, Sun Cong
Art Directors: Huang Yong, Sun Cong
Character Design: Luo Qiuyi, Zou Yunting
Background Design: Gu Fangyu, Li Yue, Luo Qiuyi, Shi Wenjie, Zou Yunting
2D Animation: Gu Fangyu, Shi Wenjie
Editor: Zou Yunting
Genre: Kid's Fantasy

Synopsis: A little girl meets a living wish lantern and hopes that her dream will come true once she makes a wish. However, the futile lantern will leave the girl and go back to heaven.

Miss Rope and Mr. Can

CUC Anima, the Animation and Digital Arts School of Communication University of China, Beijing
5 Minutes
2D Animation
Producers: Lu Shengzhang, Jin Xinqing, Shi Minyong, Tan Xiao
Supervising Producers: Huang Xingyuan, Zheng Weilin
Executive Producers: Suo Xiaoliao, Gao Weihua, Chen Jie
Directors/Screenplay/Storyboard/Digital Compositing: Du Yinghan, Chen Ran
Presented by Su Zhiwu, Liao Xiangzhong
Faculty Adviser: Liu Dayu
Scene Design: Chen Ran
Character Design/Animation: Du Yinghan
Sound Design: Chang Yun
Original Music: Zhu Suoyun
Genre: Youth Culture/Love Story

Synopsis: An Otaku girl falls in love with an Otaku boy who lives downstairs in the same house, but both are too shy to communicate with each other.

A delivery boy rings at the door. A woman's feet come from the shower. She has stored a lot of tins and bottles of water in the fridge and the kitchen.

When she looks outside there is a cat playing with her clothes that she has hung on a line. Her bra lands on the bamboo-pole dryer that belongs to her neighbor living downstairs. When she tries to get it hooked on a rope, she ends outside in Harold Lloyd–like stunts. She lands downstairs and enters the room, with the neighbor's underpants in her hands. When she leaves she sees the boy upstairs at her room. He wants to return her bra. It turns out that he is her anonymous friend.

Mu

Animation School of Beijing Film Academy
8:02 Minutes
Executive Producer: Zhang Liangyuxiao
Co-Producers: Sun Lijun, Li Jianping, Sun Cong, Huang Yong
Director/Screenplay: Shao Xueqing
Voice Actors: Shao Xueqing (Xian), Cao Jinwu (Mu), Yuan Meng (Mum), Mo Jiashan (Physician)
Storyboard: Shao Xueqing, Zhang Mingxi
Presented by Zhang Huijun
Instructors: Liu Xian, Xu Zheng
Character Design: Cao Jinwu, Zhang Liangyuxiao
Background Design: Cao Jinwu, Yang Yiwei
First Key Animation: Cao Jinwu, Zhang Liangyuxiao
Second Key Animation: Yang Lei, Sun Weijun
Music: Kazuyo Lin
Vanguard-Sound Studio
Sound Effects: Li Yixuan
Genre: Kid's Fantasy

Synopsis: Xian, a blind boy, has had surgery to recover his vision.

A worried mother approaches the surgeon who is operating on her kid: "Doctor, how is he?"

"I have told you before. There is a low rate of success at that type of surgery because the kid has been blind for many years."

"Doctor, please!"

The doctor leaves.

"You cannot give up! Doctor!"

Upon leaving: "We will try our best to save him."

We hear the voice of the blind boy, who is afraid of possible failure:

"Will I be able to see again? What could I do if the surgery has failed?"

Suddenly he hears the voice of another kid.

He escapes from reality and enters his inner world.

"Why can I see you?" he asks.

The voice belongs to a little, one-eyed, bag-like monster. The little guy gives the kid a flower.

"This is my flower?! You are able to let me see what I know?"

The monster makes the boy feel well and prepares a children's room for him.

"How about I call you Mu?" Xian asks.

The monster accepts the name happily.

At home. The boy's eyes are bandaged. Mother helps him to eat his meal: "Eat some more and then we need to remove the gauze."

Xian leaves, desperate.

"What on earth is he thinking about?" Mother wants to know.

In his dream world Xian is returning to Little Mu.

Together they visit a vivid, colorful world of joy and laughter that is populated by all kind of funny, toy-like beings.

Then the forest.

After that, like Nils Holgersson, Xian is riding on back of a peacock.

Under water, both he and Mu ride in a bubble.

Mother doesn't know what's going on in the boy's mind. She knees down while he is sitting on his bed in the dark, but there is much light in his mind.

Suddenly he feels that Mu is going:

"Mu, are you going because I have to remove the gauze? Well, I won't remove it. If you are gone and I still cannot see, I will lose everything!"

Xian has tears in his eyes, but Mu leads him back into the light.

The boy realizes then that he has his mother on his side all the time and decides that it's time to go back: "Thank you, Mu!"

For a last time, they hug each other.

While Mu gently strikes the boy's face, Xian removes the gauze. First there again are images from his imagination.

"Mum!"

He sees his mother waiting for him under a rainbow, opening her arms to welcome him back into life. After seven days he has recovered, and wonders if one day he will meet Mu again.

Comment: A very poetic and sensitive plot.

Musical Chairs

Guangzhou Academy of Fine Arts

3:47 Minutes
Directors: Du Yukai, Tang Ya
Original Soundtrack: Wang Jingfei (Communication University of China)
Genre: Experimental Animation

Synopsis: The game of musical chairs is illustrated by computer graphics. The main character represents the human race. The human, in his selfish way, discovers that he can't bear the consequences of his own actions. The whole setup of this simple game tries to depict a society in which people want to get more and more to fulfill their insatiable desires. Maybe humans will win, but perhaps on the route they will lose something of greater importance.

My Grandpa

CUC Anima, the School of Animation and Digital Arts of Communication University of China, Beijing
4:36 Minutes
2D Animation
Supervising Producers: Huang Xinyuan, Zheng Weilin
Producers: Lu Shengzhang, Jia Xiuping, Shi Minyong, Tan Xiao
Executive Producers: Suo Xiadong, Gao Weihua, Chen Jie
Director/Screenplay/Animation/Digital Compositing/Editor: Hu Yuhan
Presented by Su Zhiwu, Liao Xiangzhong
Faculty Advisers: Hong Fan, Zhang Yue
Original Music: Fan Weiping (Central Conservatory of Music)
Voice Actors: Hu Yuhan, Dong Siyuan
Genre: Family/Kid's Memory

Synopsis: "Hand in hand, with love till life ends, was not much reflected in my grandparent's life."

"I would leave him if I were twenty years younger!" Grandmother said during a family party. Grandpa and Grandma, as I knew them, got along just fine despite some small quarrels they had from time to time. For the most part, it was due to Grandpa's slightly fey personality. Grandpa often ignored the fact that he was not allowed to smoke for health concerns. He thought we couldn't do much as long as he never admitted it. To avoid direct confrontation, Grandpa went to great lengths to hide cigarettes in various places. Finding those was never so difficult for Grandma, who after all had lived with him for more than half a century. I couldn't imagine how unbearable life was going to be for Grandpa without smoking. But there was more than just smoking. Grandpa's consciousness about saving money was somewhat extraordinary. Expired food? There was no such thing. Sometimes, to save food, he could be incredibly vigilant and agile."

As Grandma lets fall some food to the ground, we see him using his chopsticks and pick it up.

"Having said that, Grandpa was actually a very generous person to others. Coming home from shopping, Grandma was often greeted by all sorts of surprise guests." (Drawings include a blind person, a brontosaurus, an extra-terrestrial.)

"To his family, Grandpa's expression of love was more elusive. Every Saturday he would call us at six in the morning and tell us that everything was fine, then quickly hang up. Strangely enough, Grandpa had always been very quiet every time we visited him. He just fell asleep for the most part. That said, after many years I figured that Grandpa must have enjoyed those moments in his own unique way. After dinner Grandpa would wake up, as everyone was about to leave. Seeing him and Grandma looking at us through the window became my fondest memory of him. I would always look back, waving arms in the air and shout to them: See you next week! Just like this, day after day, like a petal in the wind. One day, I realized Grandpa was no longer with us."

Comment: The student devoted this short to the memory of his grandfather who in caricature resembles UPA's *Mister Magoo* and in his own right seemed to have been quite a character: "This work tells stories about my grandpa, who was a stubborn and odd man but had a very kind and generous heart. His unique way of expressing individuality and feelings was elusive and sometimes brought headaches to the family. But there was always bliss and completeness in the family when he was around. Many years have passed since he left us; we all still miss him very much." Like many other sentimental pieces, this one uses piano music.

My Little World

CUC Anima, the Animation and Digital Arts School of Communication University of China, Beijing
6:06 Minutes
2D Animation
Supervising Producers: Hang Xinyuan, Zheng Weilin

Producers: Lu Shengzhang, Jia Yinqing, Shi Minyong, Tan Xiao
Executive Producers: Suo Xiaoling, Gao Weihua, Chen Jie
Directors/Animation: Chen Mengqian, Liu Jiao
Screenplay: Chen Mengqian
Storyboard: Liu Jiao
Presented by Su Zhiwu, Liao Yiangzheng
Faculty Adviser: Liu Dayu
Music: Fu Leng, Chen Sha, Yang Shihan
Genre: Kid's Story

Synopsis: "Everyone is a star in the sky.

Some are shining, lighten up in the sky in one place or another.

Others don't. But they still exist, only hiding under the quilt, didn't make a sound."

A shy girl introduces herself: "My name is YunYun. I'm five years old." Her grandma has told her that she has to learn math and to prove she can, she multiplies: "One multiply three is three, one multiply four is four, one multiply five is five ... four ... five ... six ... seven ... eight." YunYun counts. "Teacher told us people are socially connected. She shows children's drawings in her book who hold hands and asks: 'Are we connected like a train? Or like a spider net?'"

"Where do babies come from? Are they falling from the sky? Or growing from the ground?"

YunYun is unable to communicate with others easily, but she likes tearing paper by herself as her way of playing with other kids. In her world, there's only the things she likes and those she doesn't like. YunYun's monologue tells things she likes and doesn't like.

"Why are there four seasons? Is it because the Earth wears a hat?"

She has drawn a friendly-faced Earth with a hat.

"He covers himself up with a white quilt when it turns to winter. When he picks off the hat, it turns to summer."

Lying on her bed: "Why do I have to go to kindergarten?" In the bathroom: "Every day, so boring. Mum says I have to go to kindergarten to learn knowledge."

Surrounded by giant birds of her imagination: "I don't like wearing the school uniform. This uniform is so ugly. Not as beautiful as that one."

She wears a yellow skirt—and the paradise birds seem to agree to her choice.

At breakfast table: "I don't like having meals. I don't like eating pumpkin. I don't like eating red dates. I also hate matrimony vine. Mum always told me there is a Miss Tomato

living in my stomach. I have to eat Mr. Cauliflower, so that Miss Tomato and Mr. Cauliflower can finally meet. Another thing: I don't like to cross the street. There are so many cars on the street. I pass the street. What about my shadow? My shadow will be run down by cars. I don't like to see right through other people's eyes because when those people look at me it seems to spur a monster to eat me. I don't like to call my nickname: Watermelon Peel. Others call me Mushroom, Little Mushroom."

She stresses her imagination and sees herself falling into the sea: "But I like playing underwater, see all the different things underwater. Turn in the light when I sleep. The light turn into a little bear. The bear will keep me company. Little bear, sleep with me, play with me."

"I also like tearing paper because I can tear paper into a little fairy. Also tear paper into a lot of animals. The sound of tearing paper is like a melody to me."

The cut-paper moves in her imagination very much like something right out of the films animated by Norman McLaren: birds, an octopus, monkeys, fish, monsters.

Suddenly three other kids turn up and ask her what she is doing.

After awhile: "I'm tearing paper."

The kids laugh, but their shadows join and float to the nightly sky.

Nature Selection

Youth Film Studio
Cofound Graduation Films
Animation School of Beijing Film Academy
9:12 Minutes
2D Animation
Genre: Fantasy

Synopsis: In ancient times a mysterious artifact appeared on earth that passed its mighty power to the chosen species: wisdom and technology that would advance upcoming generations to a new era. And it proved one thing: Everything has its own circle.

Animals are the first to plunder the artifact. The scene changes to 3,500 years later. Humanized animals, bulls, sheep and horses, have a problem as their weapons are put back to the stone age by the energy force of alien spacecraft commanded by reptile beings. The artifact throws them back in evolution.

The scene changes to 10,000 years later. An ape man finds the artifact.

Hum

The Old House Story

Animation School of Beijing Film Academy
10:21 Minutes
2D Animation
Producer: Zhang Huijun
Production Managers: Sun Lijun, Li Jianping, Sun Cong, Li Liang, Huang Yong
Producers/Screenplay: Zhu Yuchen, Mao Jianxing, Fan Xiangman, Yang Jiajie, Li Shuo
Executive Producer: Yang Jiajie
Director/Storyboard/Character Design: Zhu Yuchen
Art Advisers: Liu Xian, Xu Zheng
Art Directors: Zhu Yuchen, Yang Jiajie
Key Animation: Zhu Yuchen, Mao Jianxing, Fang Xiangman, Li Shuo
Sound Designer: Lv Xiaoxiao
Editor: Zhu Yuchen
Dedicated to Ren Nuyi
Genre: Parable
Synopsis: In a small, old house located near an atomic power plant in a shabby area of town, there live four families. But they hate each other. One night, something magical happens that is going to change their lives. An electrical charge is hitting the house. The old man goes to look into the mirror when he wakes up, and is shocked to see a dog face, with his own dog barking. When he opens the door he finds out that everybody living under the roof has changed too. One man instead of his head wears a complete toilet; another, a big hammer; a boy, a football. After a while the house begins to collapse. But the changed people seem to be happier than before.

The Other Side of the Trestle

CUC Anima, the Animation and Digital Arts School of Communication University of China, Beijing
7:04 Minutes
2D Animation
Producers: Lu Shengzhang, Jia Xiuqing, Shi Minyong, Tan Xiao
Executive Producers: Suo Xiaoling, Gao Weihua, Chen Jie
Directors/Character Design/Animation/Editors: Jiang Ning, Bao Haojun
Screenplay: Jiang Ning, Wang Zhuoxi
Presented by Su Zhiwu
Faculty Advisers: Gao Weihua, Li Wei
Scene Design: Bao Haojun, Wang Zhuoxi
Music Guide: Fu Long
Music: Sun Yuming, Liu Hao
Sound Design: Zhang Yue, Suo Yun, Wang Zhuoxi
Genre: Fantasy

Synopsis: A little girl living in the mountains falls down a cliff on the way home from school and dies. Her soul is a ferret passing through the door of life and death, and thus able to be reborn. A dream boy with green eyes helps and carries her back to life. The boy cannot follow her back into life, but there are her parents, who find her.
Comment: Inspired by Hayao Miyazaki.

Red

Beijing Normal University College of Art and Communication/Media Lab
12:12 Minutes
Stop Motion
Executive Producers: Tao Zhiqiang, Liu Shaolong, Zhu Peng, Hao Duan
Director/Producer/Screenplay/Art Director: Tao Zhiqiang
Supervisors: Lv Bing, Meng Zhao, Shan Liang, Zhou Pengbo
Production Managers: Cao Yan, Xia Xin
Music: Ma Yuan, Sun Xiaosong
Genre: History
Synopsis: Set during the Japanese occupation of Shanghai.

"My name is Xiao Tian, from Nagasaki. My father died in Northeastern China in the warfare. Now only my mother and my little sister are at home. I was sent here to be the supplementary soldier from Shanghai last week."

He is wounded and would prefer to go home. He gives a girl a red scarf. In war there is love and hate.

Chinese people protest: "Beat Japanese imperialism. Beat Fascism. Return our territory."

Chinese soldiers are executed by Japanese. Xiao Tian is slain by a Chinese soldier with a stone.

The Song for Rain

CUC Anima, the School for Animation and Digital Arts of Communication University of China, Beijing
8:11 Minutes
2D Animation
Producer: Lu Zhengshang
Executive Producer: Gao Weihua
Director/Screenplay/Storyboard/Art Direction/Animation/Editor: Zheng Yawen
Presented by Su Zhiwu, Liao Xiangzheng
Faculty Adviser: Li Zhiyang
Genre: Fantasy

Synopsis: A rainy city. A boy with an umbrella sees a little fox trying to gather falling rain into a leaky bag. He decides to help the fox. When the fox takes a red umbrella, they find out that it works better for collecting water than the leaky bag does. So the boy wins the confidence of the animal and discovers the magical place the animal has traveled from in search of rain. The fox uses the rain to water some flowers in a garden. Somehow the boy loses the fox, but he is glad when he comes home and finds a flower besides the umbrella.

Comment: "Dedicated to Nature."

A Star-Spangled Journey

Animation School of Beijing Film Academy

2D Animation

10:04 Minutes

Producers: Sun Lijun, Li Jianping, Sun Cong

Executive Producers: Sun Ping, Yu Feng

Director/Screenplay/Character Designer/ Scene Designer/Storyboard/Backgrounds: Zhang Xiaojue

Voice Actors: Hou Wen (Jojo), Liang Sida (Cantonese), Qi Wanning (Teacher), William Back Wu (Victor), Jeffrey Schwab (Waiter), Stanley Seiden (Student)

Art Supervisors: Li Jianping, Hui Zheng, Huang Jianfeng

Layout: Liu Ji, Yu Feng

Action Designer: Yu Feng, Zhang Xiaojue

Animation Supervisor: Zhang Yi

Animation: Liu Ji, Zhang Jing, Zhai Jingcheng, Huang Jiangfeng, Zhang Yi, Liu Yiaoying

Visual Effects Supervisor: Zhao Wenzhu

Sound Designer: Wang Shuangshuang

Original Soundtrack: Dai Huazhang

Genre: Student's Life

Synopsis: A female Chinese exchange student visits the United States. We hear her voice as she prepares for the stay: "The distance between Beijing and San Francisco is 10,301 kilometers." Then takeoff, landing, passport control, heavy luggage. "It's your first time in the U.S., isn't it?" "Hm." "Congratulations, you are in the most beautiful city of the country. People sleep quite early here, unlike the nightlife in China, so vibrant. Your landlord is Cantonese. But don't worry, she is very nice. If you go to school, walk downhill along the street. Turn left when you reach Holloway Avenue. The school is full of people. Sleep well."

Next morning in a class at the Fine Arts Department of San Francisco State University. They clap when the new one enters the classroom. She feels at the center of attraction. Fireworks, you name it. But actually, it's just imagination. Nobody really takes notice of her. Eventually the teacher introduces her: "Morning everyone. This is Jojo. She is an exchange student from Beijing Film Academy. Jojo, are you ready to introduce yourself to the class?" Jojo looks around, obviously terrified, missing the words. "Oh my god, she told me yesterday that I didn't need to do this." Then recovering and gaining some courage: "Ok, good morning, everyone!" In stylized images she introduces herself: "My name is Jojo. I come from China. I'm studying in Beijing Film Academy. My ... er ... my ... animation." "Major." "Yeah, my major is animation. I will be here for this semester with you guys. Okay, that's all." She is finished.

Next day a fat black boy wheels on his chair towards her to make contact: "Hey Jojo, how's it going? I like you." "What?" "Because you are the new one here. I know all the other classmates way too long. It's kinda boring, actually." Then a question: "So do you like Superman?" "I did see the film, but ..." "Ok," the boy interrupts. "That means you like the comic book?" "Actually, I haven't read them." The boy produces a picture of Superman: "See... Look what I have here? Superman, yeah. Batman, yeah. You are Superwoman. Ok, stop. I can loan it to you if you want. By the way, I'm Victor." He wheels away shouting: "Superman!" Another day, another guy turning up in the cafeteria while she studies the menu: "Hi, my name is Jeffrey. I will be server tonight. Are you ready to order?" He recommends "surf and turf kebab and beer crackling chicken. Personally I would choose the beer crackling chicken because people love it. But my wife tried it and she hated it because there is ..." Another customer agrees: "Yeah, my mom says it smells like too much garlic." Jojo makes her choice: "Ok, I'm ready. Can I have one of these?" "Ok, no problem. Which sauce would you like. We have BBQ Sauce/ketchup/mustard/mayo/ranch/honey mustard." "...er ..." She feels like she is packed in ice. "Mustard," the server decides himself. "How do you like your eggs? Scrambled or sunny side up?" "What?" "Scrambled," he decides again. "Oki doki, scrambled. How do you like your steak cooked?" Finally I got one that I understand, Jojo thinks and orders: "Six to seven." "Sorry," he sings. "I mean rare/ medium rare/medium well/well done."

Pause. "Medium well, thanks. Excellent. Coming right up."

It's so difficult to get accustomed to an unknown world, from people to food to architecture.

Comment: Personal account of an animation student's trip abroad, handled in a very colorful style with nicely done background art. From the images, we know that the student enjoyed her stay greatly.

Subwars

CUC Anima, the Animation and Digital Arts School of Communication University of China, Beijing
5:10 Minutes
Producers: Lu Shengzhang, Shi Minyong, Jia Xiuqing, Ye Jing, Zheng Weilin
Executive Producers: Gao Weihua, Suo Xiaoling
Director/Layout/Storyboard: Sean Soong
Presented by Su Zhiwu
Supervising Producers: Liao Xiangzhong, Huang Xinyuan
Animation: Sean Soong
Animation Advisers: Li Wei, Cheng Teng
Inbetweening: He Dongxin, Sean Soong
Ink and Paint: He Dongxin, Zhang Zhe, Xie Xiaoyu, Sean Soong
Digital Composition: Sean Soong
Composition Adviser: Ai Shengying
Faculty Advisers: Xue Yanping, Hong Fan, Yang Xiaojun
Editing: Li Xia, Sean Soong
Original Music and Sound Design: Ayo Chen
Genre: Macabre Fantasy
Synopsis: An old, bearded man, wearing a cap with a Red Star but otherwise looking like Father Christmas, enters a subway car. Suddenly he produces a laser sword, right out of *Star Wars*, and attacks the passengers, causing panic and bloodshed. Some young people try to oppose him but are beaten. Some cartoon characters turn up, including Inspector Black Cat, R2D2 and martial arts figures, and fire with machine guns, but nothing can stop the old man, who seems to command supernatural powers. In the end it turns out to be a kid's dream—or is it?

The Thief and the Hat

LX Studio
The School of Media and Animation, China Academy of Art
3:12 Minutes
Executive Producers: Han Hui, Huang Dawei
Director/Screenplay/Character and Scene Design: Liu Xinxin

Guidance Teachers/Tutors: Huang Dawei, Yu Jin, Yang Mai
Animation and Color Style: Liu Xinxin, Shen Yaqiang
Sound Design: Ji Hang
Sound Director: Liu Xiaoshan
Genre: Fantasy
Synopsis: A fight between three persons—a tall, slim one, a short, fat one, and a boy—and the moon. Apparently the moon has stolen one of their hats, so the three decide to go there and get the hat back. They try various methods but all fail. Finally, the tall one jumps up and gets the cap, but the moon, changing to human proportions, protests and takes it back.
Comment: Inspired by the Pixar short *La Luna*.

Wall

Zhen Yuan Animation Studio
Animation Department of Communication University of China at Nanjing
7:58 Minutes
Executive Producers: Liu Jinan, Ding Haiyun
Producer: Zhang Huilin
Co-Producer: Xu Dingkai
Producer: Shen Da
Director/Storyboard/Art Supervisor/Editor: Gu Zhihai
Screenplay: Gu Zhihai, Zheng Hao, Liu Xinlu, Shen Da, Liu Lei
Instructor: Hu Wei
Design: Zheng Hao, Liu Xinlu
Animation: Gu Zhihai, Liu Lei
Special Effects: Shen Da, Gu Zhihai
Music and Sound: Wang Siyun
Genre: Childhood Memory/History
Synopsis: A simple story of a father and son that takes place in the 1970s and 1980s, with some relics of the Cultural Revolution still around and a red flag providing some color. Some misunderstandings between the father and son are like an invisible wall. With the development of society, this wall experiences a series of changes from new to old, from being dismantled to being reconstructed. But with time passing by, it just fades away.
Comment: "This short film is specially dedicated to our hardworking parents!"

A reflection about the changes in people's lives as well as their spirits. Black-and-white computer animation with color spots worked in.

Who Touched the Feather

10:20 Minutes

Beijing Institute of Fashion Technology
Directors/Screenplay: Xu Zheng Yue, Yu Xiao
    Guang
Modeling Design/Background Design: Yu Xiao
    Guang, Xu Zheng Yue
Movement Design: Yu Xiao Guang
Recording: Wang Xin
Guiding Teacher/Tutor: Chang Wei
Genre: Nature
    Synopsis: The story of a late autumn forest,
with wind whistling. Several different bird
characters are introduced.
    Comment: Cut-out animation and Chinese
paintings combined with stop-motion tech-
niques.

Wine Woman
3:55 Minutes
2D Animation
    Synopsis: A story that occurred in the
Shanxing pubs tells of a timid young man
with a lean old lady. He has come to have a
drink beforehand, sweating, as he is afraid of
women. Then she turns up, a beautiful girl,
but when he tries to touch her an old lady intervenes.

A Wolf in the Tree
9:30 Minutes
Director: Lin Jiaxing
Genre: Fantasy Comedy
    Synopsis: Little Red Riding Hood wants to
seduce the Wolf but he's not very interested.

Zombies vs. Plants
Jilin Animation Institute, Animation and Car-
    toon School, Changchun

7:54 Minutes
3D Animation
Producer: Zheng Liguo
Associate Producer: Rita
Directors: Jackie Liu, Jacob
Screenplay: Jackie Liu
Storyboard: Jackie Liu
Character Designer: Li Peng
Scene Designers: Li Peng, Feng Man
Production Designer: Jackie Liu
Animation Supervisor: Jacob
Textures and Lighting Supervisor: Jackie Liu
Modeling Supervisors: Jacob, Alvin Zhang
Effects Supervisor: Rita
Animation: Wang Yitao, Wang Guanxiang, Li
    Yang, Zou Fen, Sun Jinyi, Yu Zhixin, Zhang
    Yingjie, Windy, Adam, Doven, Liu Shiqun,
    Zhou Ze, Adrain, Fu Yijin
Music and Sound Effects: Jackie Liu
Editor: Jackie Liu
Administration of Networks: Lin Yanqiang
Genre: Sci-Fi Comedy
    Synopsis: We see in what might be a desert
town a zombie worker fleeing from giant
flowers, then arrested by them. There are
other zombies in cages, and the plants are
experimenting. But the worker resists, slaps
the plants in the face and frees the others. A
battle between zombies and plants follows.
It looks as if the zombies will make it, but
suddenly their march is stopped by a gigantic, man-eating plant. Then there is a fight
between the man-eating plant and a robot
that is radio-controlled by the zombie worker
and beats the plant. In the end, they get the
worker, who is brainwashed, and his essence
is absorbed to the benefit of the plants.

≫ Selected Animated Science ≪
and Educational Films

2011

Interesting Lecture About Time and Space
6 Minutes
Creator: Li Wei
    Synopsis: Jil and his friends bring audi-
ences a joyful learning experience.

The Result of Carelessness
Xiamen Thumb Animation Co., Ltd.
1:57 Minutes
    Synopsis: Tiantian uses an automatic bar-
becue machine brought from Big Devil Lord
to celebrate Duoduo's birthday, but unfortunately the machine doesn't work. Although
the Big Devil Lord repairs the machine,
Tiantian is still angry. Her friend Rui tells her
about detailed legal regulations and reminds

her that when buying products, she should check their safety in order to protect herself and others.

    Comment: Encourage children to protect their rights.

Thumb Education Series
Xiamen Thumb Animation Co., Ltd.
3 Minutes Per Episode
    Comment: An amiable grandpa tells children about the things of life; for instance: What is blood circulation?

 # Selected Animated Commercials

2009

Laughing in Jianghu: The Rising of Magic Religion
Perfect World Media Center
1:37 Minutes
    Comment: CG spot promoting the company's net game of same title.

2010

The Adventures of Star Cat: An Advertisement of Adventure in Ancient City
3 Minutes
Directors: Jin Bo, Hu Yingzhi

    Comment: An advertisement broadcast that is popular throughout China.

BMW Spot
1 Minute
Creator: Duan Fei
    Comment: Demonstrates the advantages of BMW cars through animation software.

Laughing in Jianghu: The Final Fight
Perfect World Media Center
2 Minutes
    Synopsis: Fight between the leader of the Sun and the Moon Religion Oriental Undefeated and Lin Huchong.
    Comment: Second CG spot to promote the

Opening of Jilin Animation Museum in September 2011. *Left to right:* **Rolf Giesen, Anna Khan, Chang Guangxi, Zheng Liguo (courtesy JAI).**

Internet game of the same title. Lots of Chinese-ink special effects.

Subaru WRC

1:46 Minutes
Director: Wei Chunming
   Comment: When talking about sports cars, Chinese fans first will think of Subaru.

When You Believe

4:33 Minutes
Director: Luo Ke
   Comment: MTV music video.

2011

Alcoholic Alcohol

1 Minute
Creator: Yang Dengyun
   Synopsis: All friends gather to taste precious alcohol.
   Comment: Advertisement for Hunan Alcoholic Alcohol Co., Ltd. It adapts traditional Chinese ink animation, using Chinese painting as the background, to present the characteristics of both Chinese alcohol culture and the local custom of adoring Ghost God in Western Shanxi.

Bathe

10:30 Minutes
Director: Wei Wenjun
Screenplay: Li Wanqing
   Synopsis: Blue Elves cross time and space and arrive in a magic bathing world.
   Comment: Promote ideas for future products of Glory Water Heating Group by using the cartoon images of the company, the Blue Elves.

Continent of God and Devil

2:16 Minutes
Director: Wang Xiao
   Comment: CG animation based on Continent of God and Devil, produced by Perfect World Net Technology Co., Ltd., Beijing.

Fortune Center

2:47 Minutes
Creators: Zhang Yi, Lin Xiaojun
   Synopsis: By accurate analysis, aliens search on Earth for the best working platform and eventually focus on Fortune Center.
   Comment: Spectacular visual language creates a vision of future that sets the theme of "The Green Leads the Future," presenting the advantages of "green" architecture.

The Yitian Sword and the Dragon-Killing Knife

Beijing Perfect World Net Technology Co., Ltd., Media Center
2:14 Minutes
   Comment: Promoting the company's Internet game.

Mobile Content and Webtoons: A World in Flash Animation

Nearly eighty percent of Chinese animation is Flash animation. Basically, Flash is cheap animation. It is used for mobile content that is spreading like wildfire all over China.

But there is more to Flash than just opening new venues for business. Mobile content is provided on the Internet largely by industry, but also by individuals.

Wu Weihua and Steve Fore ask,

How does the Chinese animation industry move beyond the dichotomy between political and commercial orientations in the context of a contemporary postmodern, postsocialist culture? An answer might lie in the brief history of Flash in China, its origins as a decentralized Internet-based medium, and in the motivations of its practitioners and fans....

Flash animators have faced some of the aesthetic and socio-political dilemmas that have been common to innovative Chinese artists in all media since early in the XX century: how to articulate (and rearticulate) the grand narrative of China's modernization, and how to deal with the pressure to create nostalgic images of China that may be more comforting to overseas audiences, but are in fact little more than orientalist mythologies. Since the mid–1980s, China's Fifth and Sixth Generation film directors and reform era avant-garde visual artists have explored avenues of self-expression and artistic experimentation in ways that had been explored by some Flash animators, and these journeys of discovery have taken place in a public arena far closer to the center of contemporary popular culture trends and aspirations than most Chinese fine artists and art filmmakers have been able to venture. In a very real sense, to understand Chinese Flash is indeed to understand the postmodern turn of cultural identity in the digital era.[23]

These words seem exaggerated when viewing some of the amateurish work. Nevertheless, there are new approaches visible.

⇒ Selected Mobile Animation ⇐

2010

Animation Show of Qizhi Meeting Da Bing
Episodes Totaling 777 Minutes
Directors: Qizhi, Da Bing
　Synopsis: Qizhi and Bing are the representatives of Southern Crosstalk. They perform in the Hunan accent and create unprecedented comedy effects.
　Comment: The series set a new record for domestic animation sale price per minute.

The Awkward Marriage
Gold Leopard Animation
1 Minute
　Synopsis: Funny, absurd marriage story illustrated with cute images.

Awkward Twelve Constellations
Gold Leopard Animation
3 Minutes
　Synopsis: The twelve constellations combined with absurd action.

The Black Box
1:20 Minutes per episode
Director: Chen Liaoyu
　Synopsis: A compendium of clips.
　Comment: Composed of 2D, 3D and mobile facial expressions. Each edition includes several short films.

Mobile Man: Love Plugin
2:31 Minutes
Director: Zhao Yu
　Synopsis: A love story of mobile man Aska and his girlfriend Kemi.

Mobile Man: Memory Can't Be Deleted
2:47 Minutes
Director: Zhao Yu
　Synopsis: More about Aska and Kemi.

On the Way
Director: Chen Lijiang
　Synopsis: The daily affairs of three white-collar colleagues working in the same company and taking the same bus.

Star Cat's Opusculum
6 Minutes
Director: Fan Xiaoning
　Comment: Star Cat looks somewhat like a simplified version of Garfield.

A Warm Couple
5 Minutes per episode
Director: Chen Ningpei
　Synopsis: Sweet love stories.

2011

Bao's Fashion Life: Ceremony of Becoming Buddha
2:23 Minutes
Director: Zhou Ruilan
　Synopsis: Xuanzang, played by Bao, arrives with his three disciples in Heaven after going through many difficulties. Buddha holds a grand ceremony in their honor so that they will become like him. While feeling happy, Xuanzang and his disciples leave as tragic figures.

Children Say What They Like

1 Minute
Director: Zhou Zhizhong
Synopsis: The adult world in Loli's eyes.

Clap Your Hands

1 Minute
Director: Zhu Tengbin
Synopsis: Several children sing the song "Clap Your Hands If Feeling Happy" in English and Chinese and dance to it.

Crazy Hedgehog

2 Minutes
Director: Huo Wenxian
Synopsis: Stories about the crazy hedgehog family and its friends.
Comment: Cross-media content that includes Microsoft MSN, Tencent mobile, and Guangdong TV mobile.

The Dream of a Potato Man

1:20 Minutes
Director: Lin Zhi
Comment: The short mainly reflects the choices many young people are going to face in their lives. The little episode tells about the contradiction of social dreams and private, personal demands.

The Evolution of Word "Dust"

72.8 Seconds
Director: Hu Jun
Synopsis: By a new interpretation of the word "dust," the short shows environmental changes. Overcutting of trees reduces the number of deer (which are the preferred method of transportation), and the overuse of cars instead of deer will destroy the green homeland, create more dust and pollute the environment.

Fish and Net

Xiamen Thumb Animation Co., Ltd.
4:06 Minutes
Synopsis: A story of how unity makes strength, told by using the example of a fish and a net. One small fish is caught by a net of Cat Happy. The fish pursues the net lines to loosen their grip and escapes with its friends. The cat, realizing what has happened, is upset.

Flower Tower Elves

Xiamen Thumb Animation Co., Ltd.
19 Seconds
Synopsis: Spring is evident everywhere. Beautiful flower tower elves, dressed in costumes, smile while bathing in an endless sea of flowers. One elf picks a bunch of flowers that ride on the wind and flies with the other elves, through the quiet forest and on the warm spring wind.

HI-13

Boxin Animation
20 Minutes
Synopsis: A young guy wants to be cool and leave a good impression on his girlfriend, but mainly fails to do so.

Lovable Unnamed Women

Boxin Animation
20 Minutes
Synopsis: The hard blind-date experience of a woman, above the average age for marriage, who wears a Cherry Tomato headgear.

Love as This

2 Minutes
Director: Hu Guilin
Synopsis: What is love? You separate and make peace again, on and on, finally returning to the starting point: If we were like at the first sight...
Comment: This animation doesn't tell people anything. It just wants to provoke and make them think.

Nomo's Travel in Fujian

Xiamen Xiangfong Information Science and Technology Co., Ltd.
7:43 Minutes
Synopsis: The Nomo are a couple of Flash-animated octopuses that live under the sea. They love each other and are not bothered by materials. They come to the beautiful southern part of Fujian and want to live there as husband and wife but on the way have quite a few adventures.

Selfish Giant

Xiamen Thumb Animation Co., Ltd.
5:20 Minutes
Synopsis: The story of a giant who has the most beautiful garden in the world, which he doesn't allow anyone else to play in it. The birds are unhappy and tell the Northern Wind, Snow and Hail. They decide to punish the giant and let him always live in winter. One day spring comes and the giant sees the

children secretly coming to his garden to play. Finally he realizes that kids are the most beautiful flowers. Therefore he pulls down the wall and lives with the children happily every day.

Comment: Based on a story by Oscar Wilde that has been turned to animation repeatedly.

Stop When the Light Is Red, and Walk When Green

Net Dragon Company
2:23 Minutes

Synopsis: Pipi Monkey's mother knows how active her son is and reminds him repeatedly to be careful when crossing the road. Mother also tells him to walk on the Zebra when crossing and above all to obey the main traffic rule, "Stop When the Light Is Red, and Walk When Green."

The Stupid Thief and a Telephone

3 Minutes
Director: Yang Luonan

Synopsis: A gunman wants to kidnap and blackmail but fails again and again when using a telephone.

Two Naughty Guys

Net Dragon Company
2:01 Minutes

Synopsis: Wangwang Doggy and Taotao Rabbit are always quarreling and fighting noisily in kindergarten. Suddenly in the washroom, they fall to the ground. At lunch they fight over the hot soup. Wangwang Doggy's nose is burnt and he is sent to the hospital.

You Can Choose

1 Minute
Director: Cai Min

Synopsis: Different choices made by people facing nature. Let's make the earth more beautiful. Greedy demands might pollute earth and destroy our living environments.

Comment: The two main characters are designed according to finger's image, meaning that everything starts from your hand. So does environmental protection. In style, it is like children's paintings.

 Selected Webtoons

2001

Xiao-Xiao/Xiao Xiao Zuo Pin

Director: Zhu Zhiqiang

Synopsis: Part 1 shows two kung fu character fighting. The next parts are more ambitious as they involve more characters: Part 2 has the main character face interactive challenges. Part 3 puts Xiao-Xiao against endless, successively greater numbers of opponents. And so on. Xiao-Xiao's perpetual nemesis is The Boss, a gang leader, who commands the enemy sticks.

Comment: Series starring simple kung fu stick figures that parody Hong Kong martial arts films. Xiao Xiao, the protagonist, is an elite assassin. Done in the Adobe Flash format.

2004

The Paradise of Bandits/Qiangdao de Tiantang

Director: Jiang Jian-Qiu

Comment: Debuted on "Flash Empire," a popular platform.

2007

Flee at Night/Lin Chong Ye Ben

Director: Zhang Zhen-Xing

Comment: Traditional Chinese ink and wash painting, combined with computer techniques.

2007–2009

Kung Fu Bunny/Shaolin Rabbit and Wudang Dog

Director: Li Zhi Yong

Synopsis: An invincible cartoon rabbit fights his artist creator and a dog.

Comment: Li Zhi Yong is known to his students at the Animation School of Communication University of China as "Vincent." So far he has produced three entries with a highly popular character, Kung Fu Bunny, a mix of 2D animation and tabletop stopmotion that obviously is inspired by early Max Fleischer *Out of the Inkwell* cartoons.

The first was made while Li Zhi Yong himself was still a student and shows the title character and creator changing roles, with the creator shrinking into the cartoon world and the bunny growing to human proportions.

This is how "Vincent" describes his recent work:

> The phone rings. I talk with my friend about basketball.
> I draw a bunny and play tricks on him. The revengeful little bunny attacks me. I use the drawn lines to scratch him. He moves swiftly. Dropping into a drawn tooth glass, the little bunny kills a fish and jumps out. A dog, drawn by me, shall arrest the rabbit. A long chase is the result.
> The dog is ready to beat the hateful bunny. The bunny, however, splashes ink to my glasses. A war between kung fu bunny and myself breaks out. After several rounds I am beaten to the ground.[24]

See Through/Da Da Ga Da Sci Gua

16 Minutes
Director: Jokelate
Synopsis: During a war two hostile fighter pilots find themselves alone together on a remote island.
Comment: 3D anti-war satire.
The artist explains:

> I have always liked drawing since I was a child, but I had no training. I always practiced by myself. However, ten years ago in China it was very difficult to make a living from painting. So I entered the West China Medical University. You know, it is an easier living to be a doctor but I have not given up painting. Then I heard that 3D animation can make money. I think the greatest happiness in life is making money by my own love. So I started learning 3D MAYA software. When I graduated a year later, I also finished the basics of animation. I made a short experimental film to apply for a job in a small AD company.
> However, a year later I found that cus-

tomers, professional situation and some other objective conditions didn't meet with my own aspirations. My space was limited. So I quit and returned home. I spent three and a half year on this short film (soundtrack and score not included) and devoted entirely to it. It's a story of two "potatoes" from different alignments in a big war. They were abandoned in the battlefield and met each other by accident. They finally saw through war and recognized that it was meaningless to function as bandits for autocrats. They didn't want to be victims in a political frenzy anymore.

> I tried to highlight my original concepts with CG techniques to achieve a new level of expressive forms and styles which indicated my inner world. In this film I want to present my thought: Besides mainstream there should be a different sound. People deserve more time and space to think about themselves. We are supposed to see the truth through the mist in the world, then make the choice of fate by ourselves and not commanded by some bigwigs.

> Well, a short film is a short film. I wish I could have put everything in it but that would have been far beyond my ability. So I had to simplify the artwork.[25]

2008

West Lake Fish/The West Lake Fish Cooked with Vinegar/Xihu Cuyu

4:50 Minutes
Producer: Jiang Lian
Director: Chen Xi
Story: Zhang Liang
Animation: Chen Fan, Liu Bo
Synopsis: Two famous characters of the Ching Dynasty: One, slim Liu Yong, is obsessed by art, while the other, fat He Shen, is only interested in food. Together they fish on West Lake with a grotesque outcome.
Comment: Distinctive Flash animation combined with traditional Chinese elements that has originality and is fun to watch. Chen Xi graduated from Beijing Film Academy.

2009

Adventure of Li Xianji

20 Minutes
Director: Li Yang
Synopsis: An experimental work about Chinese youth lost in the digital world of New Media.

Comment: A stream of consciousness is used to narrate the story, in addition to inner soliloquy. The rich, fantastic plot, full-fledged application of techniques, and dazzling effects make this film unique among recent Chinese entries. The short took the Web by storm at the end of 2009.

Freud, Fish and Butterfly

Haiyang's Animation Studio
3 Minutes
Director-Animator: Haiyang Wang
Editor: Wang Ying

Synopsis: A myriad of associations fly through a strange world of even stranger fantasies. Freud anyone?

2010–2012

Reflection of Crescent

Great Demon Nation Production Co.
TV anime series announced on the Internet
1:22 Minutes Teaser

Synopsis: The young protagonists reflect on these questions: What is happiness? And what is love? And find a fulfilling "career" in the demon world. Starring Demon King successor: Kai Yalun. Distinguished descendant of the Elites: Sal Weagal. A Half Demon Youth: Weyi.

Comment: China-produced anime. Comments by anime aficionados on the Internet seemed to react positive to the teaser that was released to promote the project: "So I click play ... and I was speechless!! THIS?!! CHINESE ANIMATION!!?? THIS WILL NOT BE A PHONY I HOPE!!!" "I hope the anime will have this quality for real!"

"I came across Reflection of Crescent while looking around youtube and it looks amazing. It's supposed to be a boy love anime that was produced in China. I understand that it is not made by a professional studio and

won't air on TV, but it was said to have come out fall 2011."

"GAWD this BL-anime made by a Chinese animation studio has been reeking havoc upon fangirls and fanboys!!! I really want to see the ova, don't care if it's in any language, I'll still watch it! The trailer is SOOOOO good and I really want to watch it! They say it was supposed to debut in 2011, then it got postponed to 2012, on who-knows-when!"

2011

Ketchup

7 Minutes
Producer: Shui Bo Wang
Director: Yan Bai Shen
Screenplay: Guo Chun Ning
Photography: Wen Lan Wang, Wu Gong Hu
Musical Score: Yan Bai Shen

Synopsis: In 1984 a boy lives with his parents in the countryside. There are tomato plants growing everywhere, and as every year, Mom prepares ketchup. One day soldiers arrive and the boy becomes witness to the execution of a group of men. On the street their blood mixes with dust and looks like ketchup.

Comment: Part of a trilogy titled *Fledging Memories* written by Yan Bai Shen's wife, Maggie (Chun Ning) Guo. The other parts are *The City of Youth* and *A Kiss of a Mosquito on the Foot. Ketchup* is based on the artist's childhood and deftly conveys the way small events in memory become intertwined with bigger ones.

Yan Bai Shen was born in Lanzhou City, Gansu Province, in 1977. His father worked in a top-secret military factory on the Loess Plateau, in northwestern China. Sequestered from the rest of the nation, his family remained untouched by the changes that swept through the country in the 1980s and '90s.

Afterword

The Digital Future in Cartoons and Interactive Games

In the past years Chinese animation has increasingly moved into the digital age, with a number of state-of-the-art computerized studios emerging, including some with motion-capture capacities. The hundreds of animation training programs that have sprung up also focus on digitalization.

Although computer-generated animation has a number of benefits, some of its principles and modes of operation are contrary to what existed during China's golden era. In the beginning there were critics in China and abroad who pointed out that digital animation is more formulaic, less spontaneous, and not as open to experimentation as traditional animation. They also bemoaned the tendencies of 3D to be additive—too detailed—in an art form that traditionally reduced things to their essentials, and the marginalization of the animator who no longer feels as though he or she is creating the character, but instead is part of a collection of people and programs.

However, if there was any resistance, it was short-lived. Chinese animation experienced a "subversive revolution in visual narrative followed by the spread of Flash websites, independent animation, and computer graphic activities such as the animation design of computer games, special effects in film and television, and animated messages for mobile phones."[1]

Currently, concerning online games, China is number two in the world.[2] But the demand for interactive games will make it number one. Online games in China will be successful, as Harvey Lee, a specialist in gaming, says, because they produce on spec, and if they get one million users or more they can break even because of advertising.

China will have a pretty good chance in the future as media are defined anew. Actually, we are in the Stone Age of virtuality. We have said Chinese are not good at straightforward storytelling, but the new media don't rely on straightforwardness. That, in the end, will work for Chinese entrepreneurs. So young is the Internet and mobile culture and so eager are Chinese users that it could become an Asian medium.

A New Era

My good friend, twice Academy Award–nominated stop-motion artist and painter Jim Danforth, wrote in the foreword to his wonderful life account, *Dinosaurs, Dragons, and Drama*: "I believe that 'mass entertainment' doesn't need to mean mindless entertainment."[3]

I had never dreamed of going to China,

but when I did and traveled around cities from the north to the south, visiting cartoon festivals that seemed to be the same all over, from Dalian to Hangzhou and to Xiamen, with interesting but sometimes incoherent scholarly talks, award ceremonies without films being screened publicly, and stages filled with cheap merchandising items, I saw many problems but I remained hopeful.

The various entrepreneurs were mostly capitalists who were interested not in content but in grinding out large quantities.

Raymond Chow, head columnist of *China Daily*, reported in November 2009 about a cartoon festival in Guangzhou and quoted me. I had compared Chinese animation with fast food, "without roots in their own culture or emotional exchange."[4] I still like this comparison. And I am grateful that I was allowed to publicly speak about it in China, although not everybody liked it. I feared they couldn't stand constructive criticism at all because it would make them lose face. But they let me talk, and they listened.

It's hard to find a way through, and this book is the proof. I knew a lot about animation history, for many years saw each piece and clip of Chinese animation to make myself familiar with it (and sometimes suffered through it), and read about Chinese history—but the new media are a jungle, at least at the first glimpse.

You need a bushwhacker to pass through it.

Raymond Chow continues:

Can you call it a "boom"? On the surface it appears to be. But like many things in China, it is artificially inflated. Sometime in the past decade, people, including the government, realized that animation is big business. Central government launched drives, local governments dangled incentives and capital flowed like red wine at a party.

The only caveat is, nobody is buying. Most TV stations do not pay for such programs. If the major companies do pay, the fees are so minimal it's not even worth the producers flying to Beijing to make a deal.

This leaves just one way forward. Use television exposure as a promotional tool, like Hasbro did in the late 1980s when it offloaded without charge some *Transformer* series to Chinese TV channels. It recouped its investment by selling toys at astronomical prices. But those who follow this route are ambushed by bandits, who snatch earnings by illegally associating their names with a hit show, or selling pirate products.[5]

But in producing merchandising even Chinese companies are pirated. The producers of popular Xi Yang Yang series were forced to issue the following statement: "Recently, we found there are some fake 'Pleasant Goat and Big Big Wolf' consumer products in the market and their qualities are very poor. These fake products did do harm to our brand 'Pleasant Goat and Big Big Wolf.' Apart from the issue of no quality assurance, fake products are also contradicted to our concept of bringing laughter to the world."[6]

As a historian I naturally adore early animation. I was proud to have brought original artwork by the godfather of animation, Winsor McCay, to China: inked drawings on small white cardboard of Gertie the Dinosaur (1914) and the Sinking of the Lusitania. Some of my Chinese colleagues never had heard about McCay, but when they realized what his work meant to animation they began to adore and cherish it.

This is an indicator that the main obstacles to better quality in Chinese animation are the present decision-makers themselves. But I am sure that new quality-conscious entrepreneurs will emerge in the rise of the new virtual age we are facing, and transform the media to their own demands. There certainly is creativity spreading all over China. And digital media are growing up, maturing and separating from the toy industry and the commercialized taste of small children.

The format will be totally different than what we were used to in regular animation. Animation has already adapted to every new medium, as to film, sound, and television, and now to the mobile market.

New Chinese animation will not come from traditional studios. It will reflect the pattern of Chinese society and have its roots in the new youth culture of the big cities (although two-thirds of the country is rural).

Chinese society is moving—and so is animation. It is only a question of time. There are scholars who tell us that in a few decades China may lead the world.

The Chinese are preparing to become the biggest competitor in a fierce rivalry for global markets with the former champion, the United States. That transformation process may not always happen peacefully, but in the end the pendulum surely will swing back to the East.

Here is an interesting commentary by Thomas L. Friedman that deals with a question brought up in the introduction to this book:

> One of the standard lines about China's economy is that the Chinese are good at copying, but they could never invent a Hula-Hoop. It's not in their DNA, we are told, and their rote education system reinforces that tendency. I'm wondering about that: How is it that a people who invented papermaking, gunpowder, fireworks and the magnetic compass suddenly only became capable of assembling iPods? I'm wondering if what's missing in China today is not a culture of innovation but something more basic: trust.
>
> When there is trust in society, sustainable innovation happens because people feel safe and enabled to take risks and make the long-term commitments needed to innovate. When there is trust people are willing to share their ideas and collaborate on each other's inventions without fear of having their creations stolen. The biggest thing preventing modern China from becoming an innovation society, which is imperative if it hopes to keep raising incomes, is that it remains a very low-trust society....
>
> China is caught in a gap between its old social structure of villages and families, which created its own form of trust, and a new system based on the rule of law and an independent judiciary. The Communist Party destroyed the first but has yet to build the second because it would mean ceding the party's arbitrary powers.[7]

Not all believe in China's rise, and some forces are even working against it: "Has China's rise peaked? If one were to pose this question a few years ago, he would probably be laughed out of the room. The conventional wisdom then was that China's rise was certain to continue. But today, this question is very much on everybody's mind."[8]

There is another question. It's about creativity used to create a better environment. I heard an interview with a former German minister of interior, Gerhart Rudolf Baum,[9] who said that without culture there will be no creativity. China will have to find a way out of the jungle of cultural industries back to its cultural roots to find its own style of creativity.

Chapter Notes

Introduction

1. *China Daily*, Monday, April 3, 2007.
2. State Administration of Radio, Film and Television, ed., "Several Suggestions for the Development of the Chinese Cartoon, Film, and TV Industry," SARFT Beijing, April 20, 2004.
3. *The Wall Street Journal*, February 17, 2012.
4. "'Cultural Imperialism' in China's Film Market," *Claremont Journal of International Relations*, June 9, 2011.
5. "Oriental DreamWorks," *Animatoon World Animation Journal* 18, no. 96 (reprinted by permission of Mr. Nelson Shin, publisher, Seoul, Korea).
6. "Dream Works and Chinese Protectionism: A New Joint Venture Shows the Barriers to Investment in China," *Wall Street Journal*, February 17, 2012.
7. *Los Angeles Times*, April 11, 2012.
8. Colin A. Ronan and Joseph Needham, *The Shorter Science and Civilisation in China*, vol. 2 (Cambridge, MA: Cambridge University Press, 1985), 123–124.
9. Francis T. S. Yu and Suganda Jutamulia, "Holography: Origin, Development, and Beyond," in *The Art and Science of Holography: A Tribute to Emmett Leith and Yuri Denisyuk*, ed. H. John Caulfield (Bellingham, WA: SPIE—The International Society for Optical Engineering, 2004), 7.
10. Rolf Giesen, "ChinAmation," *film-dienst* (Cologne), June 1, 2005, 58–60.
11. Internally circulated information published by Beijing International TV Week 2000, p. 46.
12. "Chinese Animation Industry Box Office Up in 2011," *Xinhua*.
13. "China Encourages Private Investment in Animation," *Xinhua*, July 12, 2012, ChinaDaily.com.cn.
14. Robert Lawrence Kuhn, "China Can Produce. Can China Create?" *China Daily*, October 5–11, 2012, 8.
15. "China's Collapse 'will bring economic crisis to climax in 2012.'" *The Guardian*, January 11, 2012.
16. Bruno Bettelheim, *The Uses of Enchantment: The Meaning and Importance of Fairy Tales* (New York: Knopf, 1976), 236.
17. *China Daily*, April 7, 2012.
18. Liu Lu, Wang Chao and Fu Jing, "Message and the Medium: Nation Needs to Mobilize Its Soft Power Resources to Win More Hearts," *China Daily*, Saturday, April 7, 2012, online edition.

Chapter 1

1. Richard Fleischer, *Out of the Inkwell: Max Fleischer and the Animation Revolution* (Lexington, Kentucky: University Press of Kentucky, 2005), 26.
2. Richard Fleischer, *Just Tell Me When to Cry: A Memoir* (New York: Carroll and Graf, 1993), 95.
3. Fleischer, *Out of the Inkwell*, 29.
4. Marie-Claire Quiquemelle, *The Wan Brothers and 60 Years of Animated Film in China* (Annecy, France: JICA Diffusion, 1985).

Chapter 2

1. Wan Brothers, "Talking About Cartoons" (Shanghai: Mingxing Production, 1936).
2. Marie-Claire Quiquemelle, *The Wan Brothers and 60 Years of Animated Film in China* (Annecy, France: JICA Diffusion, 1985).

Chapter 3

1. Kosei Ono, "Tadahito Mochinaga: The Japanese Animator Who Lived in Two Worlds," *Animation World Magazine* 4.9 (December 1999). Online edition.
2. Ibid.
3. *Sovietskoye Kino* 1–2 (1933): 10.
4. John A. Lent, "Te Wei and Chinese Animation: Inseparable, Incomparable," *Animation World Network*, March 15, 2002.
5. Liu Qing Fang, *When Chinese Animations Meet Globalization* (Rotterdam: Erasmus University, 2007), 30.

Chapter 4

1. David Ehrlich with Tianyi Jin, "Animation in China," in *Animation in Asia and the Pacific*, ed. John A. Lent (Bloomington: Indiana University Press, 2001), 10.
2. *Shanghai Animation Film Studio: 1957–1987* (Shanghai: Shanghai Animated Film Studio, 1987).
3. *Shanghai Animation Film Studio, 1957–1987* (Shanghai: Shanghai Animated Film Studio, 1987).

Chapter 5

1. Obituary. "Zhang Songlin," *China Daily*, May 14, 2012.
2. *Saiyuki*, directors, Daisaku Shirakawa and Taiji Yabushita with the participation of Osamu Tezuka; producers Goro Kontaibo, Hiroshi Okawa, and Hideyuki Takahashi (Toei); cinematographers, Komei Ishikawa, Harusato Otsuka, Seigo Otsku, and Kenji Sugiyama; art department, Koichi Maeba, Hajime Numai, and Masaaki Yano; animation director, Yasuji Mori; animators, Akira Daikuhara, Hideo Furusawa,

193

Masao Kumagawa, Osamu Tezuka, and Yasuo Otsuka; background artists, Kazuo Ozawa, Kimiko Saito, Eiko Sugimoto, Mataji Urata, and Saburo Yoki; photographers: Komei Ishikawa, Harusato Otsuka, Seigo Otsuka, and Kenji Sugiyama; released by American International Pictures in the United States as *Alakazam,* with the voice talents of Frankie Avalon, Sterling Holloway, Arnold Stang, and Jonathan Winters.

3. Pressbook for *The Monkey King—Uproar in Heaven 3D* (Shanghai: Shanghai Media Group, 2012).

4. *Animation Resources,* directed by Stephen Worth.

5. Pressbook for *The Monkey King—Uproar in Heaven 3D* (Shanghai: Shanghai Media Group, 2012).

6. Pressbook for *The Monkey King—Uproar in Heaven 3D* (Shanghai: Shanghai Media Group, 2012).

7. Pressbook for *The Monkey King—Uproar in Heaven 3D* (Shanghai: Shanghai Media Group, 2012).

8. Pressbook for *The Monkey King—Uproar in Heaven 3D,* (Shanghai: Shanghai Media Group, 2012).

9. Te Wei, quoted by Ehrlich, "Animation in China," in *Animation in Asia and the Pacific,* 15.

10. Yan Dingxian, quoted by David Ehrlich, "Animation in China," 14.

Chapter 6

1. Updated version of Giannalberto Bendazzi's *Cartoons: One Hundred Years of Cinema Animation,* unpublished manuscript.

Chapter 7

1. Justin Sevakis, *Buried Garbage—Chinamation.* October 25, 2007. Anime News Network, online.

2. Liu Qing Fang, *When Chinese Animations Meet Globalization* (Rotterdam: Erasmus University, 2007), 29.

3. Ehrlich, "Animation in China," 19.

4. Rolf Giesen and J. P. Storm, *Animation Under the Swastika* (Jefferson, NC: McFarland, 2012), 116–117, 119–120.

5. Anipages Web site, Monday, May 9, 2005.

6. Manfred Durniok, http://www.durniok.com.

Chapter 8

1. Zou Chin, interview by John A. Lent, *Animation in Asia and the Pacific.*

Chapter 9

1. Liu Yuzhu, interview by author, Changzhou, China, 2005.

2. Qu Jianfang, "On the Development Future of Chinese and Foreign Animation Collaboration," presented at the International Animation Artists Salon, Wuhan, China, November 4, 2006.

3. Ibid.

4. "Chinese-Japanese Three Kingdoms Anime on Air in June," The Asahi Shimbun, *Bizchina,* Anime News Network, April 29, 2008.

5. "A Glaring Case of Plagiarism on Chinese TV," France24 International News, September 18, 2009.

6. Paraphrased from a CCTV press release.

7. Press release, Alpha Animation and Culture Co., Ltd., Guangzhou.

8. Press release, Alpha Animation and Culture Co., Ltd., Guangzhou.

9 *China Daily,* May 7, 2012.

10. Hong Kong Film Archive, "Frame After Frame" (Hong Kong, 2006).

11. Hong Kong Film Archive, "Frame After Frame" (Hong Kong, 2006).

12 Hong Kong Film Archive, "Frame After Frame" (Hong Kong, 2006).

13. Giannalberto Bendazzi, *One Hundred Years of Cinema Animation.* Updated version, unpublished manuscript.

14 Li Wanran, "Chinese Cartoon 'Kui Ba' Strikes a Pose," *CNTV.cn Culture Express,* July 14, 2011.

15. Keen Zhang, "'Kuiba' Sets Chinese Animation on a New Path," *China.org.cn,* June 29, 2011.

16. An Wei, "Behind China's Domestic Animation Slump," *China.org.cn,* November 22, 2011.

17. Author's synopsis from a subtitled version of the film.

18. Program brochure published by the organizing committee of the Sichuan Television Festival.

19. *The Standard* (Hong Kong).

20. John Willett, *Alienation Effects in Chinese Acting* (New York: Hill and Wang, 1964), 91.

21. Antony Tatlow, Tak-Wai Wong, eds., *Brecht and East Asian Theatre,* in *Proceedings of a Conference on Brecht in East Asian Theatre Hong: Kong 16–20 March 1981* (Hong Kong: Hong Kong University Press, 1982), 39.

22. Synopsis by the filmmaker.

23. Wu Weihua and Steve Fore, "Flash Empire and Chinese Shanke: The Emergence of Chinese Digital Culture," *Animation Journal* 13 (2005) (Santa Clarita, California): 28–51.

24. Animation School, Communication University of China, Beijing.

25. Jokelate, e-mail to author, October 26, 2009.

Afterword

1. Wu Weihua, "Independent Animation in Contemporary China," *Cartoons,* Winter 2005: 21–25.

2. Chinese Online Game Market Roundup.

3. Jim Danforth, *Dinosaurs, Dragons, and Drama: The Odyssey of a Trickfilmmaker,* vol. 1: *The Outward Journey* (Los Angeles: Archive Editions, 2011), xi.

4. Raymond Chow, "Original Pirate Material," *China Daily,* December 11, 2009, Online edition.

5. Ibid.

6. See *TOON EXPRESS,* Toon Express International Limited (TE Group), Hong Kong, online.

7. Thomas L. Friedman, "In China We (Don't) Trust," *New York Times Global Edition,* Thursday, September 13, 2012, 7.

8. Minxin Pei, "Superpower Denied? Why China's 'Rise' May Have Already Peaked," *The Diplomat,* August 9, 2012.

9. *Im Dialog,* Phoenix TV (Bonn, Germany), November 11, 2012.

Bibliography

Bendazzi, Giannalberto. *Cartoons: One Hundred Years of Cinema Animation*. London: John Libbey, 1964 [Updated version unpublished].

C for China Content: Animation Special. H2 2010. Beijing: CMM Intelligence, 2010.

CCTV Animation. Promotional brochure.

Chang, Hong/Xu Yuzhong. *30 Years of Artistic Animation in China*. Hangzhou: Zhejiang University Press, 2009.

Chaozhu, Wu. "A Good Film To Be Loved by Children—See Color Animation 'Little Trumpeter.'" *Hunan Daily*, December 6, 1973, 3.

Dingxian, Yan. *Forty Years of Film Animation in the People's Republic of China*. ASIFA Animafilm, Winter 1987.

Ehrlich, David. "Animated Couples: Yan Dingxian and Lu Wenxiao." *ASIFA News* 1 (1994): 5–6.

_____. "Chinese Animation." In *Hawaii Film Festival Catalogue*. Honolulu: Hawaii Film Festival, 1992.

_____. "Chinese Animation." In *Animation in Asia and the Pacific*, John A. Lent, ed. Bloomington: Indiana University Press, 2001.

_____. "Profile in Courage: Te Wei." *Annecy 95 le Quotidien*, no. 2, May 31, 1995.

_____. "Te Wei." *ASIFA News*, no. 2, 1993.

Fang, Liu Qing. *When Chinese Animations Meet Globalization*. Rotterdam: Erasmus University, 2007.

Farquhar, Mary Ann. "Monks and Monkey: A Study of 'National Style' in Chinese Animation." *Animation Journal*, Spring 1993, pp. 4–27.

50 Years of Chinese Animation and Comics, 1949–2009. Special edition.

Fleischer, Richard. *Just Tell Me When to Cry: A Memoir*. New York: Carroll and Graf, 1993.

_____. *Out of the Inkwell: Max Fleischer and the Animation Revolution*. Lexington: University Press of Kentucky, 2005.

Gilsdorf, Ethan. "Chinese Animation's Past, Present, and Future: The Monkey King of Shanghai." *Animato!* Winter 1988, pp. 20–23.

Guanyun, Ou. "Before the Production of 'Ginseng Baby'—Wan Guchan Talks About the Experience of Paper Cut's Film Creation." *Xinmin Evening Paper*, December 1, 1961, p. 2.

_____. "Gathering Images of 'Create Disturbances in Heavenly Palace'—Wan Laiming Talks About the Characteristics of Modeling Figures of Zhang Guangyu." *Xinmin Evening Paper*, June 5, 1962, p. 2.

Hong Kong Film Archive, ed. *Frame After Frame*. Hong Kong: 2006.

Hui, Jiang. "First Domestic Color Puppet Film 'Little Hero' Achieved Original Success in Production." *Popular Film* 14 (1952): 13.

Lent, John A., ed. *Animation in Asia and the Pacific*. Bloomington: Indiana University Press, 2001.

Liuyi, Wang, ed. *March: Chinese Animation Enters New Century*. 10 volumes. Beijing: Sunchen Publishing House, 2013.

McLaren, Norman. "I Saw the Chinese Reds Take Over." *McLean's*, October 15, 1950, pp. 73–76.

Ming, Jia. "Neza on Screen (Color Animation 'Neza Stirs Up Sea')." *Film Stories* 2 (1979): 25.

Mochinaga, Tadahito. *Animeshon Nitchu koryuki: Mochinaga Tadahito jiden*. Tokyo: Toho Shoten, 2006.

"Nominees for Cyber Sousa Award of 2011: The 4th Xiamen International Animation Festival." Program Brochure. Organizing Committee of Xiamen International Animation Festival, 2011.

Qin, X. J. *Zhong Guo Dong Hua Pian de Chan Ye Jing Xie Yan jiu*. Beijing: China Market, 2006.

Quiquemelle, Marie-Claire. *The Wan Brothers and 60 Years of Animated Film in China*. Annecy: Festival d'Annecy, 1985.

Roffat, Sébastien. *Propagandes Animées: Le dessin animé politique entre 1933 et 1945*. Paris: Bazaar, 2010.

Shanghai Animation Film Studio, 1957–1987. Shanghai: Shanghai Animation Film Studio, 1987.

Shangyi, Han. "A Magical Flower in Art Garden—Appreciate the Artistic Treatment of 'Neza Stirs Up Sea.'" *Liberation Daily*, October 16, 1979, p. 4.

Shuchen, Wang, et al. "Conduct Literature and Art Creation with Party's Basic Line—The Experience of Making the Animation 'Little

Trumpeter.'" *Wenhui Journal*, December 12, 1973, p. 3.

Su, Li Yin. "A Cultural Explanation of Contemporary Animation Art: A Comparative Analysis of Chinese Ghost Story, Mulan, and Lotus Lantern." *Film Art* 3 (2001): 87–90.

Wei, Te, and Jin Tianyi. "The Contemporary Situation of Chinese Animation and Perspective: Policy and Market." *New Film* 4 (1997).

Wikipedia. *Chinese Animation: History of Chinese Animation, Pleasant Goat and Big Big Wolf, AI Football CGO, Xiao Xiao, Astro Plan, Calabash Brother*. Memphis, TN: General Books, 2011.

Yi, He. "Be Immersed in the Poetic Sense and Painting Flavor: Jottings on 'Fishing Boy,' 'Little Carp Jumps the Dragon Gate' and Other Animations." *Film Art* 6 (1959): 25.

_____. "Try Hard for the Development of Children Film Cause: See Puppet Film 'Little Hero' and Others." *Popular Film* 22 (1954): 12.

Yin, Zhan. "New Space for Free Made Sound Creation." *New Films*, September 1999, 48–50.

Index